Modern prison w...ing
selected and edited by
PHILIP PRIESTLEY

Jail
Journeys

The English prison experience since 1918

R
ROUTLEDGE
London and New York

For D.G.W.

First published 1989
by Routledge
11 New Fetter Lane, London EC4P 4EE
29 West 35th Street, New York, NY 10001

© 1989 Philip Priestley

Typeset by J&L Composition Ltd, Filey, North Yorkshire
Printed and bound in Great Britain by
Biddles Ltd, Guildford and King's Lynn

British Library Cataloguing in Publication Data
Priestley, Philip
Jail journeys: the English prison
experience since 1918
1. England. Prison life, since 1918
I. Title
365'.6'0942

Library of Congress Cataloging in Publication Data
Priestley, Philip
Jail journeys.
Bibliography: p.
Includes index.
1. Prisoners—England—Biography. 2. Prisons—
England—History—20th century. I. Title.
HV8657.P75 1989   365'.941   88–30666

ISBN 0–415–03458–2

(Jacket illustration by Ralph Wolfe-Emery)

CONTENTS

'A community is infinitely more brutalised by the habitual employment of punishment than it is by the occasional occurrence of crime. . . .'

Oscar Wilde, 'The soul of man under Socialism'

ACKNOWLEDGEMENTS

Jail Journeys is the second in a projected three-part series of titles that deal with prison life in the British Isles over the past two centuries. The first of them, *Victorian Prison Lives* (Methuen 1985), reported the subjective experience of the English prison from 1830 to the outbreak of the First World War. The present volume brings that story up to date. I am grateful to the Nuffield Foundation for continuing help with the costs of research for this project.

I have been greatly helped by the staff of the following libraries: Bodleian Law Library, Oxford; British Library; Bristol University Library; Cambridge Institute of Criminology; Cambridge University Library.

An especial and voluminous debt of gratitude is also due to those booksellers who have supplied most of the volumes from which the extracts that follow have been selected; principally Mr J.C.G. Hammond, the late Basil Donne, Camille Wolff, and Clifford Elmer. Others all over the British Isles have helped in individually smaller but collectively equally important ways.

For other advice, encouragement, suggestions and material I am grateful to Professor Terence Morris, Una Padel, Jim Little, Don Woodman, Denise Harris, Bill Eyre, Tony Parker, and Nigel Gray.

I would like to thank all the publishers, authors, and agents who have given permission for material to be used in this book, and I would be very grateful for information that would enable me to contact copyright holders whom I have not been able to trace.

Thanks are also due to the following for permission to reproduce photographs:

Johnathan Bayer – Dartmoor Prison p 1; Pentonville Prison p 15; Oxford Prison p 29; Pucklechurch Prison p 38; Blundeston Prison p 159; Long Lartin Prison p 178.

Radio Times – Hulton Picture Library – Holloway Prison p 63; Strangeways Prison p 77; Strangeways Prison p 127.

Educational Explorers – in the cell p 61.

© *The Estate of Bill Brandt* – *by permission of Noya Brandt* – Wormwood Scrubs Prison p 33.

MPP
Rosscarbery
August 1988

PROLOGUE

The English Prison

Dartmoor Prison

⇒ The nineteenth-century legacy ⇐

Between 1916 and 1919 two and a half million men were conscripted into the British Army to fight the infantry and artillery battles of the First World War.[1] Nearly six thousand of their compatriots – a handful against the millions – served sentences of imprisonment in English gaols rather than answer the call to the colours.[2] These were the conscientious objectors: most of them Christian pacifists; some of them socialists opposed to the war on political rather than moral grounds. Stephen Hobhouse was a Quaker, and Fenner Brockway had been editor of *Labour Leader*, the newspaper of the Independent Labour Party. Both served extended sentences of imprisonment during the war and they joined forces afterwards to write a report entitled *English Prisons Today*, which was based on testimony collected from more than four hundred former prisoners and prison staff.[3] It is an important document in the history of the English prison: magisterial in scope and meticulous in detail – a picture of society's most coercive institution taken at an instant of profound crisis in the national life. Even more importantly for what followed in the twentieth century, their report depicts a system which in its broad essentials had survived virtually intact since the time of Sir Edmund Du Cane. 'To the first offender,' they concluded, 'the peculiar and distinctive feature of prison life is the sense of being in the grip of a huge machine which is felt to be repressive at every point, inhuman, aimless, tyrannical.'[4]

Sir Edmund was Chairman of the Prison Commission from its inception in 1878, when he presided over the amalgamation of the national 'convict' prisons and the local gaols. The buildings he inherited from a previous era had been designed for, and were originally dedicated to, the spiritual regeneration of prisoners. But within them Du Cane had proceeded to construct a regime of 'salutary terror' that owed virtually nothing to reformist sentiment and almost everything to repression and deterrence.[5] And what Sir Edmund built, he built to last.

THE GLADSTONE COMMITTEE

There is nothing in that to surprise any but the most cursory student of Victorian public affairs. But what *is* surprising is that between the construction of Du Cane's regime and the experience recorded in *English Prisons Today* there intervened – in 1895 – the report of the Departmental Committee on Prisons; the Gladstone Report. In terms of historical neatness the timing of the report could hardly have been bettered. It reviewed the state of the penal system at the end of the nineteenth century and came to the conclusion that although it possessed many administrative features then thought to be positive, it remained the case that

> the prisoners have been treated too much as a hopeless or worthless element of the community, and the moral as well as the legal responsibility of the prison authorities had been held to cease when they pass outside the prison gates.[6]

Because of ill health, Du Cane gave only limited evidence to the Committee, but its findings cast a retrospective shadow of criticism over the whole of his life's work and he resigned from the public service forthwith. Gladstone proceeded to point the system in the direction of the twentieth century with an admonition to do better, and a recommendation for reformative elements to be added to those of deterrence by then so firmly embedded in the daily life of the late nineteenth-century prisoner. But the general guidance it gave was not that different in spirit from what had informed Sir Edmund's handiwork. And it was, from the moment of its enunciation, almost equally fatally flawed. Gladstone declaimed a policy in which 'deterrence and reformation' were to be the 'primary and concurrent objects', and a new chairman was appointed to carry out the necessary work.[7]

Sir Evelyn Ruggles-Brise had served alongside Sir Edmund in the Prison Commission, although latterly in silence, since his chief refused to speak to him for some years following a minor altercation between them.[8] An urbane and intelligent man with politically radical leanings, Ruggles-Brise was the first non-military head of the English prison service and he set to work with a will to give organisational expression to the contradictory wishes of the Gladstone Committee. The most tangible result of his efforts was to be seen in the creation of the Borstal institution – a fresh way of dealing with young offenders. It sought to minimise the criminal contamination of young men during periods of imprisonment served alongside more sophisticated or more depraved criminal companions, and to replace it with more wholesome influences. 'To the exhortation and moral persuasion of a selected staff,' said Sir Evelyn, 'we added physical drill, gymnastics, technical and literary instruction; inducements to good conduct by a system of grades and rewards, which, though small and trivial in themselves, were yet calculated to encourage a spirit of healthy emulation and inspire self-respect.'[9] The innovation was enshrined in the Prevention of Crime Act of 1908 and became, in the years that followed, the envy of penal administrators all over the world.

But so far as the male adult prisoners were concerned, twenty years went by and the conscientious objectors of the First World War arrived in their hundreds at Wormwood Scrubs, Wandsworth, and other prisons up and down the country, to find regimes as harsh and as destructive in their effects on human beings as anything the Gladstone Committee had felt moved to criticise. Ruggles-Brise had done his best, starting up the Borstals and creating a climate of cautious optimism about the work of the prisons, but beneath it all virtually nothing had changed.

Despite assertions to the contrary by Sir Evelyn himself, and the genuinely liberal interventions of Winston Churchill during his brief stay at the Home Office, the rule of silence still prevailed in English prisons.[10] Penal servitude prisoners still spent the first six months of their sentences in what amounted to solitary confinement. Oakum was still picked in cells; mailbags were still sewed eight stitches to the inch; the food was insufficient in quantity and of a uniformly awful quality. Staff and prisoners remained locked in a state of undeclared war that occasionally boiled over into overt violence. And the elements of reform so strongly urged upon the Commissioners by the Gladstone Committee amounted, in 1918, to little more than the nominal presence in prisons of the Church, some minimal education, and the accidental influence for good of individual prison warders. It is difficult to interpret the publication of *English Prisons Today* as anything other than a reminder to the Home Office to implement what its own Committee had recommended to it more than twenty years before.

To try to understand some of the reasons for this deep-rooted resistance to change it is useful to look back at the historical origins of the English prison, and to trace its development from the unreformed state of the eighteenth century to the disciplinary solidities discovered by Hobhouse and Brockway in the early years of the twentieth.

CORRUPTION

It has become a convention of the 'progressive' school of English penal history to locate the origins of reform in the indefatigable programme of visits to Bridewells, Houses of Correction, Gaols, and Prisons made by the Sheriff of Bedfordshire, John Howard. The prisons he visited were the responsibility of the justices of the peace for the area in which they were located. They exercised these responsibilities as County Benches convened in Quarter Sessions, and they exercised them, as may be imagined, in ways that varied from place to place, and from time to time. Howard's travels to these dark and diseased repositories of vice and sin were the outward and publicly visible signs of an inward and spiritual journey in search of grace and, like the Quaker diarists before him, he wrote down everything he observed on the way. The flavour of his findings can be quickly conveyed.

> Bridgwater Town Gaol. 1774, September 10. Prisoners none. Only one middle sized room: and one of the two windows stopped up. In this room at Midsummer Quarter Sessions 1774 were shut up twenty-seven prisoners. At Summer Assize the same year, thirteen; two of them, Women.[11]

> Worcester. The Castle Yard. The day-room for Men and Women-felons is in the middle of the area; only fourteen feet by twelve. Near it is a Hand-Ventilator for airing the Men-Felons dungeon, which is twenty-six steps under ground, and circular, about seventeen feet diameter, with barrack bedsteads. ... Mr Hallward the Surgeon caught the Gaol-Fever some years ago, and has ever since been fearful of going into the dungeon; when any Felon is sick there, he orders him to be brought out.[12]

From these and hundreds of similar observations, Howard compiled a contemporary likeness which he published in 1777 as *The State of the Prisons*. Amongst its influential readers the book evoked a sense of horror, but more importantly it also provoked the beginnings of a movement of penal reform that was to revolutionise the purposes and practices of the English prison over the next sixty years. For Howard and his horrified readers, as well as for all of his and their successors in the field, the principal problem of the prison, apart from the purely physical squalor of the place, lay in the unregulated congregation of so many malefactors in one place. By even the most unsophisticated view of the matter such an arrangement could lead only to the corruption and further criminalisation of the incarcerated. It was not possible to conceive of any degree of moral reform being achieved in such circumstances.

And in truth, that was not the purpose of the 'unreformed' prison. Many of its prisoners had been committed there for debt and other civil difficulties that could only be resolved by payments of necessary sums to debtors or the due authorities. In criminal cases it existed mainly to hold the accused until they could be 'delivered' by the Quarter Sessions or a visiting judge of the Assize. After trial, the guilty were consigned to the condemned cell, ordered to be whipped or transported, and occasionally sentenced to periods of punitive imprisonment.[13] The infrequency of this last sort of sentence can be explained partly by a traditional preference for more brutal and typically more terminal disposals, and partly by the costs of the operation, which county benches of justices were reluctant to take on themselves. Nor was central government, such as it then was, inclined to pay the bills. In Howard's time, the gaolers of the local prisons paid rents to the justices for what amounted to concessions that allowed them to make money by extorting charges from those they held in their custody. The precise conditions of a person's imprisonment depended therefore largely on the size of his or her purse.[14] For the well-off it represented no more than a restriction on their ability to move freely in the world. For the very poor, who were a majority of those in prison, it could mean a sentence of death – a slow one by starvation, relieved only by the generosity of fellow prisoners or such charities as might be available. For the more fortunate it might mean a sudden exit in the grip of the 'Gaol Fever' that had made the surgeon at Worcester so fearful.

The first priority, therefore, of Howard and his helpers was to physically clean up the *squalor carceris* of the places he had visited and to remove the sources of graft and corruption so clearly at work in their management. But around these originally simple impulses towards cleanliness and good order there soon grew up a complex web of philosophical exposition and religious enterprise, replete with contending factions and schools of thought that were prepared to fight tooth and nail over the earthly bodies as well as the eternal souls of prisoners. Some of these ideas were the subject of small-scale practical trials in Gloucestershire and other parts of the country during the later years of the eighteenth century – but their time was not yet.

TRANSPORTATION

Since Elizabethan times, the shipment to the colonies of both male and female convicts had been a favoured mode of disposal for an English government apparatus that lacked the physical means to confine more than a handful of 'State Prisoners' in places like the Tower.[15] The American Declaration of Independence of 1776 effectively closed off the ports of that part of the world to this branch of the slave trade. As the unwanted convicts accumulated in the Old Country they were placed on ships that were destined never to set sail. These were the hulks, permanently berthed in the Thames and on the south coast.[16] Conditions on board these vessels were, if anything, more unsatisfactory than those of prisons on dry land, and their presence was a standing reproach to the pretensions of an age that liked increasingly to think of itself as enlightened. 'To show my readers how we were treated,' says Mark Jeffrey, who was kept on the hulks prior to being transported, 'I may mention, as an actual fact, that one man dropped dead from starvation!'[17]

The recently-discovered subcontinent of Australia – empty to European eyes that simply did not see the 'savages' scattered across its vast spaces – came as a heaven-sent solution to the problem. In 1787 seven hundred and fifty-nine convicted felons were assembled from around the country, placed aboard the ships of what came to be called the First Fleet, and despatched to the southern hemisphere.[18] It was an audacious enterprise, and for a time Australia appeared to be the answer.[19] But not for long. Judicial hanging, which had been the mandatory punishment for more than two hundred offences at the end of the eighteenth century, was under attack. Reformist sentiment was mobilised to reduce the categories of capital offence to those of murder and certain classes of treason only. As a result the prisons henceforward had to hold offenders who would have been previously hanged and who now became additional candidates for exile. Transportation was increasingly expensive to administer and, as time went by, not a little difficult to reconcile with the wish to encourage ordinary civilian emigration to the new colonies. The hulks remained full to the brim with their unsavoury human cargoes.

THE PENITENTIARY

Into this prolonged historical hiatus in the treatment of offenders there now stepped the singular figure of the English philosopher Jeremy Bentham – or, to be more accurate, a mummified version of some of his ideas. As the foremost exponent of the doctrines of Utilitarianism, Bentham was less concerned with the welfare of an individual who had committed a crime than with the well-being of 'the greatest number' who had not. His plans for what he termed a 'Panopticon' embodied a vision of perfect order that was to be achieved by a passive architecture of separation and restraint on the one hand, and an economical use of supervisory staff on the other.[20] At the heart of Bentham's design was the 'lantern', a watchpoint from which one person could supervise hundreds of prisoners locked in individual cells. So keen was he to construct his patent machine for 'grinding rogues honest' that he purchased with his own money a marshy site at Millbank some hundreds of yards to the west of the Houses of Parliament. Funds from the Exchequer were actually voted to the project but delays and diversions prevented Bentham from making a start on the building. The land was eventually donated to the state, which used it for its intended purpose in the early years of the nineteenth century.

The National Penitentiary at Millbank was completed in 1816. It was the first purpose-built prison establishment ever to be paid for by central government and was intended to provide a preliminary period of solitary 'probation' for offenders sentenced to be transported. Men and women were held there in conditions of separation and complete silence for up to eighteen months and then loaded onto transports bound for the Antipodes.[21] The building, a warren of octagons, staircases, and courtyards quite unlike the classic simplicities of Bentham's design, proved to be inadequate to the tasks set for it.[22] Constant disorders amongst the convicts were followed by a lethal outbreak of cholera, and the experiment was terminated.[23]

For new inspiration, and for an answer to the basic penal problem of contamination, English prison reformers next looked across the Atlantic where two alternative models of the penitentiary were to be seen in proper working order. The 'separate' system was in operation at the Walnut Street Penitentiary, Philadelphia; it relied on the total physical separation of prisoners into individual cells, where they worked and received visits from the staff of the prison. At the Auburn prison in New York the regime was equally silent, but it allowed prisoners to work and exercise together. The silence was maintained by a system of strict surveillance and discipline. Of the two systems – and both had their adherents in England – the separate system prevailed, and was translated into resplendent concrete reality at a site on the Caledonian Road in north London. Pentonville Prison was the new National Penitentiary, and when it opened its gates to prisoners in 1842 a new era in penal history opened with them.[24]

To begin with, everything went according to plan. The prisoners were housed in their separate cells, each with its own toilet facilities and its mechanically advanced system of hot-air central-heating – criticised by one contemporary as a 'costly extravagance'.[25] Each was furnished with a supply of improving tracts as well as with the Holy Bible. There were daily religious services in the chapel, a place so cunningly contrived that the individual members of the assembled congregation could see none of their neighbours but each had an excellent view of the chaplain in his pulpit. Simple work was undertaken in the cell. Exercise took place in individual airing yards. And whenever prisoners had to move from their cells their faces were hidden by special hoods, or they were instructed to turn their faces to the wall when other prisoners approached or passed by. The whole was a miracle of construction and organisation, and magistrates all over the country rushed to build similar establishments to deal with the burgeoning crime rates of a newly industrialising society.[26]

But quite soon, things began to go wrong. Stories began to be heard that the separation and the silence, salutary as they might be in spiritual terms, were more than ordinary flesh and blood could stand.[27] Symptoms of mental disorder appeared in numerous cases, and when batches of convicts came to be moved to Millbank for embarkation to the penal colonies, their condition caused a stir amongst the people responsible for their transportation – some of whom were naval captain-surgeons.[28] There was a considerable public outcry against this mental cruelty, led, in part, by novelist Charles Dickens, who had visited the American experiments in separation and written lurid accounts of their effects on the prisoners exposed to them.[29] The authorities found themselves in a dilemma. The much-trumpeted new system, far from casting out the sins of the captive criminals, appeared to drive them out of their minds instead. It would clearly have to be abandoned in favour of some other, less damaging system of containment. The trouble was that Pentonville and all the other prisons built so precipitately along similar lines were designed for one purpose only, namely, to hold prisoners under the 'separate' system. And because the buildings were so durable, and had cost so much to build, they form a substantial part of the Victorian legacy to the twentieth century.

An equally durable and equally intractable aspect of the legacy is to be found in a fundamental failure of the penal imagination. This has consisted of an inability on the part of prison administrators, both then and now, to conceive how people could be held together in any way that avoids the possibility in all cases – and the strong probability in many of them – that criminal contamination will be the principal outcome of a prison sentence. There is a sense in which the whole history of prisons in this country, from the failure of Pentonville onwards, consists of a tacit coming-to-terms with that impossibility – relieved here and there by sporadic and generally unsuccessful efforts to do something about it.

THE LOCAL PRISONS

Alongside the development of the National Penitentiary and the continued transportation of convicts to the South Pacific there was a constant effort on the part of central government to influence the local administration of prisons by the justices of the peace. It began in earnest with the findings of a select committee of the House of Lords in 1835. It took evidence about the state of the 'Gaols and Houses of Correction in England and Wales' – which it concluded had changed little in many respects since the days of John Howard – and recommended the appointment of Inspectors of Prisons.[30] It was the beginning of a process of inspection by officials, and exhortation by select committees and other parliamentary bodies that are recorded in a remarkable series of reports – the famous 'blue books'.

The local gaols presented different problems from those encountered in the convict establishments. They dealt with very large numbers of petty offenders committed to prison for very short periods – during the nineteenth century there were more than twenty million receptions into them.[31] But they reproduced in miniature all the great issues of moral theory and practical control that plagued the administrators of the national prisons. The answers they came to – regimes that embraced silence and separation in different proportions; dietaries (sometimes yoked to so many turns of the handle on the 'crank') that varied according to locality and the 'scientific' predilections of individual medical men; 'hard labour' that ranged from the uneconomic picking of oakum to the killing daily ascent of 19,000 feet on the endless staircase of the treadmill – satisfied their critics on neither side of the argument.[32] Reformers continued to think them too punitive, and a vocal section of 'public opinion' continued to castigate them for favouring undeserving prisoners at the expense of the 'honest poor'.[33] The inability of the local gaols to rationalise their approaches to these and other penal matters led to increasing pressure from central administrators to bring *all* the prisons in the country under unified control.

The high hopes of the early prison reformers were shipwrecked on the obdurate realities of a human nature that proved incapable of bearing the religious and moral burdens of their visionary schemes. Two men took on the task of rescuing something from the debacle and attempted to create from the wreckage that was washed ashore a more enduring system. The first of them, Major-General Sir Joshua Jebb, had helped to build Pentonville and was therefore one of the architects of his own misfortune.[34] The Penitentiary had been intended to prepare convicts for the voyage to Australia, but as the practice of transportation came to an end, it became imperative to devise some alternative destination for them. Jebb's answer was to construct a system of 'penal servitude' to replace the lost opportunities of the bush and the outback. It consisted of setting up, from 1849 onwards, what amounted to 'labour camps' on British soil. In them, offenders who would otherwise have been transported were to serve long sentences engaged in heavy and unremitting toil on public works – digging out the great dock basins at Chatham, building the breakwater at Portland, reclaiming the unsuitable land of High Dartmoor for agriculture. The reformative value of this work was nil, and acknowledged as such. It represented punitive hard labour pure and simple.

The entire experience was terminated by a period of conditional release known as the 'ticket-of-leave' system, adapted from the Australian experience. Released convicts were required to report regularly to their local police offices, and although many of them failed to do so, the element of control built into this procedure was intended to allay public feeling about the release into their midst of these long-term prisoners.

SIR EDMUND DU CANE

When Jebb died in 1863 he was succeeded by Captain (later, Sir) Edmund Du Cane, another Royal Engineer, another architect, and a man with practical experience of penal administration in Australia.[35] But whereas Jebb had started his professional life with a positive and hopeful theory of the possibilities of prison discipline, Du Cane had to start from a position where that optimism had been confounded in practice. Jebb had never publicly renounced his earlier attachments to penitentiary ideals; and Du Cane did not distance himself explicitly from those principles until he had established a system of draconian discipline that drove out all hope in the hearts of those subjected to it. He did this first in the convict prisons, and, after the Prisons Act of 1877, he applied it to the local prisons, which had previously been administered by the justices in their idiosyncratic and inefficient fashions. The decision to nationalise all the prisons in the country followed several decades of unsuccessful attempts by central government to urge on local justices some uniformity in the administration of their separate establishments, in the form of common penal aims and standardised conditions of treatment. When they all came under the control of Sir Edmund he wasted no time in imposing his will. Several of the smaller prisons were immediately closed down;

the rest were swiftly incorporated into a national system of which a later Commissioner could boast that he knew exactly what was happening minute by minute, day by day, and week by week, in every prison under his command.[36]

The framework of this disciplinary timetable rested on two organising principles. One was an unacknowledged adoption of the 'silent' rather than the 'separate' regime, and the other was the institution of 'progressive stages' through which longer-term prisoners moved, earning by their good behaviour – or forfeiting if they were badly behaved – minute 'privileges' that slightly ameliorated the severity of the conditions they were forced to endure. The whole system was administered by a gentlemanly class of governors recruited principally from the commissioned ranks of the army or navy, and by subordinate 'officers' drawn principally from the 'other ranks' of the same services. And to the immense and unconcealed self-satisfaction of Sir Edmund Du Cane, the erection and perfection of this 'vast, punishing machine',[37] was accompanied by an undeniable abatement of serious crime as demonstrated in the annual criminal statistics.

WOMEN IN PRISON

The place of women prisoners in this history is difficult to judge. Women did not really exist in the criminal law of the nineteenth century, and had been virtually unrecognised as a separate sex by legislators. Until the reform movement of the late eighteenth century, the 'promiscuous mingling' of the sexes in the prisons of the period had been taken for granted.[38] The women were seen simply as part of the criminal underworld that continued to exist without hindrance within prison walls. When Mrs Fry 'discovered' the wretched women of Newgate in 1817 she began to work with them on a voluntary basis, offering them education, and christian compassion and a more orderly way of life, which the women themselves adopted by majority vote at their mentor's bidding.[39] Other parts of Mrs Fry's mission to Newgate concerned the consolation of those women who were condemned to be hanged, and those who were waiting to be transported to Australia – a fate that for many of them resembled something worse than death. To coordinate this work, in which other like-minded women joined, Mrs Fry formed a Ladies' Society which rapidly became a model for countless others throughout the country, and later abroad.[40] Middle-class and pious 'ladies' visited their local prisons and tried to reclaim some of their lost sisters for respectable domestic service. Voluntary 'penitentiaries' flourished in some areas: places where women were encouraged to go after their release from prison to be trained to acceptable standards of domesticity as sempstresses or as washerwomen.[41] Stimulated in part by these earnest efforts and in part by the general reforms of the prisons then taking place, women were segregated from men and put under the charge of female staffs. The prison matron became as familiar a figure as the head turnkey had previously been. Mrs Fry's societies faded away after 1850, but an echo of her work remained in the officially-managed Refuges for women prisoners at Fulham, Winchester, and elsewhere. Otherwise the treatment and management of women prisoners practically ceased to exist as a separate area of concern to prison administrators.

Into this quiet backwater of penal policy there intruded from 1905 onwards an influx of politically motivated, middle-class and socially well-connected women in the shape of the suffragettes who were imprisoned for the offences they committed in the course of their campaign for votes for women.[42] The suffragettes were horrified to discover – and share the experience of – the conditions being endured by their criminally convicted sisters.[43] In their subsequent agitations and writings they drew the attention of a wider audience to what was happening in women's prisons.[44]

VOICES FROM THE CELL

The official history of this regime and its development from the disorderly prison houses of the later eighteenth and early nineteenth centuries to the mechanical marvels of Du Cane's dispensation can be read in a voluminous literature of government blue books and annual reports. But there also exists an alternative account of these proceedings. The subjective experience of the evolving prison has been documented in a rich and uniquely detailed flow of autobiographical material from the pens of prisoners and officials throughout the period. In an earlier era the voice of the prisoner had been traditionally heard from the foot of the scaffold.[45] When executions were moved indoors by a civil authority increasingly nervous of a mass audience for displays of official barbarity, this direct contact with the thoughts of the criminal classes was lost.[46] It was preserved for a while in the gallows tracts produced for public enlightenment and private profit by the clerics who ministered to condemned prisoners until the moment of their execution. Woven around these texts, and as a kind of blasphemous descant to them, there also grew up a subterranean literature of stories about famous criminals such as Jack Sheppard.[47] These were passed on by an informal oral tradition that flourished in the flash houses and drinking dens frequented by the criminal lower classes in London and other cities.[48] But beginning in the 1830s, and with growing frequency thereafter, there began to be heard the authentic and seriously told stories of prisoners and prison officials themselves. One part of this library – a set of semi-anthropological accounts analogous to the tales of travellers returned from darkest Africa – was subscribed by gentlemanly or middle-class prisoners. Edward Gibbon Wakefield, for example, a gentleman convicted of abducting a young lady he wished to marry, spent two years in the unreformed Newgate and wrote a book about it afterwards.[49] Transportation, too, produced its chroniclers, among them the Cambridgeshire burglar Mark Jeffrey, who describes his experiences in English gaols prior to being shipped off to Australia.[50] But just as autobiography itself is a literary genre rooted in spiritual experience and its exploration, so the prison biography seeks to tell and make sense of the distinct and distinctly different prison world through which the criminal pilgrim is forced to journey between sentence and release. Prison chaplains themselves wrote compendiously, particularly after the establishment of the penitentiary regimes in the 1840s and 1850s, and some of them gathered improving life-stories of sin and conversion from members of their flocks.[51]

Penal servitude – the most extreme and dramatic of the sentences ever served on English soil – produced what is perhaps the richest crop of Victorian prison biographies. Many of these were written by fallen gentlemen writing under cover of pseudonyms like 'One Who Has Tried Them'[52] and 'One Who Has Suffered'.[53] *Five Years Penal Servitude* by 'One Who Has Endured It'[54] is the classic prison biography of the nineteenth century. The author's real name was Edward Callow, and he later gave evidence to the 1879 Royal Commission of Inquiry into Penal Servitude.[55] There were also frankly sensationalist and money-making efforts produced in the penny-dreadful format and aimed at the same market. And some biographies combined elements of all the types of the genre – that of George Bidwell, for example: sentenced to life imprisonment in 1873 for a gigantic swindle on the Bank of England and released on medical grounds after serving fourteen years.[56] Political prisoners were an equally vocal set of witnesses, keen to use their experiences in prison as a vehicle for propaganda against the governments they opposed: the Chartists,[57] the Fenians,[58] and the Suffragettes[59] all made significant contributions to a growing literature.

Although the details of any particular biography may be distorted by the perceptions and intentions of its author, the whole corpus of work presents a picture in which the main outlines are clearly confirmed from many sources. The picture they present is an horrific one: an inhuman system, inhumanly administered; great mental and physical suffering redeemed by tiny glimpses of essential goodness from fellow prisoners and some members of the prison staffs. Running through the pages of the prisoners' tales, whether they are religiously, politically, or financially motivated, there is an obvious desire to understand and explain a bizarre social experience and to publicise the details of an otherwise concealed world. And perhaps most importantly of all, they constitute an attempt on the part of their various authors to redeem the years of lost time and to make them count for something – not least the possible reform of the system under which the authors had suffered. In this last aim some of the nineteenth-century authors were not unsuccessful: the strictures of 'One Who Has Endured It', and of the Irish prisoners Jeremiah O'Donovan Rossa and Michael Davitt, all contributed to the creation of a climate that led in time to the establishment of the Gladstone Committee in 1895; that in turn led to the condemnation of the whole of the Du Cane era as one of inhumanity.

Stephen Hobhouse and Fenner Brockway had been political prisoners during the First World War, and their book *English Prisons Today*, which collected testimony from former prisoners and prison staff, was consciously designed to tap into the reformist stream of prison biography. It too was successful in pointing to the absurdities and cruelties of the system still existing in English prisons as late as 1918. What happened next in the English prison system of the twentieth century is the subject of the rest of this book, which gathers together voices from the cell and from prison officials to tell the continuing story in their own words.

NOTES

1 Statistics of the Military Effort of the British Empire in the Great War 1914–1920, The War Office, 1922.

2 Report of the Central Tribunal, 1919, p. 25.
3 Stephen Hobhouse and Fenner Brockway (1922) *English Prisons Today*, London: Longman.
4 Ibid., p. 561.
5 Sir Edmund F. Du Cane (1885) *The Punishment and Prevention of Crime*, London: Macmillan.
6 Report from the Departmental Committee on Prisons. PP. 1895.(C.7702) LV 1. p. 7.
7 Ibid., p. 7.
8 Shane Leslie (1938) *Sir Evelyn Ruggles-Brise*, London: John Murray, p. 87.
9 Ibid., p. 93.
10 Sir Leon Radzinowicz and Roger Hood (1986) *A History of English Criminal Law and its Administration from 1750*, vol. V, *The Emergence of Penal Policy*, London: Stevens, p. 770.
11 John Howard (1777) *The State of the Prisons in England and Wales*, Warrington: Wm Eyres, p. 395.
12 Ibid., p. 322.
13 George Laval Chesterton (1856) *Revelations of Prison Life*, vol. II, Hurst & Blackett, p. 135.
14 Edward Gibbon Wakefield (1831) *Facts Relating to the Punishment of Death in the Metropolis*, London: Effingham Wilson.
15 William Hepworth Dixon (1869) *Her Majesty's Tower*, 4 vols, London: Hurst & Blackett.
16 W. Branch Johnson (1957) *The English Prison Hulks*, Christopher Johnston.
17 W. and J. Hiener (eds) (1968) *A Burglar's Life*, Sydney: Angus & Robertson, p. 57.
18 *The Voyage of Governor Phillip to Botany Bay* (1789) London: John Stockdale.
19 Robert Hughes (1987) *The Fatal Shore*, London: Collins Harvill.
20 Jeremy Bentham (1791) *Panopticon; or, The Inspection House*, London.
21 Capt. Arthur Griffiths (1875) *Memorials of Millbank and Chapters in Prison History*, 2 vols, London: Henry S. King.
22 Reverend Daniel Nihill (1839) *Prison Discipline in its Relations to Society and Individuals*, London: Hatchard.
23 Sean McConville (1981) *A History of English Prison Administration*, vol. I, 1750–1877, London: Routledge & Kegan Paul.
24 Radzinowicz and Hood, op. cit.
25 William Hepworth Dixon (1850) *The London Prisons*, London: John Murray, p. 10.
26 Du Cane. op. cit.
27 Michael Ignatieff (1978) *A Just Measure of Pain. The Penitentiary in the Industrial Revolution*, London: Macmillan.
28 Chesterton, op. cit.
29 Charles Dickens (1842) *American Notes*, London: Chapman and Hall.
30 Select Committee of the House of Lords on Gaols and Houses of Correction in England and Wales, 1835, XI. 1, p. 438.
31 Estimate based on judicial and criminal statistics for the period; these are not accurate for the earlier part of the century. The total includes those committed for trial, committed for sentence, on conviction, in default of fine payments, and those detained in connection with other civil matters.
32 Robert Hindle (nd) *Salford's Prison*, Salford Local History Society, p. 11.
33 Thomas Carlyle (1850) 'Model Prisons' in *Latter Day Pamphlets*, London: Chapman and Hall.
34 Colonel Joshua Jebb (1844) *Modern Prisons: Their Construction and Ventilation*, London: John Weale.

35 Lady Alexandra Hasluck (1973) *Royal Engineer: A Life of Sir Edmund Du Cane*, Sydney: Angus & Robertson.

36 Shane Leslie, op. cit.

37 Michael Davitt (1885) *Leaves from a Prison Diary*, vol. I, London: Chapman and Hall, p. 249.

38 James Neild (1812) *The State of the Prisons in England, Scotland and Wales*, London: John Nichols, p. v.

39 *Memoir of the Life of Elizabeth Fry with Extracts from her Journal and Letters* (1847) vol. I, London: Hatchard, p. 265.

40 Maria Wrench (1852) *Visits to Female Prisoners at Home and Abroad*, Wertheim.

41 Susanna Meredith (nd) *Washing for Love*, London: Nine Elms Tales.

42 Sylvia Pankhurst (1911) *The Suffragette Movement*, London: Longmans Green.

43 Constance Lytton (1914) *Prisons and Prisoners*, London: Heinemann.

44 Helen Gordon (1911) *The Prisoner – A Sketch*, Letchworth: Garden City Press.

45 Reverend C.B. Tayler (1849) *Facts in a Clergyman's Life*, London: Seeleys, p. 199.

46 Sir Edmund Du Cane, op. c t.

47 W.H. Ainsworth (1839) *Jack Sheppard*, London: Richard Bentley.

48 *Old Bailey Experience . . . by the Author of 'The Schoolmaster's Experience in Newgate'* (1833), London: James Fraser.

49 Edward Gibbon Wakefield, op. cit.

50 W. and J. Hiener (eds), op. cit.

51 Walter Lowe Clay (1861) *The Prison Chaplain – A Memoir of the Rev. John Clay*, London: Macmillan.

52 *Her Majesty's Prisons and their Effects and Defects by One Who Has Tried Them* (1881), London: Sampson Low.

53 *Revelations of Prison Life by One Who Has Suffered* (1882), Potter.

54 *Five Years Penal Servitude by One Who Has Endured It* (1877), London: Richard Bentley.

55 Report of the Committee Appointed to Inquire into the Working of the Penal Servitude Acts, PP 1878–9 (c.2368) XXXXVII,1.

56 George Bidwell (1888) *Forging his Chains. The Autobiography of George Bidwell*, Hartford, Conn.: Scranton.

57 Thomas Cooper (1872) *The Life of Thomas Cooper. Written by Himself*, London: Hodder and Stoughton.

58 Jeremiah O'Donovan Rossa (1882) *Irish Rebels in English Prisons*, New York: D.J. Sadleir.

59 Helen Gordon, op. cit.

BOOK ONE

Into Prison

Pentonville Prison

'Take him down,' said God, and it's nine-steps down to the holding cell beneath the court. Up above, pomp, dignity, the majesty of the law. Directly underneath, accumulation of dirt and litter and hard-backed benches and hobgoblins of creation. If only the people in the public gallery could unzip the floor and look at us now. They'd see past the pompous acting of wig and ermine, maybe. Up there polished oak and no dust anywhere. Down below, a devil's brew of atmosphere, dirt, lads and men – all shut away from the searchlight of public knowledge. At midday a warder unlocked the holding cell door and two more warders came in carrying a tray loaded up with stale cobs of bread and butter and a bucket of near-cold tea. They poured the tea into paper cups – a thin, watery brew – and the bread was tossed at us like fodder to cattle. Such was lunch; and two more hours had to pass before judge and barristers and solicitors worked their ways through five-course lunches and bottles of claret at a nearby hotel. (Archie Hill, *A Cage of Shadows*, 1973, pp. 232–3)

'Oh God, nine months ...'

The temporary accommodation for prisoners sent up for trial appalled me. The whole of the court is a glare of unnecessary electric light, but these cells are left almost in darkness, and, as one passes along the corridor, one can just see white anxious faces peering out, dim as fish in an obscure tank. The cells are scrabbled over here and there with declarations of human misery. I noticed one scratched on the open door of a cell whose occupant had gone up to stand in the dock – *'Oh God, nine months. What will my poor wife do?'*

How such accommodation for prisoners about to stand their trial can be reconciled with the parrot-cry that the English law presumes the innocence of the accused until he is found guilty, I leave readers to decide. (Compton Mackenzie, in *Walls Have Mouths*, W.F.R. Macartney, 1936, p. 44)

A Black Maria

The prisoners, about eight in number, were taken out to the back of the building, where stood a motor vehicle with the engine purring. It was a Black Maria, familiar to most Londoners by sight. Few people stop to realize the load of anguish and despair which it carries daily.

The prisoners filed in, and were locked up in narrow compartments hardly big enough to hold a fully grown man. I am about 5 feet 10 inches in height, but my head touched the roof, and there was not sufficient room to enable me to stretch my legs. The cell had no light of its own, and the window consisted of wooden shutters the slats of which sloped abruptly to the ground, so that only the roadway immediately below was visible. To anyone subject to claustrophobia this experience must be terrifying, and the close confinement following the mental torture of the trial nearly drove me crazy. (Richmond Harvey, *Prison From Within*, 1937, p. 13)

When we at last passed through Pentonville gateway, and I heard the doors clang to behind us, I thought to myself: 'Hello, back at it once more!' The dreary, depressing prison atmosphere gripped one immediately; the grim silence and bleakness of it all. (Trevor Allen, *Underworld*, 1932, p. 145)

Pentonville gateway

We were led up to a desk where sat a heavily built, black-moustached warder who had just been handed the number of 'body-receipts' corresponding to the total of the men admitted. He then called the name of the man on each receipt and asked from what police court they had been remanded, and for how long. As each man answers the warder checks his statement, and tells him to 'sit down on that form and be quiet'. (F.A. Stanley, *A Happy Fortnight*, 1938, p. 310)

Body receipts

'Name!' bawled the reception officer.
'Gordon James.'
'Gordon James, What?'
'Gordon James, man, just Gordon James.'
'Not just Gordon James you stupid black twat! Gordon James, sir!'
'Gordon James, sir.'
'What religion, James?'
'Church of God.'
'Church of God? Church of God? What the fucking hell's that?'
'Well, sir, it's ...'
'Don't tell me what it is! I don't want to know what it is! You've got no religion! You're a fucking Moss Side Ponce! That's your fucking religion! ... We got fucking hundreds of you bastards in here ... every one a fucking ponce! It's a fucking religion with you blokes. If I had my way, I wouldn't nick you, I'd fucking well top the lot of you! While you're here you'll be Church of England and like it! Empty your pockets!' (Ron Phillips, 'The Black Prisoner's Subjective View,' *Race Today*, June 1974)

Name!

'And 'old up your 'ead, when I speak to you.'
''Old up your 'ead, when Mr Whitbread speaks to you,' said Mr Holmes.

'And 'old up your 'ead.'

I looked round at Charlie. His eyes met mine and he quickly lowered them to the ground.

'What are you looking round at, Behan? Look at me.' ...

I looked at Mr Whitbread. 'I am looking at you,' I said.

'You are looking at Mr Whitbread – what?' said Mr Holmes.

'I am looking at Mr Whitbread.'

Mr Holmes looked gravely at Mr Whitbread, drew back his open hand, and struck me on the face, held me with his other hand and struck me again.

My head spun and burned and pained and I wondered would it happen again. I forgot and felt another smack, and forgot, and another, and moved, and was held by a steadying, almost kindly hand, and another, and my sight was a vision of red and white and pity-coloured flashes.

'You are looking at Mr Whitbread – what, Behan?'

I gulped and got together my voice and tried again till I got it out. 'I, sir, please, sir, I am looking at you, I mean, I am looking at Mr Whitbread, sir.' (Brendan Behan, *Borstal Boy*, 1958, pp. 41–5)

Touch my toes   I vaguely remember the ordeal of the reception where I was told to strip in front of an officer and, while standing behind a screen completely naked, was ordered to touch my toes. Not quite knowing why but half afraid it meant a beating I asked the officer the reason, only to be told, 'To look up your arse for contraband of course, boy. What do you bloody well think?' (Andrew Keith Munro, *Autobiography of a Thief*, 1972, p. 19)

'He must be   I was told to undress and have a bath. No door to the bathroom –
queer.'   just a bath. Smells of carbolic. A scrubbed board with slats in it lay on the floor and a well-used rough towel waited for me to dry myself. They had stripped me off and searched me; some old lags often hide tobacco or hashish on themselves, so a thorough search was necessary for every new prisoner before he was allowed into the confines of that hallowed place of rationed tobacco and no drugs. It was a little embarrassing, and it was necessary to cast off a little more of my individuality in order to cope with the situation. Why the officer wanted to chat with me while I had my bath I didn't know; maybe it was to make sure I didn't escape. My first thought at the time was that he must be queer, so I had a very modest bath and clambered into my prison clothes as quickly as possible. They stank. They were rough and hard. They were too big and too small. They had holes. They could have had W.D. printed on them with arrows and it would not have seemed out of place. As it was, I was glad to get anything on. (Roy Catchpole, *The Key to Freedom*, 1974, p. 21)

When the prisoner is admitted, he receives one shirt which he wears, and another which he takes with him to his cell. This does not mean, however, as at first sight appears, that he is, in fact, issued with two shirts. One of these must serve as his nightshirt. He is permitted to change one dirty shirt for one clean one each week. (He does this at his weekly bath.) He is intended to use one shirt for sleeping in his first week. At the end of the week, he is to exchange his day shirt for a clean one, which he is to use for sleeping; the shirt in which he has slept during the previous week serves as his day shirt for the ensuing week. Thus, during the whole period of his sentence, he will never be able to wear a clean day shirt. (Norman Howarth Hignett, *Portrait in Grey*, 1956, p. 101)

Two shirts

On your arrival Governor Hawkins (ex-RN retired) makes it quite clear that he is not running a pleasure-boat. But it is a boat, a ship, there is no doubt in my mind about that. A world of numbers and steel and the heavy crash of iron doors and boots ringing up and down the companionways, the bridges, and decks of this ship sailing nowhere. The steel is not only cold but clammy to the touch. The cells are of whitewashed stone with scrubbed floors and a half-moon grille. Each deck is prefixed by a letter followed by two sets of numbers and each peter has an odour of disinfectant pervading over the spreading corrosion of flesh and brick. Everything is grey, the walls, faces, uniforms: except at night when a pilot light burns in the well of the hall and the steel becomes gunmetal blue, gleaming in the webbed catwalks and netting like some giant armoury with the guards awaiting the signal to open fire. ... (Jim Stockton, *Runaway*, 1968, p. 135)

A world of numbers and steel

This is Civilisation, the compass and ruled lines of a draughtsman, making exact uniformity, each segment of the orange alike, each filled with silent solitary souls. Damn the psychic vice of such a designing brain. Little need now for flogging, dungeons and foulness. You can do it with clean air and light. Just make everything the same – so silent – so solitary – so inhumanly civilised. (Jack Hilton, *Caliban Shrieks*, 1935, pp. 108–9)

This is Civilisation

A second warder, who had been champing by a linen-room hard by, came up and took me. He was allowed to do no other service while waiting for me to be bathed. He was tight-lipped, tubby; his neck rolled up shinily to the bald ball of his head-back like a snapped old grapefruit; he waddled as he led me to an oblong hall splatted with ducky little cell doors. By them nestled buckets as friendly as milk bottles on the early morning steps. From the

Ducky little cell doors

buckets scrubbing brushes stuck out like elbows. The figure of the warder himself was something like a champagne bottle in a bucket, not that I ever saw one outside the pictures. He led me to the top landing up three stair flights, and pushed me into a cell. 'Remember your number,' he said. 'O.K.,' I said, but as he cracked the door shut I forgot it. It had something to do with A, but as that was the letter for the whole top landing, that did not help. (Hippo Neville, *Sneak Thief on the Road*, 1935, pp. 298–9)

 The cell

A prison cell is not an attractive pied-a-terre nor does it contain the accoutrements for gracious living. As I stood with my back to the door I faced an expanse of painted brick wall, the only break in it being the sole source of light, a small and heavily barred window set high up. On my right was the bed, a stout tubular steel and wire contraption hinged to the wall, and over in the far corner a triangular table bearing an enamelled bowl and jug and beneath it, on the floor, that relic of Victorian bed-rooms, a pisspot. Against the left-hand wall stood a small but sturdy wooden table with a matching chair, and that was the lot. The decor was Home Office green and light brown, embellished with graffiti some of which, when I got round to studying it, was highly erudite. But it was the door that was the monster, a massive barrier with a peephole covered from the outside, a steel and wood Cyclops that came to life when a large key was thrust into its ancient innards. That door was my enemy. On the other side of it was freedom, fresh air and sunshine, golden sands and a warm blue sea, woods and green fields and the open sky. On my side was the breeding ground of despair and hopelessness. Fuck it, I thought, now is the time to make the best of a bad job. (Charles Kray, *Me and My Brothers*, 1976, pp. 115–16)

The sudden click

At night-time the officers are supplied with felt slippers in which they creep round the landings and spy upon the prisoners to see whether they are doing their cell tasks. The only warning one has of their presence is the sudden click of the tiny shutter. This is usually only heard after the officer has finished his inspection, as he opens it carefully and without sound. It is most unnerving to look up suddenly and see an eye staring at one. (H.W. Wicks, *The Prisoner Speaks*, 1938, pp. 27–8)

Into prison

Like sitting in a room with rough-cast bricks, a barred window and a door that is locked from the outside.

What is it like to be locked in a cell?

I once wrote that a prison cell was 'like a hole in the wall, like a world of thought, like an optical illusion, a place where men die, where men are born. It always takes something away from you, mostly that which is good.' Being locked in a cell is one of the unhappiest things you could imagine. There is no way out, it's a frustrating thing to experience.

One guy said to me years ago: 'If you want freedom, you can get it in a cell – all you have to say is, "There must be a better place than this."' A nice thought, but hard to visualise, doing twenty-five years. (Jonathan Marshall, *How to Survive in the Nick*, 1974, p. 29)

Sometimes the smell in these triple cells becomes so offensive that the convicts try to smother it by placing their own clothing over the chamber pots at night. The result is that their very clothes become impregnated with the smell. It is quite revolting.

Mass filth campaign

At Pentonville and Wandsworth the lags got so disgusted that they decided to organise a mass filth campaign in an attempt to bring about some improvement in the vile conditions. In a mass demonstration of protest they began hurling the contents of the chamber pots out of the cell windows until the exercise yards and grounds looked like laystalls.

Some lags went even further and tipped the contents of their chamber pots over the heads of the screws. This is all quite revolting, but if the prison authorities take the last vestige of human decency away from men how do they expect them to behave? How a supposedly enlightened Home Office and conscientious Prison Commissioners can tolerate such an abominable state of affairs without taking drastic steps to remedy it is beyond my comprehension. (Robert Sykes, *Who's Been Eating My Porridge?*, 1967, p. 96)

⤜ First night ⤛

'Get your bed down at once,' he ordered. 'In fifteen minutes I'll turn the light out, whether you're ready or not,' and with that he shut the door, and I was alone.

There was no time for the moment to think of my situation. I had no wish to be caught in the dark, and without more ado I turned my attention to bed-making. Three planks attached to two pieces of scantling stood against the wall, together with a hard coir mattress, on which reposed a pillow of the same material, two sheets, and two blankets. The whole formed a bed raised about two inches from the floor. An electric light burned dimly above the door, but its feebleness only emphasized the general depression of the place and the weariness of my own mind.

The warder was as good as his word. Within fifteen minutes his footsteps could be heard approaching, there was a loud click outside the door, and the cell was plunged in Egyptian darkness. But sleep was out of the question. The day had been too eventful, and my nerves and brain were strung to a pitch which precluded rest. Moreover, the bed was abominably hard and uncomfortable, and I tossed and turned about, vainly endeavouring to banish the thoughts that kept clamouring for admission. (Richmond Harvey, *Prison From Within*, 1937, pp. 19–20)

Chinese water-torture

All the events of recent weeks surged over me, I knew grief and horror and remorse, but could not and would not cry. Hours later – it could have been days later – the light went out; and, during the whole night, it kept on being turned on again at regular intervals while I heard someone at the spyhole. It was as though uncountable harriers had been despatched to follow and watch

Into prison

and mock me. It was only two years later that I learned that the authorities had put me on half-hourly special watch for the first week, because they feared I would do away with myself. Actually nothing was ever further from my mind.

As the days, the months and the years wore on, I was to learn of the pointlessness, the weariness and the monotony of a seven-year sentence. I was to learn that the greater punishment falls upon those outside, the wife and children who wait. I was to learn of the wicked waste of time and opportunity. Although during those years I saw vast improvements in the atmosphere, organisation and amenities of our prisons, wasted time continues to provide a sort of temporal Chinese water-torture that only those who have been captive can comprehend.

But that was all to come. The only lesson I learned on first impact was that, while the punishment, the test of character, the rehabilitation, may all be, as some men say, in the slow passage of a seven-year sentence, the greatest bitterness and shock are concentrated in the first seven days.

And the epitome of the complete, puzzled desolation is in the first night. (Peter Baker, *Time Out of Life*, 1961, pp. 12–13)

⤛ Slopping out ⤜

A hopeless, endless first night. Then the morning. Tolling bell. Door flung open. 'Empty your slops!' Porridge and bread. Spoon, prayer-book, educational book, prison number. Great bare halls, radiating from central hall like spokes of a wheel, iron staircases and balconies enclosed by wire netting, like the gangways of a ship's engine-room. Heavy doors studded with bolts and locks. Hollow-sounding footsteps. Continuous clinking of warders' keys. 'Stop talking there!' (Trevor Allen, *Underworld*, 1932, p. 146)

Presently, my own cell was unlocked. I took a tentative glance *I turned away* outside. Men carrying chamberpots, basins and buckets, trooped past. Emptying my slops into the stinking chamber, I followed them and joined the long queue that was forming at the recess in which were a lavatory and a large sink, with a cold water tap, into which the men emptied their chambers. The stench was nauseating and soon the stone floor was swimming with spilt urine and water.

'The f——er's stopped up again!' one of the prisoners told me. 'Some c——t's thrown 'is cob darn it!'

By the time I reached it, the sink was filled to the brim and overflowing. On the top of it floated a layer of human excreta. Retching, I turned away and threw the contents of my pot down the lavatory. (Anthony Heckstall-Smith, *Eighteen Months*, 1954, pp. 20–1)

One or two deprecatory observations

Criticism of these arrangements centres first on the disadvantages of the chamber-pot, and then on the nature of the recesses and WC provision generally. As to this, one or two deprecatory observations may be ventured. Prisons were not designed for those from whom this sort of criticism most generally emanates; and while we should no doubt do better if we were building today, the normal habits of large numbers of the prison population still fall short of refinement. And making all due allowance for this, is either the standard of fitting or the cleanliness of a modern prison WC *much* below the average of similar accommodation in – say – railway stations and public places? As for the chamber-pot, the difficulties of dispensing with it have already been discussed, and it is after all not peculiar to a prison cell. The principal objection is to the unsavoury process of 'slopping out' on morning unlocking, when the prisoners line up to empty their slops at the recesses. This objection must be sustained; but the slops must also be emptied. The solution of the problem, in spite of constant thought, has not yet emerged. (Sir Lionel Fox, *The English Prison and Borstal Systems*, 1952, pp. 228–9)

And the smell ...!

And the smell ...! Try to imagine several hundreds of men who have been confined in their cells for periods of up to fourteen hours and so unable to get out to obey the call of nature – imagine them all emptying their chamber pots at seven o'clock in the morning. Three men in a cell means three chamber pots. The occupants have to sleep with this stench all around them. In recent years the recesses where the pots are emptied have had the walls tiled instead of being whitewashed, and in some cases an exhaust fan has been fitted into the window bars; but no exhaust fan yet invented can entirely take away this lingering smell.

And still they preach about prison being educational and reformative, fitting the wrongdoer to take his place in civilised society when at last he is released. Short of shitting on the carpet twice a day and leaving it there, I can't see how any ex-prisoner can dutifully practise outside what he has learnt inside. (Harry Houghton, *Operation Portland*, 1972, p. 133)

Hard labour?

Wandsworth Prison had an association where prisoners, sitting a couple of feet apart, engaged in the production of mail bags. It was a large hall, with a cutting table at the end opposite the doorway. Midway on either side was a platform on which a discipline warder sat, keeping a watchful eye on all that went on. Another two warders were in charge of the work and, in general, took no notice of whether or no the prisoners engaged in conversation. 'No Talking' had been a very strict rule here, but shortly before we arrived the rule had been withdrawn. We were therefore at the mercy of the discipline warders. You might exchange a few remarks with a neighbour, and then hear the warder shout: 'That'll be enough talking!' If you continued, you'd be for it, not for talking but for disobeying an order. (That's how it worked when we were in: I don't know if it is still the same.) (William Gallacher, *The Last Memories of W. Gallacher*, 1966, p. 207)

The 'Tin Tailors' was almost entirely composed of 'old lags', chiefly (though not exclusively) of the elderly variety. Every type of criminal, every type of crime, was represented. My first reaction to them had an element of that which Fox expresses: an instinct of repulsion, of the sort which Francis of Assisi overcame in embracing the leper. But I was one of them; my previous motoring offence had caused the Commissioners to assign me to their company; and I could do nothing about it.

My first dirty mail-bag

I took my seat amongst them, on the metal chair, in an atmosphere pregnant with silently excited curiosity. I received my first dirty mail-bag, and made my first essay into the mysterious art of darning. I shall not attempt to express the fabric of my mind. But I became suddenly conscious of a sense of warmth, of friendship, of sympathy; I ventured a quick look round, and I saw in the eyes of these men messages which they could never have articulated even if freedom of speech were to have been accorded to them. I was profoundly moved: I felt something of that depth of feeling which, for me, is always most deeply stirred by powerful music in a church setting; I felt that I was in a holy place as realistically as I also knew that I was in a place of ugliness and squalor.

As we formed to go in for my first midday meal, one of these 'hardened recividists' pressed into my hand two thinly rolled cigarettes, a piece of matchbox, and two split matches. He was an old man with white hair; I never knew his name; but if ever it could be that these words reach him, I hope that he will realise my abiding and grateful remembrance of his Christian and generous gift. (Norman Howarth Hignett, *Portrait in Grey*, 1956, pp. 254–5)

Stone-breaking Fog and rain had prevented us going outside the prison walls for labour, so we were ordered stone-breaking in the weather sheds. This meant sitting down on wooden benches at one-yard intervals and facing a long stone platform. With iron hammers we reduced granite pieces to small flints. To prevent eye injuries each of us wore a pair of close-mesh wire goggles, but the wearing of them made the surroundings assume semi-darkness. With the heavy fog, damp atmosphere, and the roar of the stone-crushing machine behind us, the job warped our very souls. (W.G. Davis, *Gentlemen of the Broad Arrows*, 1939, p. 128)

Hammered into dust 'C' wing was out of commission. During the war it received a direct hit from a bomb, and had since been uninhabitable, even by prison standards. The bomb had cleaved through the building, and left a sixty-foot gap between the sections. It was now possible to stand in 'D' yard and see through to 'C' yard. The task allotted to the 'D' yard contingent was to collect salvage bricks and stone from the rubble of 'C' wing, break it into smaller pieces, and load it into wheelbarrows. The reduced rubble would then go to the hammer party, who would hammer it into fine chips. The fine chips were then hammered into dust, and rolled into the paths by the roller gang.

This ridiculous task went on for several years, because I've spoken to people who did it long after I had left. (L.J. Cunliffe, *Having It Away*, 1965, p. 58)

Going to be ripped out Sudbury used to be an American army base and the conditions were appalling. Each billet had an antiquated stove and the coke fumes affected prisoners' chests. While we were there, a firm of contractors installed a warm air duct system. The senior medical officer condemned it as inadequate, but the contract had already been signed. The workmen told us that when the contract was finished all the ducts were going to be ripped out and a new system built. They were working on the lump. They were laughing about it all and commented: 'Whoever was in charge of these contracts at the Home Office must be Father Christmas.' (Des Warren, *The Key to My Cell*, 1982, p. 88)

The silence of the roaring looms To my great satisfaction and joy I was told to join the power-loom party. Here in the weaving shed I felt happier, following my old trade, and I was able to study again whilst working, writing on the steel of the breast-beam. I was cut off, too, for a large part of the day by the clatter of the looms from the empty or obscene chatter of some of the convicts, which I found was not always a boon and privilege to hear, on the contrary often being humiliating and degrading in the extreme.... Here in the weaving shed I enjoyed the silence which reposes at the very heart of the steady, monotonous roar of machinery – the silence of the roaring looms which I learned to love as a boy. (William Holt, *I Was a Prisoner*, 1934, p. 52)

My time was spent in the tailor's shop, where I passed my hours *Bearable* making civil defence jackets for women, and boiler suits and other rather unglamorous garments. But it was the tailoring instructor, Mr Millman, who perhaps did more than anyone else to make life bearable. He made one's life that little bit better, always trying to be amusing and seeing the funny side of any crazy new regulation that suddenly emanated from the Home Office. (John Vassall, *Vassall – The Autobiography of a Spy*, 1975, p. 160)

In the workshop we painted toys. I was on Bugs Bunnies, which *Bugs Bunnies* in those days had green shoes with red bows on them, and that was my job, painting their shoes. I quite enjoyed it, mainly because the officer in charge of us was the nicest screw I'd met, a chap known as 'Ginger'. Everyone respected him. He had a bunch of tough villains on his hands, but he knew how to get the best out of us and there was never any trouble in his workshop. (Frances Finlay, *Boy in Prison*, 1971, p. 28)

The problem of prison labour is a microcosm of what is, perhaps, *The last and* the last and greatest problem of democracy: how to produce a *greatest* nation of willing and intelligent workers, for work waiting to be *problem of* done, in a mechanized age. If prison experience is aught, the *democracy* 'conscript State' is no solution. Pressed labour and good citizenship do not go together. And it seems to me that the whole argument of Karl Marx is vitiated by his lack of imagination to foresee the scientific and mechanical achievements of the twentieth century.

If a man is deprived of all personal power over the material world of things, of all personal freedom in his economic life, he becomes the slave of society and the State, which will deprive him as well of the freedom of thought, conscience and speech, of the right to move about and even the right to live. (Nicolas Berdyaev, *The Destiny of Man*)

(James Leigh, *My Prison House*, 1941, pp. 116–17)

Into prison

Exercise

You have most likely seen a dart board, well an exercise ground is similar. It is rings inside one another. These rings are made of stone flags; it is like walking on the flags in the street only you walk round and round. The young and energetic walk on the outer rings briskly, and the proportionately less mobile crawl on the graduating inner small rings. The energetic squad on the outer ring move round and round ever turning to their right, those moving in the ring just inside of them, walk the reverse way, those inside them keep walking right and those who are the slowest crew crawl along the innermost ring continually turning left. You see you are always walking away from the men inner to you. This prevents it being the companionable stroll of four deep. To check you from holding conversation with the men traversing the same ring as you, you are spaced about three yards away from one another. As a further precaution two screws are watching you from points opposite to each other. The most you can snatch with your fellow prisoner is about two words a stroll round, and by the time you've finished a sentence, your exercise time is about up. If you happen to get too near the man in front, the screw puts up his hand and you then have to stop until there's a sufficient distance between you to prevent talking. (Jack Hilton, *Caliban Shrieks*, 1935, pp. 116–17)

Exercise yard

EXERCISE YARD

```
        d a n d r o u n d a n d r o u n d
       n                               a
      u                                 n
     o                                   d
    r                                     r
   d                                       o
  n                                         u
 a                                           n
d                                             d
 n                                             a
  u                                             n
 o                                               d
 r                                                d
  o                                              n
   u                                            u
    n                                          o
     d                                        r
      a                                      d
       n                                    n
        d                                  a
         r                                d
          o                              n
           u n d a n d r o u n d a n d r o u
```

Malcolm J. (28)   Offence: fraud   Sentence: 4 years
(Tony Parker (ed.), *The Man Inside*, 1973, p. 111)

Into prison

Oxford Prison

✦ Food ✦

After a time it opened again and a warder shouted at me to take
my breakfast, brought round by another prisoner. I was handed a
large stone jar of the kind that holds jam or marmalade. It was
nearly full of a greyish-looking thickened liquid which I presumed
was called porridge – a description which should have made any
Scots-born official in the place rise in wrath. Along with it came a
small canister of milk. As soon as the door closed I tried the milk.
It was sour, a type which was quite a familiar food in poor
Scottish homes. I could not drink it and though I tried the
porridge my stomach would have nothing to do with it.
(Emmanuel Shinwell, *Conflict Without Malice*, 1955, p. 69)

The' was one day the party was called to the gate house to offload   *Pig-meal*
porrige. It used to come in sacks, hessian sacks. Ah got a bag an'
ah carried it into the part one store an' it was stamped 'Canadian
pig meal Grade One' an' that's the truth. An ahve also off loaded
tins of bully beef with the government stamp, the arrow, an'

'1941', '1942', on, thats what we had to eat. That's what we had to eat. Shite. The food was like crap, mass productive, steamed. It didn't do anybody any good, ah kna it didn't dee me any good 'cause that's the way me stomach is today, through prison grub.(*Nee Gud Luck in Dorham Jail*, 1985, p. 37)

Sea pie   The next thing the prison authorities do is to publish a false prospectus in the shape of a menu given to every convict; and how pleasant to read the various dinners! – 'treacle pudding' (it's like a dirty old rubber sponge); 'beef-steak pudding'; 'savoury bacon'; 'sea pie'; 'beef stew'; 'pork soup', etc. The vile concoctions masquerading under these honest names might make a hungry pig vomit with disgust. 'Sea pie' is a mess in a filthy tin, defying analysis. The top is a livid scum, patterned with a pallid tracery of cooling grey grease, and just below this fearsome surface rests a lump of grey matter like an incised tumour, the dirty dices of pale pink, half-cooked carrots heightening the diseased anatomical resemblance. The stuff looks as if its real home were a white pail in an operating theatre. The foregoing description, with suitable variations, applies to all the dinners except bully-beef, or, as the menu calls it for one day's diet, 'preserved meat', and for another day's diet 'meat preserve'; with pickles, mark you! – one small onion if you're lucky; a few skins is the usual amount.

    For breakfast: tea (1 pint to one lag), ½ pint of porridge, 8 oz of bread, and 1 oz of margarine. Year in and year out this never varies. For supper, the last of the three meals of the day, served at 4.30 p.m., 1 pint of cocoa, 10 oz of bread, 1 oz of cheese, and 1 oz of margarine; and this meal also persists throughout a man's sentence, whether it be three years or twenty. (W.F.R. Macartney, *Walls Have Mouths*, 1936, pp. 122–3)

Smelling of the urine   At twelve or soon after, the bell rang for dinner, followed once again by the shout of 'Orderlies'. The procedure was much the same as for breakfast. Each prisoner, as his cell was opened, received a round can on top of which rested a smaller tin. The small tin contained potatoes cooked in their jackets with many unwinking black eyes – quite frequently they were uneatable – and cabbage, stringy and gritty, and quite often still smelling of the urine sprinkled on it by the prison cats as it lay in the kitchen yard. In the bottom tin was a portion of dinner, bacon and beans or shepherd's pie, hotpot, haricot mutton, roast beef, boiled beef and dumplings, stewed steak or corned beef. Once every ten days there was treacle pudding as well. With the day's dinner came two ounces of bread, the whole meal not exceeding twenty-eight ounces per prisoner. Usually it was eaten out of the tin with a spoon while still warm, then the tins were wiped round with the fingers, which were licked clean by the tongue. The tins did not need much cleaning when returned to the kitchen. (Richard P. Maxwell, *Borstal and Better*, 1956, p. 89)

The fact is that the prisoners' rations are 'milked' a dozen times between the store and the cell. What is not sold outside the prison by screws is bartered inside by tobacco-hungry lags. When food rationing was most strictly in force the rations provided to the civilian population by the Ministry of Food were generally considered to be the minimum required to keep a person in health. Yet prisoners did not and do not get even these basic rations. (George Dendrickson and Frederick Thomas, *The Truth about Dartmoor*, 1954, p. 180)

'Milked'

At the foot of each cell door there was a nine-inch gap, so that if a strap broke on the hammock during the night you could ring the bell and push the hammock strap under the door so the night warden could renew it without opening you up for security. You could also put your pudding under the door for syrup at dinner time, so the prisoner on orderly duty called out to me the first day. I pushed my pudding out, and he ate it. I only saw his feet otherwise I might have committed violence. (J.W. Fletcher, *A Menace to Society*, 1972, pp. 62–3)

'Put your pudding under the door ...'

BOOK TWO

The Men in Grey

Wormwood Scrubs Prison

In Dartmoor I found five distinct types of men and criminals. The professional criminal who finds himself in Dartmoor is judged a failure. I discovered in Dartmoor men of refinement, men of the highest intellect, and also men whose very contact was contamination. To describe the last as lower than the beasts would be an insult to the beasts. I should therefore divide my five classes as follows.

Class I. – Men of good education, in trouble through bad luck and force of circumstances. Thus, Major ——— had helped a friend by going surety for him in a loan. The friend let him down, and Major ——— had to pay. The major had a small business, trade grew bad, and he found himself in debt. This was the beginning of the end.

Poverty is one cause of a certain number of men being in Dartmoor, and I contend that Dartmoor is a possibility for thousands of English citizens who have never yet seen its portals.

Class II. – The most highly respected of Dartmoor's inhabitants. In this class we find the professional crook, the burglar, the forger, the 'con' man, and his host of touts and dupes. These 'lads' cling together like the ivy. If a newspaper is smuggled into prison, it goes the whole round of Class II. I've seen ten of them sharing a piece of tobacco the size of a pea. And (let me whisper this) I found the majority of this class decent men, good sportsmen, who did not squeal at their sentence.

This class make crime a profession. Many a crime is hatched in Dartmoor Prison; many new recruits are sent to reinforce the gangs at liberty; many a meeting is arranged years ahead. Brown, the murderer of P.C. Gutteridge, met a convict at Dartmoor's gates two years after Brown himself had been released.

Class III. – My third class comprises men in for crimes of passion and jealousy. There is always a woman in the background here. The majority I found illiterate and of low intellect, and in some cases their jealousy was quite unfounded. You generally find this type vowing terrible deeds of vengeance when they are liberated. No one takes very much notice, as the threats seldom mature.

Class IV. – The moral degenerates, the practitioners of horrible vices. They should never be in Dartmoor at all. Men in this class are the tale-bearers of the prison. Woe betide you if one of these spots you breaking a regulation, or knows you are in possession of contraband! They are the informers who bring punishment down upon their fellows, and they generally display sufficient cunning not to be found out.

Yet one must feel a great pity for such as these, because they are not normal human beings. Some have merely been unfortunate enough to have had a temporary mental lapse. Others have committed the same offence repeatedly, and I claim they should not be in prison.

Class V. – The petty thief, the cheap-crook, the jackals of the criminal, and the border-line mental cases.

In this class one finds human beings stamped with the mark of brute-beasts. To make myself perfectly clear, let me draw you a simile. You have seen a huge ape at the Zoo, and instinctively thought to yourself, 'I wouldn't like to meet that fellow in the dark.'

One might trace these unfortunate men as the progeny of criminals – 'the sins of the fathers' – brought up in the slums and hot-beds of vice of our great cities, they steal or starve. There is no hope for such as these. (Ex-convict No.:—, *Dartmoor From Within*, nd, pp. 31–3)

The least troublesome of the prisoners were the small body of professional criminals known as 'The Chaps'. 'The Chaps' were respected by the others, for they were regarded as the cream of London's underworld. Their numbers included the expert cracksmen, the clever confidence trickster and the thief who went in for the big money. Such men regarded prison as an occupational risk which they took in their stride, almost philosophically. Their one aim was to get their sentences over with as quickly as possible so that they could return once again to their old ways. They had more sense than to get involved in escape plots or in riots, and were often given responsibilities with privileges because the officers knew they would not abuse them. (B.D. Grew, *Prison Governor*, 1958, p. 47)

The Chaps

In a cell just up the catwalk from mine were three yobs. Three toughies, barons of lesser power. One had a scar running from eyebrow to chin, and another had a zigzag pattern on his cheek. Gang carve-ups, apparently earned in London. Two nick terrors, these were. Hard cases. The screws gave them extra privileges and blind-eye treatment rather than have trouble. But one day I was passing their cell with just the two of them inside, and their door part open. One was sitting on his stool and the other was working on him with a razor blade. Scraping the blade over his mate's face scar to make it blare out harsh and livid. When he'd finished, he sat down and let his mate work on him. I started to laugh and they came to the door blustering angry. Guilty as kids caught with their fingers in mom's purse. The one with the razor blade in his hand lifted it at me, but I'd got his measure.

Gangland war scars

'I'll tell the whole nick,' I told him. And they both knew I meant it, that I'd put it around that their 'gangland war scars' were self-inflicted, and not for real. They couldn't stand that sort of loss of face. It would take their armour away, leave them no hiding place.

'It's none of my business, this,' I said. 'All I'm looking for in life is a swig of hooch now and then.'

They got my meaning. And the drinking mug inside my chamber pot got filled up with prison hooch every morning, in the lavatory recess. I was satisfied, if not happy. (Archie Hill, *An Empty Glass*, 1984, pp. 85–6)

Magical dexterity

'Been a pickpocket all my life, I have. There were three of us boys, and I don't remember when we weren't taught to pickpocket from our earliest days. Father was a dip, and his father before him. "That's why you was born with your fingers the same length," he used to tell us, "otherwise you're going to poke somebody in the stomach when you're after his watch. Then before you know where you are you're in the nick ."' Observing my fascination he proceeded to give an exhibition of his skill, which had been handed down to him in the fullest sense of the term. My pencil, pocket-book and fountain-pen vanished from my inside pocket in a flash and not a touch of Shorty's fingers did I feel. I wanted to know how he had acquired such magical dexterity; apart from his natural attributes, he must have learned in an exacting academy. 'Oh, Father used to hang a dummy from the kitchen ceiling by a piece of string, dress it up as a man and then we three boys in turn used to have to nick the watch or wallet inside the figure's waistcoat or jacket or trousers hip-pockets. And if the old man saw you move that dummy the least little bit, you knew you were in for a walloping. We boys got so smart at it, we could pinch the milk out of a blind man's cup of tea.' (The Rev. Baden P.H. Ball, *Prison Was My Parish*, 1956, p. 98)

Natural anarchists

In among the common ruck in prison one comes across 'originals' (not necessarily dangerous or violent men), ultra-nonconformists who do not wish to live within our moral frames of reference. These are the natural anarchists, the non-accepting incorrigibles, the disturbers of our common law-abiding round. Such men often possess the virtues of their vices; they have insights and qualities of mind not always too evident in those who have to restrain and teach them. Some rehabilitors might even learn from their pupils, and certainly one thing – that in superimposed monolithic conformity there is no solution at all to the problem of crime. (Robert Roberts, *Imprisoned Tongues*, 1968, p. 167)

The men in grey

Tony Dunford, a double lifer; he'd stabbed one boy when he was sixteen and killed another kid while he was in prison. He had been sentenced to death but had been reprieved and was still only twenty-one or twenty-two. Tall, about six foot two inches, a stringy but sleek 168 pounds, a good-looking boy, bespectacled, thick black curly hair, smooth, olive skin – faintly Byronic. He was very intelligent and read poetry and the ancient classics, very articulate, and as we were both passionate self-educators we'd engage in marathon arguments and discussions that the others found totally unintelligible. More often than not he would get the better of me. He would sulk if upset and sometimes withdraw completely to his cell. Not a committed or socialized criminal, and for all the enormity of his offences, perhaps the easiest of the bunch to reform.

A double-lifer

He was twisted emotionally, and burdened by the conviction that to be worth anything he must be tough and courageous. This was alien to his basic nature and he couldn't cope with the resulting conflicts in trying to adapt himself to society. The tragedy for him, and for his second victim, was that society demands retribution and can only exact it in an environment which enshrines, and operates on, the same anti-social subculture morality which originally precipitated his delinquency. Placing him among its most skilled exponents, and what is more, its most well-adjusted ones, only reinforced what was worst in him. (John McVicar, *McVicar by Himself*, 1974, pp. 74–5)

I catch sight among the convicts seated at the tables of a man playing draughts. Something in his face first chills me and then horrifies me, something that is evil and yet inexpressibly sorrowful. I ask about him. The answer I receive hits my heart like a hammer. I am looking, then, at the cruellest man that ever lived, a man whose crime is surely worse than that of Judas Iscariot. So unspeakable is his crime that he is shunned by the other convicts. Tonight some one has taken pity on him, and is playing draughts with him, neither speaking.

The cruellest man that ever lived

'He must be mad,' I protest.

The Governor turns to me. 'Not mad,' he replies, 'but bad. B-a-d, bad; don't let's be afraid to use that word. There's no greater danger to the nation than the modern tendency to find excuses for badness.'

*   *   *

It is past three o'clock when we go to bed. I cannot sleep for some time, thinking of the face of the cruel man shunned by all those other convicts. Surely there is something in human nature

Pucklechurch Prison

which has to be burned away, and surely there is need of a surgery of the soul as well as of the body. (Harold Begbie, *Punishment and Personality*, 1927, pp. 79–80, 84)

Man-next-door type of thing

Before I got weighed off I carried part of the public image of what a prison, a prisoner, and a warder was. A prison was a place of correction, a place where crooked men were straightened out. Warders were dedicated men who protected Society by keeping villains locked up, men who lived in constant danger of having their lives crippled for them by stubble-chinned monsters who

The men in grey

had raped half the children of England and murdered the other half, or were planning to.

I looked around me and was amazed at what I found. Ar, there were men doing time for murder and rape and violence – but not so many as I expected to see. Most of the blokes were the man-next-door type of thing; the feller from the next work-bench, the bloke sitting next to you on the bus, ordinary fellers who'd have benefited more from a kick up the arse than a lagging in prison. They – and the rest of the country – would probably have been better men in the long run if they'd been sentenced to a couple of dozen week-ends painting Old Age Pensioners' houses.

Christ Almighty, if only a bloke could describe what a prison *is*; what it *does* to you, despite what *you've* done to that Fool's Paradise called Society. (Archie Hill, *A Cage of Shadows*, 1973, p. 240)

It became clear to me that people's happiness depends, not so much on what is happening to them, but how what is happening relates to their expectations. For example, a young man who had been sentenced to seven years came back from court as happy as a sand-boy because he was expecting to get fifteen. Another lad was suicidally depressed because he got twelve months when he was expecting only three.

Sweeping the floor

One thing you have to realise is that values inside are topsy-turvy in relation to the world outside. A new arrival is always asked two questions: 'What are you in for?', 'How long have you got?' When I first met my three cell mates, it went like this:
'GBH. Ten years.'
'Dealing smack. Eight years.'
'Attempted murder. Twelve years.'
Me: 'Arrears of maintenance. Twenty-eight days.'
I could see the contempt spread across their faces. Oh, shit! I thought. Guess who's going to be sweeping the floor. (Nigel Gray, personal communication, 1987)

I have described a few of the interesting characters whom I met in prison. But of course, the majority of prisoners are not interesting. A considerable proportion of them have obviously been handicapped by natural defects of intelligence or character. Many prisoners – the bulk of the recidivists – seem constitution- ally incapable of getting away from crime. (Raymond Blackburn, *I Am an Alcoholic*, 1959, p. 179)

Not interesting

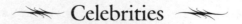

Celebrities

STINIE MORRISON

Stinie Morrison was another well-known man in the prison. He had been there since 1911, and although one could not often get him to talk, I had an occasional conversation with him about the Clapham Common murder that had led to his being condemned to death and subsequently reprieved by Mr Winston Churchill, owing to the grave doubts that arose as to his guilt.

I never saw him laugh. He swore to me, not once but a dozen times, that he had not killed Leon Beron. Times innumerable did he attempt to have his case reopened, but the Home Office uncompromisingly refused. He became one of the hunger strikers and died just about the time I was being released. Sometimes he would go for days without speaking to anyone and then everyone left him severely alone. There is no doubt, of course, that he was found guilty on the most appalling evidence. In Scotland, he would never have been convicted. The verdict would have been 'Not Proven'. ('George Smithson', *Raffles in Real Life*, nd, p. 122)

Communist by nature

And he turned good people against him as a communist. His political opinions was the cause really of him being in the position he was in. He was always talking to me about politics in prison. Morrison was a communist by nature, because he believed in communism. I wasn't very well up in communism, I knew what anarchism meant, but not communism. Communism wasn't a common name then. It was anarchist, people used to talk about that. I think people dropped the word anarchist, 'cos it sounded too much of the bomb-throwing and the shooting. Myself, I think that the left-wing people who were half and half decided that the best thing was to wash out 'anarchist' 'cos it frightened people, and adopt the word 'communist'. They say 'Christ was the first communist', he was undoubtedly. Sometimes Steinie would talk about communism – that things would never be no good till we wiped them all out. It didn't appeal to me. I didn't have any political opinions at all. For me it was too much to scheme to live. (Raphael Samuel, *East End Underworld*, 1981, pp. 172–3)

Zeppelin raid

Inspector Ward, of Brixton, who with Superintendent Wensley arrested Morrison, was killed in London by a bomb explosion during a Zeppelin raid. I shall never forget Morrison's face when the news trickled into Parkhurst. He said to me:

The men in grey

'I had become convinced that there was no God, but I think I shall alter my opinion after this.' (Charles George Gordon, *Crooks of the Underworld*, 1921, p. 20)

Then the kitten walked in. She strolled over to a corner near the furnace and curled up on a bag which was kept as her bed. Ginger-coloured, she was the pet of all the men except Morrison. He had several times lashed out with savage kicks at her when she had passed near him and this had led to rows and threats of fights. But no one was anxious to have a show-down with Morrison. He was too big, too broad-shouldered, with fists like hams, and a maniacal look in his eyes. One might as well tackle a mad bull.

The men went on moulding the loaves when, without motive or reason, Morrison suddenly rushed across to the kitten, grabbed it by the neck and, pulling open the furnace door, threw it far back into the flames. It was all done so quickly that no one had time to do a thing. Immediately there was a roar of angry shouts from the other bakers, followed by a concerted rush. But Morrison was ready for them. Picking up a heavy iron poker, he threatened to brain the first man that came near him. And there's no doubt he would have done it. (L. Merrow-Smith and J. Harris, *Prison Screw*, 1962, p. 75)

Then the kitten...

He was reported and punished.

No. 1 punishment, bread and water, very tough; that was what Stinie got. He felt wronged, and started cutting down on his food. For ninety-one days, while they tried to force him to feed, he ate almost nothing. They fed food into him through a rubber pipe down his throat. I saw them do it. Stinie just got weaker and weaker.

They put him in a padded cell, but there he refused to eat anything. Because of this a doctor ordered him out and into the prison hospital ward where I was working on special duty. He was too ill to be dangerous to himself or anybody else. Poor Stinie, they put him on a mattress on the floor and took the straightjacket off him. One of the screws told me to lift his head up. He looked up at me, sort of puzzled as if he didn't know where he was. That was how he died, in my arms, peaceful as a kitten. The man who'd murdered an old man, and a cat. He died for the cat. (Wally Thompson, *Time Off My Life*, 1956, pp. 47–8)

He died for the cat

HORATIO BOTTOMLEY

The first person I saw was Horatio Bottomley. Enormously stout at that time, he puffed and panted around a small patch of grass, alone. He was purple with the cold, wore two clown-like capes, a little comic cap and a pair of enormous shapeless gloves. (Jail gloves have no fingers. I still do not know why.)

From time to time a warder in a white coat appeared at a door and peeped out at Bottomley. Sometimes he stood for a moment, watching the solitary old man, but mostly he oscillated between the door and somewhere inside. The building was apparently a hospital.

More than anything else, I think, this circumstance decided me to try and build a life for myself. In theory, I knew, I was to be watched for every second of my existence till I died: and I wouldn't have wanted to live that way for long. But so was Bottomley supposed to be watched unceasingly. Yet here were intervals, some even as long as a whole minute, in which he was unsurveyed and could be Bottomley instead of an animal in a cage.

I watched him, unobserved. There was a distinct difference in his demeanour when the warder was absent. A naïve pathos was manifest in the alteration of his ponderous strut at such moments, in the slapping together of his hands, once or twice in his placing of a foot, daringly for a second, on the grass. (Jim Phelan, *Jail Journey*, 1940, pp. 12–13)

Sewing? (I)   'He was in this shop,' he continued. 'One day, Bonar Law paid a visit to the prison. Bottomley was working the stitching-machine, and Bonar Law saw him. "Hullo, Bottomley," he greeted him. "Sewing?" "Sewing?" said Bottomley. "No, sir, reaping!"'

I thought this was a very good story, and repeated it to all my friends as the best authentic prison story, until I read Julian Symon's life of Bottomley, in which the same incident is related as having occurred between Bottomley and the padre at Maidstone, where Bottomley was sewing mail-bags. Later, it was even quoted to me as being the answer Oscar Wilde gave to a prison visitor. (Peter Baker, *Time Out of Life*, 1961, p. 35)

Sewing? (II)   Most famous prisoners do a quiet lagging and are fairly treated. Legends about them are numerous. What a good fellow was Masterman; how polite to everybody was Bevan; what a rotter in prison was Bottomley; how Hatry has turned out one of the soundest men who ever came to gaol, how manly was old Hooley, and how he loved sewing mail-bags and had stacks of them in his cell.

On one occasion the governor passed Hooley, diligently sewing away, and remarked, 'Sewing, Hooley?'

'No, reaping,' replied the ex-Sheriff of Cambridgeshire. (W.F.R. Macartney, *Walls Have Mouths*, 1936, p. 404)

The men in grey

During my tours of inspection the prisoners were lined up and stood at their open cell doors as I passed. One morning as I was walking down the centre of the hall I was startled to see one man advance out of his cell and take up a position on the matting directly in my path some forty feet ahead. His face was crimson and his features contorted with rage. He raised his arms menacingly in the attitude of a fighting gorilla.

Two ideas flashed through my mind as I walked on. I could pretend not to have noticed him and carefully retreat. But that would never do. I could order the two officers with me to remove him to his cell. But this would be futile, for I was aware that at the sight of any manhandling on the part of the officers pandemonium would break loose. There was only one thing to do. Go on.

I continued to walk towards the alarming figure who was now cursing and swearing and threatening my life in the vilest of terms. Then as I came within a few feet of him, he suddenly let out a terrifying scream and fled to his cell, slamming the door behind him, and there he continued to shout raucously.

It was an anticlimax to the drama – though an extremely welcome one – but the incident showed me how quickly and unpredictably trouble can blow up, and how wary a prison staff must always be, no matter how sincere its determination to avoid unnecessary severity.

This particular prisoner, incidentally, after threatening the Governor's life as well as my own, violently refused to leave the prison on the day of his discharge. He had to be escorted from Dartmoor by the local police! Some years later he was hanged for the murder of a policeman. (B.D. Grew, *Prison Governor*, 1958, p. 51)

I interviewed Browne in his cell a few days before paying the *Even in this* extreme penalty and just after he attempted to commit suicide. He *fallen creature* was in a fearfully excited state when I entered the cell, but calmed down considerably after I had had a little chat with him. I found him very bitter against the police, and this bitterness was proved by his murderous action against them. The man was in hell. I never want to see another like it. He did not so much object to paying the penalty; he wanted it carried out in his own way, and not by men in blue. . . .

I shall never forget my conversation with him, and the glimpse I had of the worst side of human nature. Yet there was some goodness even in this fallen creature. Human nature is often a great mystery and most difficult to fathom. I firmly believe if Browne's punishment for previous offences had been less severe and with more of the human touch in it, he would never have come to the bad end that he did. (Sir Sidney J. Pocock *The Prisoner and the Prison*, 1930, pp. 99–100)

RUBY SPARKS

When I went to Parkhurst in 1928, just opposite me on No. 6 landing was Ruby Sparks, who was about twenty-seven, good-looking, finely built, extremely quick, and a magnificent fighter, with a very heavy punch. He was merry in those days, his white teeth flashing and his grey eyes gleaming with fun. In 1928 he was just finishing a three-year lagging for a smash-and-grab in the north of England. While in Manchester gaol awaiting trans-portation to the Isle of Wight, Ruby made a brilliant escape from the prison, but was caught through his friend breaking a leg. Ruby was one of the most reliable men it has been my fortune to meet, shrewd, able, and energetic. He rendered me a service of almost incalculable value, a service it will be difficult for me ever to pay back. He is a type that our present society seems unable to use to the advantage of society as a whole. It turns people like Ruby Sparks into motor bandits, and makes paranoiacs like Hitler and Goering the arbiters of the destinies of millions. . . . (W.F.R. Macartney, *Walls Have Mouths*, 1936, p. 98)

STRAFFEN

He was the stereotype psychopathic killer, tall and stooped with a bald head and staring eyes. He was hated by screws and cons alike and he had often been attacked, once by dozens of pairs of sharpened scissors that thudded and cut into his thin body. He swore that he was innocent but no-one believed him and he was destined to spend the rest of his life in prison. It was rumoured that the screws drugged him every day, bringing his respite, and theirs, a little closer. I didn't believe in his innocence but I pitied him and hoped I could never be like him. (Douglas Curtis, *Dartmoor to Cambridge*, 1973, p. 59)

A sense of horror

John did not read and had no books in his cell. He spent all but about four hours of his days in his cell and used to sit straight-backed on his chair and stare at the wall for hours and hours on end. He had a bath once a week on the same day and at the same time and a hair cut once a month on the first day of the month. If anything interfered with this routine, he used to get very distressed. The security-block conditions accelerated John's deterioration.

The men in grey

The vacant dead eyes that stared out from an expressionless pallid face might as easily have been those of a corpse....

John personifies, for me, the extreme inhumanity and barbarity of the establishment. The horror of John's own crimes dwindles to insignificance in face of the relentless years of cruelty inflicted upon him. John was insane when he committed his crimes, but the establishment commits its crimes against humanity in cold sanity. Physical death would have been infinitely more merciful than what they have done to John. It is as though the soul, personality and life of this being has been amputated, to leave the carcase, able to function in an animated yet somehow strangely lifeless way. John's very existence conveys a sense of horror. (Walter Probyn, *Angel Face*, 1977, pp. 109–10)

FRANK MITCHELL

My meeting with the so-called axeman, Frank Mitchell, was something of an excitement. He came from Dartmoor to be prepared for release. Word went round like wild-fire that this tough and dangerous man was arriving. I wondered why on earth he was coming to Maidstone and whether I would survive his stay intact. He did come, and what is more he was put into the cell next to mine. I had visions of the wall partition being battered down and his doing anything from raping to beating me up. He was a colossal figure, and arrived in a white T-shirt and smart slacks, with a chest-expander under one arm and a wireless set and record player under the other. I could see he was somebody exciting and I was terribly curious to know how he ticked. It was not long before I found out. He popped into my cell the next day, saying he had heard a lot about me and was glad to have the chance of meeting me and was I really gay? I told him that I was, but discreetly so. I liked him at once. He asked me if he could sit down on my bed; I said, of course. Anyway, if I had minded I would not have been able to do much about it. We hit it off well and he was intrigued to hear about my experiences in Moscow and other exciting places. I thought he felt he had missed out on life a bit, but he said he had been well provided for at Dartmoor and certainly had not gone without the fruits of life. I knew what he meant. (John Vassall, *Vassall – The Autobiography of a Spy*, 1975, p. 162)

A society of captives

In due course I found myself enjoying the privileges of the 'second stage'. At eight o'clock, after two hours' night work sewing mail-bags and after a full day in the weaving shed, I was now free to move about for half an hour on the stone flags of the basement of 'C' wing, and to converse with the other convicts.

My cell was on an upper landing, so I had to descend the steep spiral iron staircase at the end of the wing. The sight of this deep, well-like lower landing with its swarm of convicts in chocolate-brown clothes was bizarre. Looking upwards from a top landing, the wing with its whitewashed, arching roof reminded me of a Spanish cloister, but looking down, at night, the stone-flagged bottom landing at the base of the tiers of gas-lit galleries was like a Japanese street. A dull roar of conversation came from the convicts in the dim gaslight, and grotesque shadows darted over the yellow walls. Down into this weird pit I descended, the scent of tobacco coming to my sensitive nostrils. Convicts who had completed their weekly task (soling and heeling one hundred and twenty pairs of shoes, weaving several hundred yards of cloth, or some other definite quantity of work difficult to accomplish in a week) had earned 2*d*. and bought a quarter of an ounce of tobacco which they were now rolling into remarkably thin cigarettes, or stuffing with dried leaves from the prison garden into short pipes. A swarm of convicts fastened themselves like flies around the gas-jet provided, lighting their pipes and cigarettes, whilst groups of convicts behind waited eagerly for a 'drag' at the cigarette of a comrade. (William Holt, *I Was a Prisoner*, 1934, pp. 71–2)

An education   After you come on stage, every five nights a week we used to dine out – that was what we called it, dining out, when you'd have your tea with the other stagers. Association is about an hour and a half, from six to seven thirty, when you can talk and play darts and have your evening meal together. It only happened when you'd come on stage, reached stage two, after you'd done about six weeks of your sentence.

I should think it was being put in jail like that for nine months that really got me started on a life of crime. Up to that it had been all very small stuff. But once in jail, you meet all the real criminals and you begin to hear about some of the possibilities – things you'd never have dreamt would work. I think everyone who goes to jail tends to graduate from there – it's an education on its own, going inside, a university for studying villainy. Once I'd finished my time under observation and went on stage, I started meeting and palling up with hardened criminals and mostly what we talked about was our past crimes and what went wrong and how we could avoid the mistakes next time. There wasn't any question of going straight really. We all took it for granted that as soon as

The men in grey

we got out we'd get back to thieving and screwing and villainies of all sorts. (Henry Ward, *Buller*, 1974, p. 48)

Greeted with cheers

One morning as we sat at breakfast in the Hall it was announced on the BBC seven o'clock news that Craig and Bentley had murdered one policeman and wounded another on the roof of a warehouse in Croydon. This news was greeted with cheers from the long line of men eating at the wooden tables. I looked down the hall. I felt the blood mounting to my head and my heart pounding. Together with one or two others I shouted: 'Shut up! Stop it, you bloody swine!' At that moment I was seized with blind rage against those grey rows of cheering men. At that moment it struck me as a deep injustice that society demanded that in retribution for my crime I should be forced to associate with those uncivilised brutes. It was neither the first nor the last time that I experienced such an emotion. But I disciplined myself against it for it savoured too much of self-pity, that most despicable of prison sentiments. But throughout the day the picture of those cheering men persisted. (Anthony Heckstall-Smith, *Eighteen Months*, 1954, pp. 112–14)

Taught me how to live

In later years I met a man in a London prison who had an intermittent mania for destroying things. Like Köhler's apes, his first impulse was to break, rend and shatter every destructible thing which came to his hands. He came to prison in the first place because he had never succeeded in disciplining this impulse. In prison, however, he found that immediate and severe retribution followed each destructive lapse on his part. At the beginning of his sentence he took to smashing up the furniture of the cells, and it was weeks before he swallowed the bitter lesson that if you batter yourself against officialdom, it will – uniquely terrible among stone walls – batter itself against you. But eventually he did swallow it, and gradually settled down into a quiet and apparently exemplary prisoner.

Observing all this, I became curious to know how he compensated for the loss of his former mode of emotional expression; and when I became sufficiently intimate with him to win his confidence, I learned a very strange thing. *His impulse to destruction had been systematized, not repressed.* Instead of doing his smashing impulsively and without forethought, he now broke things deliberately, with every precaution against detection. He learned, too, to destroy the *function* of a thing while preserving its outward appearance. So he would bore holes in the buckets and food utensils, block the pipes of the water-closets, hide tools in the workshops. But where he could escape detection he did not hesitate to tear and burn bedding, throw ink over the scrubbed, white tables in other men's cells, and even tell lies to breed quarrels. He did all this with a cheerful, devilish deliberateness, and at the end of his sentence he told me: 'I've *enjoyed* this stretch, it's really taught me how to live!'

The important point about this case, it seems to me, is that solitude taught the man to identify himself with an intermittent frenzy, and to cultivate it till it informed his whole life. He found that he could be more destructive if he concealed his destructiveness, and prison made him *want* to be more destructive. Prison made him want to be *wholly* destructive. By isolating him, and narrowing down the field of normal instinctual development, prison turned a tendency into an obsession. (Mark Benney, *Low Company*, 1936, pp. 286–7)

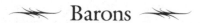

Barons

The system of baroning is based on tobacco. Smoking had been permitted in prisons and men were paid a few coppers for their labour. If they were lucky they earned enough in a week to buy about half an ounce of shag – just enough to keep the appetite alive and not enough to satisfy it. They were too weak-minded to give it up so they would borrow from one of the barons who of course, got their supplies of snout through a bent screw. Loans of tobacco were made at an interest of 100 per cent a week. It was obvious that if a man could not get through one week on half an ounce he would never be able to repay one ounce the next week, yet they went on borrowing and the barons went on doubling the debt.

The debt could only be repaid if the men wrote to relatives outside to pay money to a nominee of the baron. These letters were carried by the bent screws who had to be paid likewise. So some wretched woman trying to bring up her kids on what she could earn or get from the National Assistance Board was bombarded with letters begging her to pay up and save her husband from disaster. Those who had no means to pay became serfs of the barons and strong arm men. They slaved for them and prostituted themselves if required, but still the debt mounted up.

Finally, the wretched prisoner would be cornered by the strong arm men and beaten up, and that squared the debt for the moment.

The other way to clear the debt was to 'have it away'. It is a prison rule which even the barons recognise, that if a man runs

The men in grey

away all his debts are cancelled. So the weaker characters sometimes took this way out. They never got very far, being incapable of planning and carrying out a proper escape. The attempt usually cost them six months' loss of remission but they seemed to think it was worth it. (Shifty Burke, *Peterman*, 1966, pp. 146–7)

Snout ... Tobacco (this originates from the days of silent labour, when the sign to ask a mate for a cigarette was to lay one finger along the nose – or snout). (George Dendrickson and Frederick Thomas, *The Truth about Dartmoor*, 1954, p. 25) *'Snout'*

Grasses

I found this ex-detective sergeant, who used to help keep my books and records, a likable enough chap. He obviously had nothing but contempt, which on the whole was justified, for most of his fellow prisoners. And, faced with their open hostility, he just as obviously owed them no loyalty.

One afternoon he came to me and said: 'I think you ought to warn the fellow up above that there's something wrong with No. 13 cell on his landing.'

I went up and saw the officer on the landing above. We carefully scrutinised the cell in question, and it was only because we did the job thoroughly that we were able to discover that the bars of the window were almost severed. Together, we went to the workshop where the inmate of the cell was employed. We found concealed beneath his bench two hacksaws which had obviously been well used. Thanks to the ex-policeman's tip-off, an escape was frustrated. (Harley Cronin, *The Screw Turns*, 1967, p. 59)

So one day when this grass was at work in the bag shop one of the chap's asked the screw if he could fall out to go to the recess, having got permistion he went into the recess; had a shit in his handkerchief, holding it behind his back he went up behind the grass, (who was bisily sewing away at a mail bag, and was not expecting anything to happen to him) and emptied the contence of his handkerchief into this unsuspecting geezers bin, and then just walked away as innocent as you like, sat down in his place and carried on with his work. After a while the grass put his hand in his bin for somthing or other, and was horryfied at what he found, he went and showed the screw what some one had done, *Upraw* but the screw began to raw with laughter, at this every one else began to laugh untill the whole place was in an upraw. (Frank Norman, *Bang to Rights*, 1958, p. 85)

'You're going to be poisoned, you grass.'

It didn't take long for the word to get around Oxford jail that supergrass Maurice O'Mahoney was there. I knew that no one could actually get at me, but the mental anguish from the taunts hurled at me soon began to unhinge my mind. I would hear the slags screaming abuse in my direction from their cell windows. Things like, 'You're going to be poisoned you grass.' If I could have got at any of them, I would have torn them apart. But they were shouting their insults from a safe distance and I just had to take it.

Then threatening notes started coming under my cell door. I could hear the prisoners, who had somehow got that close, running off. I don't know what on earth the prison officers were playing at, allowing this to happen, but they did. The secret messages threatening a cruel end to me and all my family kept coming under the door and as fast as I tore one up, another would be slipped through. (Maurice O'Mahoney, *King Squealer*, 1978, p. 155)

 Nonces

Bo-Peep removed his spectacles, took out his handkerchief and began to polish them slowly. His eyes without the built-up lenses in their tortoiseshell frames were perfectly ordinary both in shape and size. As we sat there in silence I was wondering if he was really aware of another Court of Law, the inner tribunal which sits in secret to reassess his crime. Here, the thief and the condemned man are part of a hierarchy considered noble, whilst at the other end of the scale, more fearful punishments are meted out to those convicted of cruelty to children, assault on old people and informers of all kinds. (Jim Stockton, *Runaway*, 1968, p. 156)

'You're called a nonce.'

You're called a nonce because they say, 'Oh, you've been up to nonsense.' The most despised nonces are the child molesters, and then there's a sort of gradation from there upwards.

You're fixed with that image: that's it, and you are despised. It's very hurtful. Then of course they try and take it out on you physically. It was very unpleasant for me for the first eighteen months, when I was in the Scrubs – actually it was unpleasant

The men in grey

before that, in the police cells where they kicked the shit out of me, holding me down and beating me in the same way I'd beaten the girl. They kept me stripped naked in a police cell for three days with the door open and an officer sitting in the doorway. They got a policewoman to come up and verbally abuse me. They kept waking me up in the middle of the night, accusing me of trying to commit suicide, or with a doctor who would wake me up and say, 'Why did you do it? Why did you do it?' When I went to make a statement they said, 'What happened?' I tried to tell them and they said, 'Never mind all that, *this* is what happened.' And then they dictated the statement. (James Campbell, *Gate Fever: Voices From a Prison*, 1986, pp. 115–16)

'When we got into reception the first thing the screw does is to throw my record down to the con who's sat there in reception. He was sat at the table with his feet sprawled out and smoking big cigarettes. Him and his buddies, they run the place.

What have we got here?

'So he looks in the record and reads all through it. "Christ", he says. "What have we got here" and then he starts calling me names, all filthy names, you know, "fucking this" and "fucking that". He was a real rough type of bloke, a Londoner, always looking for a scrap.

'First thing that happened next morning was I was brought in front of a PO (Principal Officer) and a chaplain. The PO told me to go on Rule Forty Three. "It's all round the prison what you're in for", he said. "It's for your own good. Don't go in the shop; go behind your door." I told him I might as well go in the shop. "It's all controlled in there, there's the officers, nothing can happen."

'So I went in the bag shop and they all started pointing at me and shaking their fists. I sat down at the front and straight away there were three or four of them round me calling me a dirty bastard and kicking me. Roughnecks, the sort that like trouble. I tried to clear them away with my arms but that just made it worse. It went on all morning like that. When it was exercise the screw said: "All wash your hands." I thought "Well I'm not going into the corner because they'll fucking kill me." I hung back but the screw said "Go and get your fucking hands washed." When I got there they all got round me, fifteen or twenty of them, shouting at me. And they were hitting me and kicking me between the legs. One of them kicked me in the rupture and that caused me a lot of pain. If that had busted I would have copped me lot.

'There were three screws there and they didn't take a blind bit of notice; pretended they couldn't hear anything. One of them was filling in the work book by the door and the other two pretended to be doing things.

'When we got out onto exercise I went up to the PO in charge and said I wasn't going to walk round with the others because I'd get killed. He said "Fucking get in there." I said: "Well I can't. I want to see the governor." "Get back on fucking exercise." So I refused and he said "Well stand there then." As they all came past they were gobbing on me and taking kicks at me. The PO never tried to stop them.' (Philip Priestley, *Community of Scapegoats*, 1981, pp. 33–4)

Who the hell you pushing?

Then I saw Maxie approaching, a cookhouse moocher – in other words a prisoner lucky enough to be employed on kitchen duties, a job which is every lag's ambition when he is inside. Now Maxie was a sex offender and the average con loathes a sex offender more than he loathes the screw, particularly the sex offender who assaults little children, the creature guilty of offences so revolting that not even the sensational Sunday newspapers will report them in detail.

So when Maxie approached, looking fat and sleek in his own well-fedness, feet in kitchen clogs and ample paunch concealed by a spotless white apron, something in me snapped. (Perhaps that is part of my trouble. Something in me is always snapping.) So I stepped out of line so that this well-favoured prisoner would have to by-pass me.

It was a deliberately provocative act on my part. I felt his shoulder in my back. I swung round on him.

'Who the hell you pushing?' I asked.

I didn't wait for him to reply. I grabbed his shirt with both hands, slammed my head into his face. As he fell to the floor, blood streaming, I leathered him in the ribs.

It was a brutal attack on a man who had done me no harm. It was inexcusable. It was disgraceful. If I'd done it to a screw I would have undoubtedly been awarded the cat o'nine tails by the Visiting Committee (as I was several years later), but because it was another prisoner and a sex offender at that I wasn't even put on report. (Robert Sykes, *Who's Been Eating My Porridge?*, 1967, pp. 76–7)

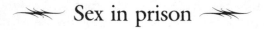

Sex in prison

I seldom have a sexual dream in the full sense of it, but a woman enters my dreams occasionally who seems to be all I have missed in life and always on waking from these dreams I feel real 'Goody Goody' because of my great respect for her and admiration,

The men in grey

totally free from sex. I have never in reality met a woman like this and I love her. (Charlotte Banks, *Teach Them to Live*, 1958, pp. 118–19)

'Lies'

In the futile attempt to prevent masturbation it was, not so very long ago, the practice to blister the gland of the penis of boys discovered in the act. The terrible suffering caused by such treatment applied to one of the most sensitive parts of the male body can easily be imagined. To what extent this revolting torture prevailed I do not know, but the statement was made to me by a prison governor, a kindly man but lacking in intelligence, who prided himself on curing the habit by this means. That his pride was justified no one who has studied boys can believe.

Nowadays a more refined but perhaps even more cruel method is adopted. A small book, well called *Lies*, is distributed among the boys, which paints in lurid colours the awful effects of the habit, ending in insanity and total paralysis. (A. Mitchell-Innes, *Martyrdom in Our Times*, 1932, p. 46)

Harmed

When I do read, however, I usually concentrate upon *The Narrow Way* or *The Pack of Lies*, both of which I have already read twice.

These are two little books issued by religious societies which afford me and all the other lads who can read much fun. Both of them discuss sex-matters and the dangers of self-abuse and other evils. *The Narrow Way* is in story form and the *Pack of Lies* is set out as Questions and Answers, or in some cases by making statements with the comment 'This is a lie' or 'This is a wicked lie' printed in italics underneath. At my age the desire for sex knowledge is a tingling flame smouldering silently and my mind sucks up anything new like a sponge. We are all more or less like this at Wandsworth. Some of the older lads claim to have experienced actual intercourse, which may or may not be true, but no matter what our age or experience we discuss these little books and laugh at the 'rude' passages, while one fellow named Chester, who knows all the bad parts off by heart, says he reads it every night in bed and admits openly that it feeds his mind with the food it likes and he gives way. He is not the only one by far, and I am, though deeply interested, a little surprised at the knowledge of sex many of my friends have and not a little shocked at their confessions. (J.W. Gordon, *Borstalians*, 1932, pp. 62–3)

Comfort and love

Last night I curled naked in the sleeping bag made out of blankets and hugged myself. I masturbated to Sarah, imagining her in different poses. It was beautifully erotic and warm, in sharp contrast to the cold outside the blankets. I love the way I am able to fall back on the richness of my inner world for comfort and love. Bed is a very attractive place to be as I can pull the blankets over my head and crawl into the total darkness. (Jimmy Boyle, *The Pain of Confinement*, 1984, pp. 290–1)

Sex on a scientific basis

I decided early in my prison life to deal with sex on a scientific basis. I use the word 'scientific' to define a process whereby I classified and recorded my sex impulses so as to get a good knowledge of what really happened to me. Every manifestation of auto-erotism was entered in my calendar. Later on, with other developments, I book-kept in the same way. I was thus able to control throughout the whole of eight years the increase and decrease of the sex urge. I may state definitely that the immediate post-masturbatory period was one of nausea and of self-distaste, and that I never got over this. For a normal man it is a wretched substitute. Miss Ethel Mannin, in an article in the *New Leader* dealing with Borstal boys, says that masturbation has no ill effects. From *Confessions and Impressions* we may gather that Miss Mannin's sex life had been too healthy for her to know anything of the effects of substitution.

The only way to master auto-erotism is to direct energy away from sex; but prison is a deliberate destroyer of all energy. The long hours in the cells, the lack of books, the apathy that grows on the prisoner, the absence of all interests and all hobbies, the hopeless outlook – these weaken the resistance. Masturbation is general in prison, and it is referred to openly and indifferently. When I went to prison, the idea of becoming even temporarily homosexual never entered my head. There are many homosexuals in gaol, and for at least four years I took no interest in them. The first knowledge that the mind was being perverted by the unnatural existence of gaol came to me through my dreams. The imagery began to change. The persistent, sharply accentuated image of womanhood became clouded after about three and a half years. Even when awake I began to find that fantastic images were pushing the original normal image out of the way. Gradually a homosexual shadow obscured the normal picture, and I began to have definitely homosexual dreams. I do not propose to enlarge further upon my own sex life, but I shall assert that within my observation the beneficial effects of such contacts upon the mental and physical health were undeniable; and my experience was that of the average man. Of course, some repressed themselves terribly and never consciously entered into this life. Others went to extremes and developed perversions that would make Krafft-Ebing's hair stand upright. Through the method of control I

The men in grey

evolved, I was able to get a good idea of the effect of different aspects of prison life upon one's sexual activity in prison. The difference between solitary confinement and association was conspicuous. (W.F.R. Macartney, *Walls Have Mouths*, 1936, pp. 419–20)

Before long I had to face a new and unexpected problem. A man serving a life sentence with whom I had been directed to work, and whom I had grown to like very much, began to develop a more than friendly interest in me. He was some years older than I, and was a bright, cheery and engaging personality, popular alike with prisoners and staff, and we had worked amicably and, I may say, efficiently, for some considerable time before I began to realise the implications of this attachment.

All the intensity . . .

My previous homosexual affairs had been adolescent and completely unsentimental, but this assumed a different aspect which I was at first unprepared to meet. All the intensity and emotions of a love affair became manifest, and I began to be alarmed at the possibility that we should both land in serious trouble. I have never been able to escape from a sense of the incongruity of a situation like this, and it was without at first any wish to encourage my friend, but to avoid scenes, that I made any response. But as time went on I became more deeply and significantly involved, and the concept of homosexual love as a complete and stable experience, was revealed to me in this way. I no longer stood in no-man's land, and henceforth my imagination and sexuality became geared to a homosexual aim and an individual object. (*Howard Journal*, 'Prison and After', Vol. IX, No. 2, 1955, pp. 121–2)

For the middle-aged and elderly pederasts and the many who had 'mucked about' with little boys, I had no time. Neither had the other prisoners, but I began to appreciate the tragic difficulties of the honest-to-goodness homosexuals. Like amiable harlots of fiction, they were soft-hearted, generous and truthful, but an even greater virtue was that they kept to themselves. They corrupted no one and never whispered 'suggestions' into the ears of the young prisoners. Furthermore they could give points to many of the 'tough' robbery-with-violence and stick-up men, and showed no trace of that mental and physical deterioration known as 'prison rot'. (*Personal Column: A Testimony of Crime*, 1952, p. 33)

Honest-to-goodness homosexuals

Two young regular soldiers, notorious for their abnormal association, both spoke with the utmost contempt for the effeminate homosexuals. On the other hand, they were on the closest terms

He only gives it . . .

with an Irish youth who spent all his spare time pursuing every possible man or youth likely to co-operate. When asked why they held such divergent views the answer was spontaneous:

'Oh, he's all right. He only *gives* it.'

This extraordinary attitude prevailed among many other prisoners, and is rather akin to the outlook of the idle youth who, while taking every opportunity to seduce willing females, at the same time sneers at his victims. (Pablo Salkeld, 'The ugly head', *Horizon*, July 1949, p. 7)

My own little dolly-bird

My own little dolly-bird was a blonde blue-eyed young con I met in the tailor's shop at Leeds Prison. At 22 he was doing five years for robbery with violence. As I was a long-timer, they gave me a job in the shop office where the men booked their daily task and piece-work in to me.

According to the number of garments – mostly overalls and GPO jackets, they made – so they got paid.

Lindsey wasn't obviously bent, but to me, a long-time observer of the weaknesses of my fellow prisoners, it was reasonably clear that there was something different here.

Although Lindsey was in for GBH, he was paradoxically the most gentle con I had ever met. He was meticulous about his work and his appearance.

Slim, of athletic build, he had that curious feature sometimes found in young men of light complexion – a total absence of facial hair.

Sometimes I looked at Lindsey and in fantasy I replaced his prison battle dress with a pretty bright-coloured sweater and his denim trousers with a mini-skirt. For his legs were in better shape than those of a lot of women I've known.

Of course I wasn't the only one to fancy him. But no one would chat him up, simply because of his record of GBH. It was known that he could use himself and therefore most of the cons left him alone.

Anyway, he wasn't very communicative. As far as I was concerned, he was the best thing that had happened to me in four years since my conviction. I sussed that Lindsey was bent, without maybe even Lindsey knowing it.

He came into the office one Thursday afternoon with his week's work. He gave me six garments and I booked him in for nine. I did this on three consecutive days.

On the third day, as he handed in his work, I looked him straight in the eyes and said: 'You've done a lot of work this week. Don't be surprised if you find yourself with a rise. You can thank me later.'

The men in grey

The following Monday he came up to me in the exercise yard and said, quietly, 'I drew top pay last week, what's it all about, you don't owe me any favours.' I replied: 'Take what's given to you, the only people being robbed are the GPO and anyway they are used to it by now.'

And so it began, that strange, exciting and sometimes frightening, inverted relationship. (Jago Stone, *The Burglar's Bedside Companion*, 1975, pp. 43–4)

Homosexuals thrive in prison like wild flowers on a dung heap. *Wild flowers*
They are despised and ridiculed by most of the other prisoners, who fear that contact with them may result in becoming homosexual themselves. But although some heterosexual inmates indulge in 'queer' relationships whilst in prison they do not continue them upon release. Masturbation is rife – for some it is their only pastime. Without the slightest embarrassment many will boast about how many times they can do it in a day. Their confessions are usually accompanied by descriptive gesticulations, which draw explosive laughter from their audience. (Frank Norman, *Lock 'em Up and Count 'em*, 1970, p. 5)

When we were unobserved he used to do a mincing little *A laughing*
provocative walk down the landing. One day I called after him, *brazen coven*
and when I said, 'By God, all you need is a skirt.'

'Oh my dear,' he laughed, 'I have one.'

'Do you dress as a woman?' I queried.

'Oh yes,' he said, 'and I bet you five pounds that if you saw me out in my skirt and bra you wouldn't know me.'

'A bra?' I laughed. 'But what do you fill it with?'

'Oh, oranges; what else? Big Jaffas of course.'

'Do you make a lot of money out of this racket?'

'Oh, about twenty or thirty pounds some weeks, some weeks none. It all depends on my clients. If they are free or not. One of them is a Labour MP and when his wife is away I stay with him for the weekend.'

'Well,' I tittered, 'at least you got the socialist message.'

He was a gentle, poor soul, unlike the other queers, who formed a laughing, brazen coven, and whom it was extremely dangerous to provoke or jeer. But after a while I began to get ashamed of having the queer for a partner as we walked round. Worse, he was beginning to bore me. Some queers are just queers, with them it's a full time job. So I began to dodge him at break times. At first he tried walking on his own. Even then he gave me little girlish waves as we passed that I had to steel myself to ignore. Gradually he got nearer and nearer to the pack, and

The men in grey

then one day he joined them openly, giggling and screaming in high-pitched voices. Then I had to hunt round for a new mate to chat to. (Brian Behan, *With Breast Expanded*, 1964, p. 162)

A *'cure'?*

Dr Landers, in any case, was not one of those who claimed that there was a psychiatric 'cure' for homosexuality. 'The Freudians,' he explained, 'may think there is, but we're all Jungians here. If a man is so obsessed by his homosexual state that he develops a neurosis about it, we can allay that neurosis and teach him, so to speak, to accept his condition without any severe feeling of guilt; but that's all we can do.'

This sounded like an admirable service for those who were in need of it, but it seemed very strange to me that a man should be sent to prison in order to reconcile himself to the condition which had caused him to be sent there.

'I don't think that's quite what I need,' I said.

'But you have said, if I remember correctly, that you are willing to be cured?'

'Yes, but if there is no cure, surely the question does not arise? Or is there some other method? What about glandular injections, or hormone treatment; is that any good?'

Dr Landers pursed his lips. 'I most certainly wouldn't recommend it,' he said. 'We have tried courses of injections on a couple of sex-cases here, but the results were far from satisfactory. One man came back quite shortly afterwards with a further conviction, and the other has undergone physical changes of a . . . a somewhat alarming nature. I am afraid that research on those lines is not very far advanced yet. It may do some good, but really we don't know enough about it.'

'Well, is there anything else you can suggest?'

'The only thing that might answer, in your case, is a course of analysis and psychotherapy which would, of course, be a very lengthy business lasting perhaps years. Even if we had time, I rather doubt whether it could be carried out satisfactorily in prison. You might, perhaps, consult a psychiatrist about it when you are discharged.'

We were back where we had started. If I had not been sent to prison, I might have been cured.

'There's just one thing,' I said. 'Supposing that I could afford a course of psychotherapy and so on; supposing I found a psychiatrist who was prepared to give it; supposing, even that it worked. What sort of person should I become?'

Dr Landers laughed. 'A very different person, I'm afraid,' he said.

'That's just what I'm afraid of, too.'

The men in grey

'Your whole personality would, of course, be altered.'

'But that,' I suggested, 'might not be a good thing? I'm a writer. For better or for worse, my work depends upon the sort of person that I am.'

'Precisely.' (Peter Wildeblood, *Against the Law*, 1955, p. 143)

Another type was the male prostitute, the filthiest brute on the market, whom you can convict the moment you hear him speak. There is but one remedy for him, as also for the gentlemen who make use of his services. Why any country should be so weak as to tolerate these creatures running the chance of their bringing into the world others like themselves – since presumably some of them are capable of normal cohabitation with a woman – is more than I can fathom, when there is a remedy to hand. If you have an animal from which you do not desire to breed, you jolly well see to it that the beast becomes incapable of breeding. These people are lower than any animals. Why not make sure of *their* not breeding, then? You would not destroy their souls – presuming them to possess any. Indeed, you might by this means assist them to find souls. ... (Lieut.Col. C.E.F. Rich, *Recollections of a Prison Governor*, 1932, p. 138)

There is a remedy

⊱ Fight, fight ... ⊰

The door to the showers opens violently, wrenched from within, and Bill comes out in a staggering crouch. His hands are up to his face, and I can see the bright red blood seeping through the fingers which are cupped in front of his face, their tips resting on his cheekbones, just below his eyes. But it is the eyes themselves which interest me most. Pain I can see, and defeat, but only as the backcloth to something else. Bill was a white-collar worker outside, and although he is a somewhat aggressive man I imagine his previous experience of fighting was limited to the ordinary 'punch-up'. He would only know from hearsay about the type of fight he has just emerged from. He is shocked and bewildered. He crosses the few paces of the hall and one of his friends pulls a chair over for him to sit on; another hands him a not too clean handkerchief, and several of them bunch suddenly in front of him as a patrolling screw is spotted moving down the hall.

Danny comes out through the open door to the showers, closes it carefully behind him, and saunters, unmarked, undisturbed, over to where I sit. He takes his place at the table, throwing one quick, contemptuous and amused glance at where Bill sits, screened by his cronies. He looks at the chessboard, and then at me.

'Whose move is it?'

I look at Danny's face for a second before letting my eyes drop to the chessmen. It is a little white but otherwise unaltered. (Zeno, *Life*, 1968, pp. 74–5)

Wallop
Exercise is another time when some of the straighteners happen. A con will hook another before the screws can get near them. It's more usually done, though, as they come out for the exercise. Someone will hide back in the little alcove and wait for his enemy and then put one on him. Generally it's the salt pot in the sock.

You've got a salt pot in your cell, a heavy sort of stone jar for keeping your salt in, and you stuff that down one of your socks. You don't leave the salt in it because you need that and anyway, it's heavy enough on its own. Anyway, you have this heavy salt pot in your sock, and you're hidden in the alcove and when the man you've got a needle to comes out, wallop, you've hit him on the head with it. This was mostly how it happened then. And it would have been so easy to stop it all by taking away those heavy old government-regulation Victorian salt pots and replacing them with modern light plastic ones, but they didn't never seem to think about things like that. (Henry Ward, *Buller*, 1974, pp. 46–7)

Spurts all over me . . .
I'm in the shop one day, and over there, I hear a fellow-inmate say: 'I wish I were at the Moor. It's a better nick than this fucking place.' At the side of the shop is a cutting-up bench .. knives lying about .. I get up off my stool .. grab one of these knives .. go over to this *Moor-lover* .. grab his hair .. pull back the head .. and *stab* .. *stab* .. his throat .. saying: '*Go back to Dartmoor*, you bastard, *but it will be in your coffin.*' The blood spurts all over me .. the man struggles .. screams .. and .. I .. I .. am jumped on .. carted off .. stripped .. thrown into the cell .. warned by the screws: '*Be sure you don't start with us, Grayson.*' *Me*, I was ready to start anything. (Victor Carasov, *Two Gentlemen to See You, Sir*, 1971, p. 118)

To make a hit
Stabbings amongst prisoners were common occurrences and there was never any great hassle or upheaval over them; the prisoners took them for granted. Prison stabbings are usually well set up events and those carrying them out would take pride in doing a neat job. I did one of these and it was against a guy from my district who had been causing some trouble amongst our group. In things like this the done thing is to make a hit and make it quick because everyone weighs these things up and if they see people getting off with things then they think you soft. So I set

The men in grey

In the cell

this deal up while walking through the corridor, the main 'hit' place, as the prisoners walk single file through dark corridors. It usually takes about four to do it, with the guy who is making the hit carrying the knife, with two in front of the victim and two behind. The guy walks up, makes the hit, then passes the knife to the guy in front of the victim and this was what I did. Before the screw can notice that someone has been hit the guy is well away, and only the victim is left, the weapon concealed by this time in a pre-arranged place. When getting to work there is a discussion as to whether it was a good hit or not. In this context, you have the art of violence in which the manner of its execution is very much appreciated just as works of art are appreciated in another culture. People in the art world understand what art is all about whereas in my world we think it's a load of balls, a big con; just as people in most sections of society view our cutting and maiming each other as hideous. The fact is that this is how we lived and if someone were to cut my face I wouldn't like it but I would accept it knowing that it was a hazard of the life I was leading. I would be intent on getting back at whoever had done it, but on the whole slashing, stabbing, shooting and death are to be expected amongst those of us who live like this. (Jimmy Boyle, *A Sense of Freedom*, 1977, p. 110)

The men in grey

BOOK THREE

Women in Prison

Holloway Prison

⇜ Reception ⇝

A woman coming to Holloway after sentence by the court is brought either in a police van or in an ordinary car. She is driven through the great gate, which clangs shut behind her and taken to the reception block. Here she is signed for: one body has been handed over and one received. The car drives away and she is taken to the reception hall, a large place with a glass roof, its area divided into small cubicles each about the size of those provided in a public swimming-bath. Here she has to undress and she is handed a dressing-gown and slippers while she waits for her issue of prison clothes. Gaily coloured turkish towelling dressing-gowns have now replaced the drab grey garments of a few years ago and the slippers are of washable plastic.

She is weighed and measured; if sentenced her fingerprints are taken; she is examined by a nurse to see if she has nits or pubic lice or scabies, and if she has any of these she is at once treated and put into a special location until it is certain she no longer offers a risk of contagion or infection to others. She is seen by a doctor; this is not usually the place or time for an exhaustive examination, but any immediate medical need can be met.

Her property is listed in her presence and she signifies her agreement by signing each page. The list is often pathetic; a typical list might be 1 dress (torn), 1 pair pants, 1 slip, 1 handkerchief, 1 pair stockings (damaged), 1 ear-ring, part bottle of make-up, 2 medallions, 1 boot lace, 1 part lipstick, 1 pair shoes (in need of repair). (Joanna Kelley, *When the Gates Shut*, 1967, pp. 14–15)

Legs wide apart ... After that you went and saw the doctor. In Strangeways in those days she used to make you get up on two chairs with your legs wide apart, one foot on each, and then jump off on to the floor. You had to do it three times, to make sure you weren't concealing anything. (Tony Parker, *Five Women*, 1965, p. 154)

⇜ Routine ⇝

In Holloway Prison the first bell clangs out at six o'clock in the morning – the signal for every prisoner to get up, dress, make her bed and tidy her cell. In winter she then remains in the cell until breakfast-time, but in summer-time she is taken out to the exercise-ground. Exercise consists of walking round silently and in single file in the little garden which fronts the hospital. Round and round and round, forty or fifty times. ...

Women in prison

Breakfast is at 7.30. Then back to the cell until 8.45, which is chapel-time. After chapel, a further twenty minutes in the cell. Then off to the workrooms, situated in a building just inside the main prison, where the prisoners labour at all sorts of occupations until shortly before noon, when they are marched back to have 'dinner'. That sorry travesty of a meal concluded, back to the workrooms until about 5.30. Then supper in the cell at 5.45. And so another weary, dreary day comes at last to an end.... (Kate Meyrick, *Secrets of the 43*, 1933, p. 107)

A dollop of porridge

I looked out and saw the other prisoners on the landings above and below, standing in the doorways holding out their plates and tin bowls. A prisoner with a red band on her arm and carrying a big pail was making the rounds accompanied by an officer.

I copied the others. Presently I was doled out a dollop of porridge and handed a small pot of sugar that was supposed to last until the following morning. A similar procedure brought me four doorstep slices of bread with a pat of margarine on top; and lastly I held out my mug for tea already mixed with milk. My door was locked again. I sat down at the table. The porridge was very lumpy, and I wondered if I could refuse it the following morning. I could hardly imagine anyone being able to consume four such slices of bread. The margarine tasted very strong. In the months to come I saved my sugar to disguise it. I could only drink a few sips of the tea; it had the same strange flavour of warm hay with which I had become familiar the night before. In time one becomes used to all these things, but for the first week I hardly ate anything. (Joan Henry, *Who Lie in Gaol*, 1952, p. 25)

'All things bright and beautiful.'

It was a very emotional atmosphere in the chapel, what with the excitement of a break in routine and being with other wings. The hymns were frequently too much for many people; some had to be escorted out, many just stood there helplessly crying. Yet week after week the girls would choose hymns like 'The Lord is my Shepherd', 'Dear Lord and Father of Mankind', 'Abide with me', which are emotional enough at the best of times. Every week we sang 'Lord of the Dance', which the Anglican chaplain used to refer to as the Pucklechurch National Anthem. Children's hymns such as 'All Things Bright and Beautiful' were often chosen. (Audrey Peckham, *A Woman in Custody*, 1985, pp. 33–4)

⫷⫷ Prisoners ⫸⫸

Granny was born in the West Country, and came to London to work as a chambermaid in one of the large hotels when she was

18 years old. A resident at the hotel was attracted by her, but for various reasons did not marry her. He kept her in luxurious apartments and lavished money on her. He sent her to a riding school, and when she became a proficient horsewoman she rode with him in Hyde Park regularly. She became a well-known figure in Rotten Row.

This new life for the simple country girl lasted for several years and then came the crash. She was cast aside and left penniless to fend for herself. She had lived in luxury and the only way to maintain such luxury ended in many convictions for drunkenness, disorderly conduct and prostitution. She spent the remainder of her life in and out of prison, but more 'in' than 'out'. (Mary Size, *Prisons I Have Known*, 1957, p. 97)

Large, blank features

One girl was too abnormal to stay out of prison for long; only prison or mental hospital staff would put up with her. She was a huge girl, of ox-like strength, with large, blank features like a piece of modern sculpture, and very low intelligence. She suffered from fits of great depression when she often became violent, and would either smash up property or floor some unfortunate person, almost at random, with a ham-like fist. In between these depressions she would try pathetically hard to please. (Joanna Kelley, *When the Gates Shut*, 1967, p. 178)

Unclean

Mildred was also unclean. It was an unpleasant experience to use a lavatory after her. The lavatory door did not of course lock, and had spaces at the top and bottom. We often used to see Mildred's feet through the space at the bottom of the door facing the toilet bowl as if she were a man. Hardly surprising that she made such a mess. She was also entirely revolting when she had her period, dripping blood everywhere, and making a sickening mess of her bed. She would often be seen walking along the corridor clutching a soiled sanitary towel, on her way to the incinerator, and no amount of shouting at her could get her to wrap up the offending object. Sometimes she would drop a used towel into her pot, and then walk along the corridor spilling a mixture of blood and urine after her, which someone else had to clean up. How can a woman get into such a state?

As a result of all this, she smelled disgusting, and also had a habit of standing as close as she could and scratching her crotch. (Audrey Peckham, *A Woman in Custody*, 1985, p. 71)

Confirmed Conservative

Had associated with criminals all her life. A serious woman who enjoyed talking politics. Like most prisoners, she was a confirmed Conservative. Although she enjoyed housebreaking she felt she was getting too old for it, and was making plans for running a brothel. (Xenia Field, *Under Lock and Key*, 1963, p. 59)

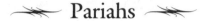

Pariahs

There are only two crimes regarded with loathing by all crooks – blackmail and child murder. This last, of course, particularly among women. Court cases are cut out of newspapers seen by the prisoners, and they are sometimes so mutilated as to be almost unreadable, but prisoners on remand have seen them, and though prisoners may never mention their own cases, it is only very rarely that the others do not know what they are in for. (Joan Henry, *Who Lie in Gaol*, 1952, pp. 60–1)

At the time I was serving three years and I was nineteen. It happened when they moved Myra Hindley onto my wing. I knew who she was but I didn't know the details of the case because it was such a long time ago. About two Sundays after she had been on the wing an article about her was published in *The News of The World*. The Deputy Governor had said that the article shouldn't be issued to us. He asked to see Myra and when she had gone off to see him I got taken into the office by the prison officer who was then in charge of the wing and another prison officer. They sat me behind the door, opened out this two-page spread and said, 'Read that.' It was quite a disturbing newspaper article. As I read it one officer stood near the door so that the article could be quickly whipped away if anyone came in. (At the age of nineteen I used to feel completely loyal to my D-wing officers – it wasn't until after my three-year sentence that I realized that prison officers didn't actually give a damn about me at all.)

'Well done, Josie.'

   Anyhow, I read this whole article and because what I had read had made me shake and tremble with horror they took me for a walk round the prison grounds. When I got back it was dinner-time, so I went up to the recess to the loo, came out and was washing my hands, when I heard someone coming up the stairs. It was Myra. I thought, 'I'll just stay here until she goes by.' But she didn't go by, she came on across the bridge. Apparently, she had been talking to the officers and she had actually been kept in the office until they knew I was in the recess. It had been all set up. It was almost immediately after I had read that newspaper article and I just couldn't handle the horror of what I'd read . . . so I went for her.

   It took the prison officers an awful long time to answer the alarm bell, and by that time she was quite a mess. I'd knocked her teeth loose at the front, she had to eat through a straw for about six weeks. Her nose was crossed to the left side of her face, I'd split her lip, her knee and her ear, and she had two black eyes. The officers treated me like a celebrity. It was: 'Here's half an ounce of tobacco, Josie;' 'Let me shake your hand;' 'Well done Josie, I've waited twelve years for someone to do that' etc. (Pat Carlen, ed. *Criminal Women*, 1985, pp. 157–8)

Love

One problem which will never be eradicated from any women's prison, no matter how 'open' and progressive, is that of lesbianism. The subject was discussed quite openly at Cornton Vale, for prisoners had heard that it was rife in jails in England. Staff were quick to stamp out any signs of lesbian liaisons, but they happened more often amongst younger prisoners who were simply lonely and searching for some kind of affection. I was always on my guard. (Sheila Garvie, *Marriage to Murder: My Story*, 1980, p. 136)

Love letters   Some more of my discoveries on the yards are Lesbian love letters, written on lavatory paper and for some reason carelessly discarded and only half torn up. I've seen enough of them to realize what they are and they all seem to me rather sad. I have been surprised at the amount of open homosexuality there is here. Girls quite often boast of being Lesbian and I'm never quite sure how much of it is a sort of bravado and wishing to be in the fashion, just as some girls at my old school told everyone they had a 'pash' on such and such a mistress or prefect because they thought it was the done thing.

Most of the declared homosexuals that I have spoken to are long-term prisoners. Some of them have children outside but they seem to have lost touch entirely with their previous life and drifted into these affairs with other girls. From all accounts there are affairs between prisoners and officers but it's hard to see how these can be countenanced. On K Wing, where prisoners sleep two to a room, the authorities have to be careful to split dangerous friendships. A rather hard-bitten fellow-prisoner asked me about K Wing when I was living there and said it must be nice in the married quarters! The officers too seem to regard the problem with a detached cynicism. When one of the girls on K Wing brushed her hair back in a boyish style she was asked by the officer if she was turning or had she turned! Cropped hair styles and boyish names are the danger signals here of course, and if a girl adopts a boy's name the other prisoners are often forbidden to use it. (Jane Buxton and Margaret Turner, *Gate Fever*, 1962, p. 115)

Work

For three months during my first year in Gateside I worked in the kitchen, from 6 a.m. until 6 p.m. This made prison life slightly more bearable for at least I had the chance to try my hand at cooking, which I enjoyed – and I got a few compliments from fellow prisoners. But there were drawbacks. Kitchen work was back-breaking, because it meant scrubbing floors and cleaning the antiquated equipment. My stint in the kitchen ended, in any event, when I had to be taken to Greenock Royal Infirmary to have an ulcerated mole removed. On my return, it was back to the long hours in the monotony of the sewing room.

I tried to be a model prisoner, for I knew that because of my background and the publicity which had attended my trial prison officers were just watching and waiting for me to step out of line. However, discipline was harder than I ever imagined it would be and there was no communication whatsoever between prisoners and officers. (Sheila Garvie, *Marriage to Murder: My Story*, 1980, p. 119)

I had hard labour – and it was hard labour too. You had to walk everywhere in single file and you weren't allowed to talk. Number 1 labour I was doing; that was outside in the prison yard. You stood in a long line down one side of some big trestle-tables with sheets of metal on them. Then the men came from the men's part of the prison, they had wheelbarrows full of rock which they tipped out on the tables for you. We had to get out the hard lumps and bash the other rocks to bits; then the bits were shovelled along to a stone slab at the end, and there they had to be ground down with other lumps of stone into a fine powder. Then you had to sweep the powder off into barrows, and wheel it over to the storerooms. I think it was sandstone, and it was made up into blocks, they were called 'Donkey stones' that people used for whitening steps with and cleaning stone floors. (Tony Parker, *Five Women*, 1965, p. 154)

Hard labour

Food

In that stoke-hole one of the women was found frying a pigeon on a shovel to eat with her beans and bacon. She had caught it without any difficulty, as they were plentiful and extremely tame. (Muriel Norroy, *I Robbed the Lords and Ladies Gay*, 1939, p. 3)

Religion

In 1962 there was an eight-day mission at Holloway, conducted by a team of two Anglican Franciscan friars and two women missionaries. The Methodist minister co-operated in the venture and the Roman Catholics had a parallel mission at the same time. The mission services in chapel and the individual visits and interviews by members of the team seemed to have a considerable impact, and gave many opportunities for further work with individuals. One of the women said afterwards, 'I'll never be clean. Too much has happened in my life and I'll always be soiled and dirty. But I know now what cleanness is like, and I shall never forget.' (Joanna Kelley, *When the Gates Shut*, 1967, p. 95)

A terrifyingly beautiful thing

'I don't think that I could adequately express just how much it means to me to have been to Confession and received Holy Communion. It is a terrifyingly beautiful thing; terrifying because I have taken a step which has taken me on to the threshold of a completely new way of life, which demands much more from me than my previous one, and beautiful because I feel spiritually reborn. I made such a mess of my old life, and I thank God for this second chance, and in my own "small way", to quote St Teresa, I hope to prove that I am worthy of His blessing. It doesn't matter whether I live in prison or outside, there is a small way wherever one is.' (Myra Hindley to Lord Longford, *The Grain of Wheat*, 1974, p. 142)

A way out

She was ill. I mean, really ill, and no one was taking a blind bit of notice.

Got no sympathy from us, I can tell you. So, what can you expect, we've got us bird to do. I mean, stone me, I've got twenty, thirty years to get thro', without coping with desperately sick

Women in prison

people. There she went on, and I mean really went on, 'I'm gonna kill meself, I'm gonna kill meself'. I'm talking about every every night when we're trying to get some sleep, y'know

Well, she's drugged up all day, they're pumping her full of drugs, but she's coming out of them at night just when the rest of us are turning in.

'I want to die, I want to die.'

She's in the strips y'know. A smock, a mattrass on the flor, and no way she can harm herself.

'If ye don't let me out of here, I'm counting up to ten, and then I'm gonna kill myself.'

I mean, night after night, for God's sake, let her get on with it.

Count to ten! We all started shouting back, ten, nine, eight, seven, six ... y'know.

If we could have thought of a way to help her, believe me, we would. Yes! I mean help her top herself!

Anyhow, she got this idea herself. She's looking at the alarm button, and thinking, 'if I pick away at the cement, and plaster, I'll be able to get at the flex, pull some out, and hang meself'. So she's picking away, and it works, she pulls a little piece of flex, then a bit more, and then some more until she's got enough to wrap round her neck.

So, with it firmly wrapped round her neck, she shouts 'goodbye everybody', 'goodbye world', and flops violently onto the floor. What happens! Another bloody two yards of flex, comes out the wall, doesn't it. So, she picks herself up, and desperately charges across the cell, hoping she'll garrot herself on the way. More bloody flex comes out. The cell is festooned with it. What's more all the bloody alarm bells are ringing all over the wing. 'Screws' are dashing round, reassuring everyone. Looking in the spy holes! 'Fault on the system Judy, don't worry.' 'Everything alright Penny, don't get upset.' Till they come to the strip cell, look in, 'Nothing to worry about Mary, ... oh, my God!'

There she is sitting in the middle of all this wiring, and she's laughing. Yes laughing! The situation struck her as being so funny, she gave up any thought of killing herself. She was cured. (Judith Ward – H Wing, Durham, in Tom Hadaway, *Prison Writers: An Anthology*, 1986, pp. 33–4)

When my baby was born soon after, they took it off me in the prison hospital and sent it out into care, they thought I was going to turn against it, I suppose. I saved up all the sleeping pills they gave me, and then I took them all at once. It was lovely, it was like being in the dead house, I was asleep for two days. (Tony Parker, *Five Women*, 1965, p. 71)

They took it off me ...

Swallowed   At intervals while in prison she was very excited, and bitterly complained of being on the observation landing. She said that the constant noise from other tenants and 'being looked at' drove her crazy with fright. One night when there was a 'full-blown concert of shrieking and yelling' from the other inmates on that landing she swallowed twelve buttons and a needle, hoping in this way to end her life, as she could not bear the state of maddening fear any longer. (*This was a perfectly true story; twelve buttons and part of a needle were recovered later after treatment.*) She was very troubled about her bowels and felt ill. She had constant pain in the region of her wounds. She felt the officers were against her. She was much frightened at the night-officer who 'creeps about and looks through the bars at her.' (*This of course is true and is part of the routine work of the night-officer.*) She knew it was silly of her, but she became so 'worked up' that she did not know what she would do next. (Grace Pailthorpe, *What We Put in Prison*, 1932, pp. 96–7)

⤐ Discipline ⤐

Some people hid treasures in their bedding, but that was dangerous, as when there was a serious search one of the first things the officers did was to rip up mattresses. In fact they were up to most of the tricks; a favourite, but not a safe one, was the sanitary towel; even this had to be confiscated frequently on suspicion, and it was no use playing outraged modesty; orders were orders. (Muriel Norroy, *I Robbed the Lords and Ladies Gay*, 1939, p. 31)

Big, masculine   One by one we were called round behind the stage, up some steps
women   and into small cubicles, where two officers stripped us down to bra and pants, which they thoroughly enjoyed, and searched each garment carefully. They looked in my mouth, and behind my ears. It was very cold, and the whole performance made quite sure that no one had any dignity left. Most of the screws doing the searching were what I later learnt to call 'butch' – big, masculine women, uneducated and badly spoken. Having been searched, we were told to stack the heavy metal tables and the chairs at one end of the hall and then line up in rows.

Shivering and utterly wretched, I was taken back to Size, where we were all locked in until 8 a.m. Monday, except for those who went to church on Sunday. (Yolande McShane, *Daughter of Evil*, 1980, p. 185)

The nearest I ever got to being put on report, in fact, was one memorable day in the sewing room when I and another woman had decided to have a fly cigarette because there were no officers there at the time. An officer came into the room, her nostrils twitching at the smell of smoke, and I could see she was out for blood.

'Who's been smoking?'

'Who's been smoking?' she yelled.

I felt I had nothing to lose, and I couldn't have cared less by this time if they'd locked me up in the 'dog box' for a year. Going on report merely meant the loss of the recreation privilege, or being locked in your cell for three days without any reading material. What did it matter any more?

I stood up. There were about fifteen women in the room at the time, most of them Glasgwegians. They all promptly stood up as well! The whole of the sewing room was on its feet and the officer was flabbergasted. Her face was scarlet with rage, for she knew she couldn't put us *all* on report. She hastily discussed the situation with a civilian officer, following which we were all marched into an office and given a stern warning.

I shall always be grateful to all those women who stood up that day. (Sheila Garvie. *Marriage to Murder: My Story*, 1980, p. 120)

⟫⟫⟫ To the scaffold ⟫⟫⟫

I heard a strange little story about Mrs Thompson, by the way. While waiting to hear the result of her appeal she passed away the time by knitting. One day a small black cat ran into the cell and began playing with her ball of wool. 'Good luck, you see,' said Mrs Thompson, brightening up. Alas for the reliability of omens! Only a few minutes later the Governor entered her cell with the dreadful news that her appeal had been refused....

Mrs Thompson's last moments, I was told, were terrible. It was said that she had to be dragged to the scaffold step by step, screaming and resisting with all her might, and that her heart-rending shrieks could be heard all over the prison. Hardened prisoners declared that to the ends of their lives they would never forget those blood-curdling cries. ... (Kate Meyrick, *Secrets of the 43*, 1933, pp. 108–9)

'Have you ever known a case in which it was too much for a woman at the last?'

'I have never known it. I have never seen a man braver than a woman.' But not the sort of glamorous bravery you used to see at

Rarely beautiful

the end of a spy film, with a disdainful Mata Hari slinking sexily to the execution post. Murderers are so often ordinary people, caught on the wrong foot. Ordinary men, without eloquence. Ordinary women, rarely beautiful. Square-faced, thin-mouthed, eyes blinking behind National Health spectacles which I have to take off at the last moment, hair scraped thin by curlers, lumpy ankles above homely shoes, in which they have to slop to the gallows because prison regulations demand that there are no shoe-laces. It is not easy to go to die like that, but the fortitude of a woman comes through. (Albert Pierrepoint, *Executioner Pierrepoint*, 1974, pp. 188–9)

 Endurance

I blame the daffodils. I blame the daffodils for the misery and depression that has suddenly been forced upon me. Who wants to hear summery sounds while they're in prison? Who wants to hear summery sounds even when they're free. Not me. I hate summer. (Marjorie Wallace, *The Silent Twins*, 1986, pp. 142–3)

Particularly brutal

The next day was a bad one for me. I could hardly get my shoe on; I was hoping for a letter that did not come; and I had witnessed a woman, goaded beyond endurance by a particularly brutal officer, empty her slop pail over her and, screaming and cursing at her tormentor, being dragged off by about six other screws to the punishment or, I should think probably in her case, to the padded cells.

I had observed that it was never the decent officers, and there were some, who were involved in these scenes. The women respected the good ones, however strict. They had to be strict, for most prisoners if given an inch took yards. But discipline is not enforced by yelling at women as though they are pigs and by taking it out on them in hundreds of small ways. (Joan Henry, *Who Lie in Gaol*, 1952, p. 49)

A pack of wild lesbians

But putting up a barricade was different. It was an act of hostility against the officers and the regime, a serious offence, punishable under rule 20 of prison regulations. June was pushed roughly down the corridor to the 'dungeon' in an annexe off A wing. 'It was like being raped,' she fantasized. 'Raped by a pack of wild lesbians.' In an anteroom she was undressed, even her bra and underpants removed, and a piece of material which looked like brown sacking was pulled over her head. She felt angry and

Women in prison

embarrassed. Her slide and rubber band were wrenched out of her hair. 'There was a sexual element in it. I almost enjoyed the whole hassle. There was I helpless, yet defensive.' One of the officers grabbed her wrists and tried to remove her silver bangle. Her grip was painful and she did not let go until June was safely inside the strip cell. (Marjorie Wallace, *The Silent Twins*, 1986, p. 173)

Governors

It is hard to believe that these punishments do prisoners much good. They support the authority of the staff and may act as a warning to others. Many governors find them the most disagreeable part of their duties. Curiously, however, a link is often forged between a governor and a prisoner in these circumstances; some of the women whom one seems to have influenced most and feels one has eventually really been able to help are those who at one time had to be punished frequently and severely. A governor has to visit each day anyone she has put in cellular confinement or on bread and water diet and often, after sitting on their mattresses with them and talking, it is possible to leave feeling that a friendship has been established; one can try to make them understand why they had to be punished and attempt to understand why they had to rebel. (Joanna Kelley, *When the Gates Shut*, 1967, pp. 22–3)

She sat very upright in the chair behind the desk, a middle-aged woman in a well-cut tweed suit. Her graying hair was drawn back in a bun. She wore glasses, and the papers on the desk in front of her were, I imagined, my case papers.

Mary Size

She exuded that air of authority natural to those who have held high positions over a long period of time. I sensed that the officer beside her was probably just as much in awe of her as I was.

My thirty-six years seemed to slip away from me, and I was about twelve, standing in front of the headmistress at my school. (Joan Henry, *Who Lie in Gaol*, 1952, p. 107)

Release

I was given absolutely no preparation whatsoever for discharge. 'The Welfare' saw me, and having ascertained that I would be met by my daughter and could go to her house, that was that. Nobody knew or cared what my circumstances were, what problems I would face, what could be done to stop me repeating the offence and returning. Only my own probation officer, who came to see me during her Christmas holiday which she had spent at Leeds with her family, seemed in any way concerned about what was to happen to me, and whether I could cope with life outside. I count myself fortunate that I had somewhere to go and someone to care for me. Nobody in Styal would have cared otherwise. Of course I had heard about the appallingness of prison aftercare, but to hear about it is one thing, experience it another. (Audrey Peckham, *A Woman in Custody*, 1985, p. 218)

BOOK FOUR

The Men in Blue

Strangeways Prison

The prison officer

I came into the service because I was bought-up in an orphanage, I went straight from there into the army, and I was captured soon after the war started and spent nearly six years in a prisoner-of-war camp. When I came home again I knew I couldn't live any life except in some kind of institution so I didn't even hesitate about applying. It's never crossed my mind to think about anything else and it never will. (Prison Officer (48), 15 years' service, in Tony Parker, *The Man Inside*, 1973, p. 57)

Disenchanting old screw

Apart from a brief course of instruction such as I had received at Hull, the training of prison officers in my early days was largely self-acquired. We were placed with older officers in charge of cells and workshops, and were expected to learn from them. At Hull these officers had been most helpful, but I was less lucky when I arrived at Parkhurst. I was seconded to a disenchanting old screw, curt in speech, morose in manner and, on occasion, downright abusive. I had to report to him on the early morning parade. The prisoners were marching out of the halls and, when I arrived at the spot where this old officer's party were forming up, I greeted him with a civil 'Good morning'. He glared at me for a moment, changed the wad of tobacco he was chewing from one side of his mouth to the other, and snapped: 'Get on with your work, mister, and don't bother me with your good mornings.' (L. Merrow-Smith and J. Harris, *Prison Screw*, 1962, p. 23)

You knew where you were

When I first went into prison as a YP (young prisoner), you weren't allowed to speak. If you showed the staff, by the look on your face, what you'd like to do, you were put down for 'dumb insolence', and given three days' bread and water. But those days were better because you knew where you stood. At the moment you don't know how you stand; the staff that's coming into the prison don't understand the psychological aspect of working with prisoners. They're two-faced, joking with you one minute and reporting you the next. In the old days there were no screws who'd have a joke with you – you knew where you were, and that's how I like it. (Ronald Lloyd and Stanley Williamson, *Born to Trouble*, 1968, pp. 152–3)

Ticket checker

To understand the experienced warder, to get the full fantastic flavour of his real task, one must imagine a ticket-checker on a railway. The ordinary checker's job is to see that people's tickets are in order; adding the jail-mentality his job would be to suspect every person whose ticket *was* in order! An experienced worker,

The men in blue

he would know that every person with an orthodox ticket was a Wide Man pulling a fast one! (Jim Phelan, *Jail Journey*, 1940, p. 339)

Fighting Fred

There was one twirl who got down the club, we used to call him fighting Fred, the reason we called him this was because he fort the war, was a black belt at judo (every blow a death blow) as he used to say, he had trained boxers, and had been a boxer his-self, he had also trained wrestlers and been a wrestler. On top of this he was once a lumber-jack, a bally dancer, a female impersonator, a brick layer, carpenter, gas man, probation officer, artist, writer, sculptor, not only had he done all these things and was a master at them, he had also done anything that you said you had done. Some times when we saw him comming we would put our heads together and try and find some thing that he had'nt done, but try as we might we never could find anything. Of course we only had his word that he had done all these things. And as I have said a screws word is law, so if Fred said he killed an Elephant with his bare hands, well that's just what he did and who were we to dispute it. After all if we did he might find some thing to nick us for and we did'nt want that.

There was only one thing that was realy true about Fighting Fred and that was his ability as an actor, he was deffinatly a througher actor and there was no doubt about that what ever. Of course he was a bigger lier than Tom Peper but we did'nt count that. (Frank Norman, *Bang to Rights*, 1958, p. 118)

The metamorphosis

The Blade was a screw in Exeter who was so thin that when he turned sideways he disappeared. Before he joined the prison service he was a milkman. It was an embarrassment to the Blade that on the landing where he worked there was a con to whom he used to deliver his gold tops. Before joining the Service, the Blade was just an ordinary working lad with a wife and kids to support on a score a week. He'd buy you a drink in the local and chat up the birds on his round and act generally like a normal human being.

The day the Blade got a uniform he changed. Overnight the metamorphosis was complete. He strutted up and down the landing swinging his keys in his right hand exposing the polished chain for all to see.

By inserting a little piece of wood underneath the peak of his cap, he could make his headgear look like something the Gestapo would have approved of. But the truth was out. We knew he was a milkman. As far as we were concerned, a milkman he would always be.

When his back was turned, some wag would bawl out 'Milko' or 'Six pints today please'.

Poor old Blade, it all got too much for him and he got a transfer to a prison where no one knew his dark secret and where the cons believed that he was exactly what he looked like – a born screw. (Jago Stone, *The Burglar's Bedside Companion*, 1975, pp. 56–7)

Cries and screams

I also remember with some bitterness and regret the treatment meted out to patients, particularly boys, who became violent or troublesome. These were nearly always shut in a padded cell and then given a severe and scientific beating-up. Although their cries and screams of pain could be heard throughout the hospital, this was always excused on the basis that the process was the best medical remedy for hysteria. My own feeling was that, on the one hand, many of the patients so indiscriminately treated were not cases of hysteria, and that, on the other hand, there must now be more humane treatment for hysterics. In many instances, these men and boys were simply difficult disciplinary cases, brought across to the padded cells especially for the beating-up. The only good I was able to do them was to stroll in the direction of the cell where the chastisement was taking place. (This was easy because the screams could be heard all over the hospital.) Fortunately, because I had been a Member of Parliament and the officers also knew that a number of people whom they regarded as influential visited me, they always feared repercussions when I was around. Therefore, as soon as I appeared outside the cell, and coughed or made my presence known in some similar way, the beating-up would be cut short; and the four, five or six officers would put their sticks back and provide a number of plausible stories as to why violence had been necessary at all. (Peter Baker, *Time Out of Life*, 1961, pp. 138–9)

'There, there . . .'

Johnston came back in charge of the mailbags, and after the Governor had gone we heard thumps and moans coming faintly from below stores, from chokey.

The Principal Officer, a thin wafer-shaven man, erect, slim and spotless and beribboned, turned his old eyes to Johnston, cocked his ear to the moaning with the air of a connoisseur, smiled and murmured appreciatively, 'Someone getting a clean shirt, Mr Johnston?'

A clean shirt was the beating they sometimes gave a prisoner beginning his punishment. They told him to strip and then when he had his clothes half-off, they would accuse him of resisting the search, beat him, baton him on the kidneys, and on the thighs.

The men in blue

Our PO was most feared. Now that he was no longer young and active enough to lead the fray, he waited till the prisoner was stripped naked by the other screws. Then he would catch him by the ballocks and twist and pull on them. Putting his weight and swinging down out of them, not abusing the prisoner or angry but rather the reverse, grunting and saying softly 'All right, all right, now, it will be over in a minute.' Grunting and perspiring with the effort. 'There, there, it will soon be over.' (Brendan Behan, *Borstal Boy*, 1958, p. 110)

*   *   *

I asked seven prison governors what they thought about bullying. Did it go on or not? With one accord they gave the same answer, almost in the same words. They could not run their prisons as they did without the co-operation of the prisoners – and this is a statement that everyone who has visited a prison will accept. The last thing they could afford to tolerate was a bullying officer. If they found one, he would go at once, and they did not believe he could exist for long without their knowing it. If you knew those Governors you would realise that it is an almost impertinent comment to say that I believed them. What then is the truth? (L. Atthill, *Spectator*, 8 October 1937, p. 575)

What then is the truth?

～ Resistance ～

Charlie eyed me speculatively. 'I've had plenty of trouble with screws during all my years in prison, don't you worry. I know how to deal with an officer who tries to score off me. Any screw who shouts at me: "Get inside your cell, stop your talking, shut your door", for instance, I know better than to argue with him, and risk losing remission, or being put on punishment diet. I gets inside like I'm ordered, I slam my cell door shut, I get down my slate and piece of chalk and I draw him on my slate, then I spits on him and rubs him out. You can't be punished for that, you know.' (P.H. Baden Ball, *Prison Was My Parish*, 1956, p. 78)

That kind of warder, who barks loudly but bites lightly, is a common variety in our prisons, but at Winson Green there was one principal officer, a man in a position one step above a warder but lower than the chief, who was what the prisoners called a super-super bastard. He was a natural born bully of the worst type; that is to say he was a coward who crumpled up when he

'You can go to hell.'

was opposed. He used to inspect the cells and find fault for no other reason than to satisfy his sadistic appetite. One day he inspected my cell.

'What's this?' he said, grabbing hold of the bundle of cleaning rags and scattering them and the brick dust about the floor. 'What have you got in here?'

I felt angry but I controlled myself well enough to say:

'Cleaning materials, as you see.'

'Then why don't you use them?' he growled offensively. 'Clean those tins! Give this floor a scrub! Make the place look less like a pig-sty!'

'I'm not a convict,' said I. 'I'm on remand.'

'You're a prisoner,' he returned. 'And you'll do as I say.'

'You can go to hell!' said I. 'I don't believe the governor would let you carry on like this if he knew about it.'

He growled something about getting me put on bread and water, but he left the cell and I heard nothing more about the matter. (James Spenser, *Limey Breaks In*, 1934, pp. 153–4)

'Backed off into a corner.'

Two mornings later I was unlocked and told to pack my kit, as I was leaving. I got my odds and ends together, said goodbye to all my pals through their cell doors and went downstairs. Davies was there with about fifteen screws. We walked out to reception where I signed the private property book. Davies was in the next room; I heard him say, 'Make him wear a jacket.' A moment later a nice sort of screw came in holding a prison jacket.

'Mac, put this on,' he said.

'You're joking,' I said. 'Tell the silly ballocks to put it on himself.'

He went back to Davies. I heard some muttering, and about four of them came back, and the same screw holding the jacket said, 'You've got to put it on, or the governor's ordered us to make you.'

'Has he? Well, I ain't putting it on.'

They started to walk towards me, and I backed off into a corner and shaped up. I look the business when I shape up, hard eyes and everything – it's one of my best effects. There was a bit of manoeuvring and then one of them, a senior screw, took the jacket from the one who was holding it and walked back to Davies. I heard him say, very emphatically, 'He won't wear it, sir.' I didn't hear Davies's reply, but they handcuffed me to a senior screw and we went out of the reception and got in a police car outside the door. (John McVicar, *McVicar by Himself*, 1974, pp. 37–8)

The men in blue

I became a bad prisoner, and refused to take orders from the *Felt power*
warders which resulted in my being manhandled one day by one
of the officers, a man who particularly disliked me. I was a strong
man, physically, and I turned on him with all my strength. I
succeeded in overpowering him and seizing his stick, and I struck
down other warders who came to his aid.

The other prisoners in the block were shouting and storming in
their cells, and my rage turned against them. Suddenly I felt power.

'Shut up, shut up the lot of you,' I commanded, and I went
down the line viciously rapping the knuckles of hands gripping
bars. This caused an even greater uproar and more warders came
rushing down. I leapt to meet them and then I remember no
more. I was knocked unconscious by a blow which affected my
brain. (John Edward Allen, *Inside Broadmoor*, 1952, p. 25)

We were concerned about what to do when the screws came back, *Did a shit*
and we felt pretty helpless. I did a shit in the middle of the floor
and started rubbing it all over my arms and body and face. I
thought that if they were going to come in then I was going to
jump on them and grab them so that they would get shit all over
them. They did come back and saw what I had done and backed
out as I positioned myself to throw my whole body amongst
them. At first Ben was reluctant to do this but he did so after
vomiting. When the screws left we sat looking at each other
throughout the night and every so often would break out in fits of
laughter. (Jimmy Boyle, *A Sense of Freedom*, 1977, p. 134)

The incessant nagging, the silence, which is not just a parenthesis *Ghastly*
between sounds, but seems as if everything has been said; the *circular saw*
exercise round and round – a ghastly circular saw that bites deep
into the nerves of even the most stolid; the working up to fever
pitch, the half-formed resolution, many times repressed and
driven deep down, there to be forced up again; the stimulation of
continued persecution, then the final irresistible impulse, the
blind half-run, the smashing blow, the shouts, the whistles, and
out of the confusion as the batons descend, 'well, I've done it
now. I may as well have my money's worth,' and fierce and many
are the blows directed at the hated jailer. Often bloody and nearly
always frog-marched to chokey, stripped naked and flung into a
cell. (Red Collar Man, *Chokey*, 1938, pp. 51–2)

❧ Collaboration ❧

Every morning about ten the Governor made his rounds of
inspection. Until he had been through the shop or just looked in

at the door as the case might be, discipline was strict. By this I do not mean that the officers were more zealous. Prisoners and officers combined to put up a good show, for should the Governor find discipline relaxed the whole prison would undoubtedly suffer. Directly the Governor departed life became normal again until the Chief Officer made his inspection in the afternoon. The afternoon inspection was merely a walk round the shop by the Chief Warder, or his deputy. He usually appeared about 4 p.m. and it was amusing to see the men keeping a 'lookout' at about that time. The shop was well lighted by large windows, and through these every side of the building could be observed. The inspecting officer might be seen behind the shop walking along the inside of the prison wall. On another day he would come from a different direction. It did not matter how he came, he could only enter the shop through the one door. As soon as he was seen in the offing the warning would be given verbally where possible to the officer on duty at the top of the shop and he in his turn would send a prisoner down to the other officer with a message of warning. Then both officers, who had previously been comfortably lazing on their chairs, would stand up and try to look efficient. Many times I have been working at the bottom of the shop and at about four o'clock have seen the senior officer on his feet at the far end of the building. To the knowing this was sufficient warning, and it was heeded. It was just another of those unwritten understandings that bind officers and men in their charge. It may seem a trivial matter to those who have never been 'inside', but this understanding between warders and men is the most precious thing in prison life. It alone makes life at all bearable. Only the blindest of fools will read into this account of everyday life in prison the need for stricter discipline. That would drive not only the prisoners mad but the warders too. (Anonymous by necessity, *Five Years for Fraud*, 1936, pp. 129–30)

Pleasing the lady

It is not unknown for a lag to have some money sent to a screw in order that he – the screw – may take the lag's wife or girl-friend out for the evening after the visit and show her such a good time as Princetown affords. Whether this is done with the idea of pleasing the lady or of pleasing the screw and thus making life easier for the lag is something which it is perhaps wiser not to debate. Whatever the reason, many prisoners adopt an attitude the reverse of that of the dog in the manger about their womenfolk. (George Dendrickson and Frederick Thomas, *The Truth about Dartmoor*, 1954, p. 176)

The men in blue

Prison officers are a curious mixture. I remember one from Wandsworth called Honeysett. Working in the censor's office he had been reading my letters and he told me that he found them chatty and amusing and that I wrote pretty well. Not long afterwards I found myself in chokey, where you are not allowed to talk or communicate with anyone and have to exercise alone. There were always four screws on duty in the exercise yard, one in each corner, and one day Honeysett was one of the four. As I passed him he did the old ventriloquism bit, speaking out of the corner of his mouth so no one could see him speaking. 'Next time round, stop and do your shoe up. ' I did as he said and he threw down a packet of Spangles, which, when you are on bread and water, is something fantastic. Screws like Honeysett are very human, others are just arseholes. (Ronnie Biggs, *His Own Story*, 1981, pp. 40–1)

Spangles

'Mr Barrabas,' he said. 'This is Sykes. A real sound man. You can trust him, make no mistake about that. So how about getting him a good number?'

Mr Barrabas

Prison Officer Barrabas gave the real sound man an appraising look.

'Better give it a day or two until we see what's going on,' he said, non-committed like. 'But I'll fix him up if he wants to do a bit of business. See you later, Sykes.'

Well, you can't say fairer than that. Even the executives of the best-run hotels are a trifle cagey until they know the strength of their guests. And I must say that Prison Officer Barrabas was as good as his word.

He arrived at my cell with a sheet of writing paper and an envelope.

I knew the drill. There and then I wrote to Manchester Freddie, asking him to send ten pounds to an address which the screw gave me.

Two days later Barrabas came to my cell again and said: 'Well, lad, your pal Freddie is right on the mark. I got the cock-and-hen this morning. How will two ounces to the pound suit you? Apart from that there'll always be the odd bit of chocolate and a few sweets and you'll be okay with me. I always look after my lads.' (Robert Sykes, *Who's Been Eating My Porridge?*, 1967, p. 80)

As I say, life wasn't so bad in Chelmsford nick. Once they realised that you were not going to give any trouble they left you alone pretty well. Me and my boys more or less ran the show to our own liking, so, apart from the trouble our relatives were put to, life wasn't so bad. My wife wrote to me regularly, and came to see

Bent screw

me on visits. It was always nice to get a letter from her but I didn't go much on those visits, they were too painful. It was through a straight screw that I knew what was going on with my mob. Once I was earning a few bob from the book I was making I was able to pay this screw to do my clerking for me. His job was to telephone a certain number in London every day and tell the person at the other end of the line any messages that I wanted to send to the mob. He also brought back information that I wanted as to how my affairs in the big wide world were running. Of course, it's not so easy running your business by remote control through the medium of a prison screw, but it was the best I could do. In fact it was an invaluable service, because from it I could prepare for a few more jobs to be done as soon as I got out. (Billy Hill, *Boss of Britain's Underworld*, 1955, p. 69)

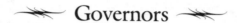 Governors

The Governor came to see me, that first day. He was tall and stringy-looking, with a face like a bad-tempered stoat, and I expected a load of the usual fanny about my having made trouble at other prisons but better not make any there, or else, sort of stuff.

We looked at each other. I could feel he was sorting me out. You can tell when a screw starts blustering that he is scared of you. Clayton didn't bluster. All he said was: 'I'm sorry about this bread-and-water, Sparks. I don't somehow think it's fair for a prisoner to bring his punishment from one convict station to another. But I can't help it,' he said, 'it's a Home Office order, and I can only hope it won't hinder you from making a fresh start with us.'

Before I realized what I was saying, I'd told him: 'That's all right, sir.' I could have bitten my tongue off. (Ruby Sparks, *Burglar to the Nobility*, 1961, pp. 79–80)

Lawton's bicycle (I)

The governor, who had been a screw himself, encouraged these sick screws to have their emotional workouts on prisoners. He was notorious for saying to prisoners who challenged a screw's word, 'If one of my officers says he saw you riding round the landing on a motorbike, then riding round the landing on a motorbike you were.' One day a prisoner made an application to the governor for permission to purchase a gallon of petrol. The governor asked, 'What do you want petrol for?' The prisoner said, 'The motorbike I was nicked for riding round the landing

The men in blue

yesterday has run out of petrol.' (Walter Probyn, *Angel Face*, 1977, p. 57)

Near the end of his service, his sadism had mellowed to a contemptuous indifference to his charges. Always he believed what he called 'my officers'.

Lawton's bicycle (II)

'If one of my officers told me you were riding round the gallery on a bicycle,' he'd snarl with Cockney venom, 'I'd believe him.' (Donald Mackenzie, *Fugitives*, 1955, pp. 198–9)

I remember a prison officer telling me that the incident that stood out from his long career was of John Vidler, when Governor of Maidstone Prison, ending an argument with an inmate by hurling a hefty book (the Rule Book, probably) after him as he turned to leave the room. The officer had remembered this as an expression of complete respect and caring. The penal reformer would probably regret the violence, or explain that the nasty old building had turned cool discussion into tension. But the concern was to make a man think, and stand up, and walk; and this aim does not really depend at all upon buildings. (Michael Sorenson, *Working on Self-Respect*, 1986, p. 107)

John Vidler

I would cross-examine the prisoner: about what he wanted, what he expected, what his attitude to the training prison was, so as to decide which group he should join. And then I would introduce the man to his future governor and suggest his having a talk with him. Nobody else on the board was allowed to talk: Miss Banks and the chaplain saw the man later. But I would emphasise to the man that everyone present meant to do as much as possible to help him and to enable him to regain his faith in life.

His philosophy

The prisoner's first reaction would often be that he wanted to go back to the nice normal ordinary prison because he knew where he was there. My reply was: 'You certainly won't know where you are here! It's for you to develop your own character and attitude. If you don't want to, you will get slung out.' In fact, only about five a year actually made life so difficult that they had to be sent back to their former prisons, and these were all recidivists. If subsequently the men got into trouble or did not work properly, I would repeat my exhortation: 'Remember what I told you at the beginning. ...' (John Vidler, *If Freedom Fail*, 1964, p. 81)

All the time I was at Maidstone I felt that John Vidler was fighting a lone battle against the relentless Prison System. I felt, too, that Maidstone will be a very different place once he retires

A lone battle

from the service, which he will shortly do. The officers themselves prophesy this. 'Just wait and see what happens when the Old Man goes!' they will tell one, with a menacing smirk. 'The men won't get away with it then!' And one knows they are thinking of the grim, rigid discipline of those other prisons where the rules are enforced to the letter and the 'Screws are always right'. For it was one of the tragedies of Maidstone that John Vidler did not realise the undercurrent of disloyalty that ran through his staff. He was, in a sense, a dictator and like all dictators, surrounded by toadying sycophants. Only a few – a very few – of his officers gave him real support because only the few understood the great value of the work he was doing. (Anthony Heckstall-Smith, *Eighteen Months*, 1954, pp. 47–8)

Governor's protest from a 'penal dustbin'

From the Governor of H M Prison, Wormwood Scrubs

Sir, As the manager of a large penal dustbin I wish to write about the latest proposal of the Home Secretary to reduce the prison population.

I am driven to write as my patience and tolerance are finally exhausted. We have before us the prospective implementation of section 47 of the Criminal Law Act 1977, which would allow courts to suspend between a quarter and three quarters of a sentence of imprisonment of between six months and two years.

The Advisory Council on the Penal System (1978) was extremely doubtful of the efficacy of suspended sentences in reducing the prison population. On part suspended sentences Mr Brayshaw, the then (1977) Secretary to the Magistrates' Association, echoed similar doubts, as did Mr Brittan, Minister of State in Parliament (1979) and the Home Office's *Review of Parole* (1981). I have great respect for Mr Whitlaw's integrity and honesty and so I cannot believe that he is satisfied with the present proposals.

From my personal point of view I did not join the Prison Service to manage overcrowded cattle pens, nor did I join to run a prison where the interests of the individuals have to be sacrificed continually to the interests of the institution, nor did I join to be a member of a service where staff that I admire are forced to run a society that debases.

I am aware of the difficulties that the Home Secretary faces in reducing the prison population, but I find it difficult to understand why, if he genuinely wishes to reduce the prison population, automatic release on licence for short-term prisoners is not introduced. However he, for whatever reason, has not done this.

As it is evident that the present uncivilized conditions in prison seem likely to continue and as I find this incompatible with any moral ethic, I wish to give notice that I, as the governor of the major prison in the United Kingdom, cannot for much longer tolerate, either as a professional or as an individual, the inhumanity of the system within which I work.

I am aware that any gesture I

The men in blue

would make would in all prob-ability be futile, but if I do not stand up I shall be like a political party putting pursuance of power before humanity.
Yours faithfully,

JOHN MCCARTHY,
Governor,
HM Prison,
Wormwood Scrubs,
PO Box 757,
Du Cane Road, W12.
November 17.

(Letters to the editor, *The Times*, 19 November 1981)

While mutiny is the biggest worry of a prison governor, escapes are the pinpricks that nag his official life. When a man makes a break the whole prison machinery is put in emergency gear and for at least twenty-four hours afterwards, until the position is properly assessed, prisoners are locked in their cells. The reason is of course that as many officers as can be spared are detailed to search for the prisoner, or prisoners, who got away.

Potentially useless

But apart from the upset to routine and the worry of the inquiry that follows, with the apportionment of blame that the Prison Commissioners will be bound to make, the governor is more acutely aware of the unrest that an escape always causes among the rest of the prisoners. It is a sort of hidden excitement that bubbles away beneath the surface and could erupt into nasty demonstrations of unrest if there was the slightest hint of a loosening of official discipline.

It is difficult to put on to paper just what tension a prison governor experiences in such moments, and it is not surprising that so many of us have at one time or another almost cracked under the strain. Because, do not forget, anyone with the responsibility of a prison governor is living an unnaturally tensed life.

It is not a normal existence to begin with. And the more I look back upon my own life, the more I realize that although it was so necessary in the past, and is in the present state of society, it is potentially useless. Unless you count the few instances when his personal intervention or counsel has helped a prisoner to make good, he contributes nothing very much to the future of mankind. I suppose he has a sort of abstract influence, if anything, like the policeman and the soldier. But as things are, you can't do without any of them. (Gerald Fancourt Clayton, *The Wall is Strong*, 1958, pp. 125–6)

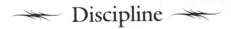

Discipline

Curious old customs still survived and on my first tour of the various parties I was mystified by the fact that if I met any party marching towards me it was at once halted and turned so that the convicts had their backs to me. When I enquired the reason for this I was told that it was to prevent the risk of any convict with a grievance spitting at the Governor or Deputy Governor. I could not see the sense in this and eventually succeeded in getting this futile procedure abolished. (Gerald Fancourt Clayton, *The Wall is Strong*, 1958, p. 51)

Lock-step

Some of the older prisoners still walked as though they were required to march the lock-step, although this had not been enforced for some considerable time. Eyes to the front, however, was still the order of the day, and at work, at exercise and elsewhere prisoners mechanically turned their heads away from each other to avoid being accused of talking. (B.D. Grew, *Prison Governor*, 1958, p. 58)

Forbidden to speak

When I first obtained permission in March, 1921, to take a weekly class for lads in Armley Gaol (euphemistically known in official language as 'juvenile adults') the old silence system still prevailed in all its rigour. Not only were prisoners forbidden under penalty to speak a single word to one another, but prison officers were also forbidden to speak to the prisoners, except to give a command or reproof or a necessary instruction. If a prison officer, on his round of inspection at dusk, who came upon a lad of sixteen sobbing in his cell at the outset of his first sentence, and away for the first time from home, were to have laid his hand on the lad's shoulder and given him a word or two of cheer, he would have been liable to be reported to the Governor and to be reproved for 'undue familiarity with a prisoner'. (T. Edmund Harvey, *The Christian Church and the Prisoner*, 1941, pp. 66–7)

'Stop that talking!'

Most officers felt they were doing their duty if at regular intervals they called out 'Stop that talking!' A supervising officer was not only liable to find himself on the carpet for permitting talk between prisoners. His own freedom to converse with a colleague, when both were on duty, was also severely restricted, and he risked a severe reprimand from the governor if found indulging in the practice. (Harley Cronin, *The Screw Turns*, 1967, pp. 20–1)

Illegal

No man was punished for talking in all my time in the English jails: it was illegal to punish people for such acts. What happened was that a man spoke, a warder told him to stop, he spoke again, and was reported: not for talking, but for disobeying an order. It was all perfectly legal and very simple. (Jim Phelan, *Jail Journey*, 1940, p. 16)

The men in blue

Discipline is not harsh at Dartmoor. There was very little trouble that I saw. Each convict is awarded eight good conduct marks per day for good behaviour. If he earns his maximum of marks, at the end of eighteen months he is promoted to the second stage and wears a black band. This entitles him to associate with other prisoners for one hour every night. At the end of two and a half years he enters the third stage, wearing a different coloured tunic. In his fourth year he enters the highest stage of all. In this stage he is permitted a tobacco and cigarette ration. He may also make small purchases of sweets and biscuits, and is allowed a news-paper. He obtains also many other privileges – is allowed to talk and permitted more visits and letters. Greater than all these, by good behaviour, a convict may be liberated on ticket-of-leave after serving three quarters of his sentence. It therefore behoves a man to obey the regulations – or at least not to be caught breaking them. (Ex-Convict No:–, *Dartmoor From Within*, nd, p. 56)

I joined the shoe-shop towards the end of the month, and just caught the monthly 'dry-bath' or search. All parties are searched once a month, and the method is most unpleasant. The search is supposed to be a surprise. When the party to be searched is marching away from the parade it must turn by the old boundary wall which bisects the prison. As the party wheels across the wall it is suddenly surrounded by jailors and marched to the bath-house. Here it is halted while most of the jailors go into the bath-house and take up their positions at the different doorways of the bath-tubs. A close watch has been kept on the men in the party in order to see that they don't drop any prohibited article. The men are then sent into the bath-house, and go into separate baths. The bath-tubs are in little cubicles. Then, with the screw watching carefully, one has to strip naked. Every article of clothing is minutely searched; the hair is ruffled; the mouth is opened; the privates are scrutinised, often to the accompaniment of facetious ribaldry. 'Got a kidney wiper there, Mac. You weren't behind the door when they were being dished out' – and so on. As these remarks were usually made by the screws who were not too harsh over discipline, one replied in kind to them, with such retorts as, 'Yes, your old woman would like to have it for a change.' The whole business is degrading, but I came to regard it with complete equanimity, except during the winter, when I got cold and sore. Only four times in nearly eight years did I hear of men being found with contraband during these 'turnovers.'

The 'dry bath' is a silly waste of time. Once I was almost caught with a newspaper, and that was the nearest I ever came to

He Questioned Me

justifying this important detail of gaol administration. (W.F.R. Macartney, *Walls Have Mouths*, 1936, pp. 87–8)

Wild beast   My name was eventually called out by the chief warder from the governor's adjudication room. Before I was allowed to enter this room my clothing was searched by two warders in case I had anything in my pockets which I might throw at the governor! I was then escorted by the warders into the room, where I had to stand behind breast-high bars like a wild beast. The governor sat at a large table about six foot away, surrounded by one chief warder, one principal warder, two ordinary warders and one chief's clerk, who is also a warder. As every one of these persons, with the exception of the governor, is carrying a truncheon, it will readily be agreed that the 'Great White Chief' is suitably protected from 'brutal and savage attack'. (F.A. Stanley, *A Happy Fortnight*, 1938, p. 270)

Astonishment   I had allowed a man a notebook to study arithmetic. The notebooks must not be used for any purpose other than that for which they are issued. This man had filled the back pages with some crude printing, and was brought (much in fear, and looking very guilty) before me, with the damning evidence, by the Chief Officer. To the prisoner's complete astonishment I told him I would put him in the drawing class where he would be taught to do lettering properly – and mildly added that he must not break the rules about note-books! – I don't know how long it took him

The men in blue

to get over it (I hope he never will), but at first it was clear that his delight was smothered by his surprise. (A. Stevens, *Father to Son*, 1952, p. 155)

For the benefit of those who know little of prison routine, it may come as a surprise to know that bread and water is still the most popular punishment of our progressive prison system, and anyone who thinks that this can do no physical harm can come and argue the point with me.

The sheer delight on the chokey screws' faces when they open the door to give you your four slices of bread has to be seen to be believed. I'm perfectly sure some of them reach orgasms over it. Many years ago I found out how to knock the grin off their faces. It is quite simple. Prison rules state that you can do three days on bread and water to be followed by three days on ordinary diet and then three days on bread and water again up to a period of fifteen days. All you do is don't eat the bread and each time they bring you a fresh lot you hand back the last lot. It isn't hard to go three days without food so long as you have water. It really winds the screws up when someone does this. You can make the remark: 'I was intending to reduce my weight anyway.' This will be guaranteed at Parkhurst to get you at least a good punch in the guts, which if you are of masochist tendencies is lovely. But if you are like me and hate pain you will wish you had kept your big mouth shut. (Brian Stratton, *Who Guards the Guards?*, 1975, p. 16)

A passage-way cut into the wall at right angles to the right-hand side of the cockpit leads to the special cells or silent cells (more generally called 'around the back'), which are used for the prisoner who for some reason or other is recalcitrant. There are seven of these cells and they are in fact cells within cells in the same way that chokey is a prison within a prison – a sort of ghastly Chinese puzzle box. Each has three thick doors and a double wall to deaden noise. They are solidly built of concrete.

To visualise these particular cells one must imagine a square concrete 'pill-box' similar to the machine-gun pill-boxes in use during the war. Its measurements were roughly 50ft in length, 20ft wide, 25ft high. Inside, this concrete shell was divided into seven cells also constructed of concrete; walls, roof, floor, all made of this material. Actually they were cells within cells for the roofs were doubled, as also were the walls, and each cell had three doors, opening outwards.

Not one of these cells had heating of any description and in winter they were intensely cold. It might be said that hot pipes ran through these cells; they certainly did run through, and in the running missed the cells, for they only ran through the passage. (Red Collar Man, *Chokey*, 1938, p. 69)

Chewed away At Dartmoor I had chewed away nearly all my wooden table in the punishment cell. Ate it, mouthful by mouthful, swallowing the chewed pulp of splinters to fill out an empty stomach.

That table wasn't anything particularly tasty. It was just a scrubbed wooden ledge, soggy from years of Dartmoor's eternal dampness. Its flavour was soap and firewood. But I'd eaten it. The lot! (Ruby Sparks, *Burglar to the Nobility*, 1961, p. 119)

Trussed up I'd had experience of canvas shirts *locked* behind your neck, but with those you *could* use your arms, you could use that pot. With a *jacket* your arms are pinioned, you are strapped *round the neck, between the legs* .. you are *trussed up like a chicken* for the *cooker* .. you are thrown down there on the rubber floor with *stiff canvas sheets* your *only* protection from the cold. The screws go out, bang that *safe-like door*. I lie there looking up at the ceiling. From where I lie I can hear *outside traffic noises*, the back of this pad abutting the outer wall of the prison. I hear motorbikes .. cars .. buses .. *roar .. bang .. crash* .. I hear children's voices .. they are *playing* out there. I'm thinking: *They will end up where I am now* one day or they will be *screws*. The light begins to fail .. there is a very small window up there .. dirty and barred .. the light seeping through. In the ceiling .. way up there .. a dark red light goes on .. I note a glass panel up there, and through that I'm *observed* by a *stealthy eye* ...

The traffic is lessening out there, no more children's voices ... But there is a tired *tweet .. tweet .. tweet .. birds* on the top of the wall about to retire for the night ... All is now *silent .. silent.*

I'm wondering: What if I want to *piss* .. shit ..? Must I do it in this *jacket*? I begin to worry. I'm *afraid* I .. I *might make a mess of myself* .. I can't get up to call for help .. I can't signal. I begin to *hate the inhuman bastards who put me in this jacket* .. careless of *what I may have to do* in the damned thing. (Victor Carasov, *Two Gentlemen to See You Sir*. 1971, pp. 76–7)

❧ Flogging ❧

... although they had robbed this poor girl of her most precious possession, her innocence, they could not have been sentenced to the 'cat' had it not been possible to prove the material robbery with violence.

The men in blue

Witnessing the infliction of corporal punishment is not an entertainment which any Governor as a rule desires, but I was present when the court's sentence was carried out upon these three young blackguards, and it gave me entire satisfaction.

Consider the position. It is scarcely safe nowadays for any woman or girl to venture along an ordinary country road, nor is a child safely to be allowed outside your door alone. And this is Old England, of which we used to boast so proudly that one could safely walk anywhere, by day or by night! Have we not got a few strong men who, instead of apologizing for being English, can be up and doing something to make England the land it was, not so long ago, when women and children were a sacred trust and respect and good manners were the general rule? (Lieut. Col. C.E.F. Rich, *Recollections of a Prison Governor*, 1932, p. 21)

I saw Eddie's back two weeks after the flogging. In the bath-house he showed it me. It looked ghastly: half-healed weals, the edges bruised blue and green, criss-crossed the white flesh of a young back, ripped and torn at the order of a Home Secretary whose party preached the brotherhood of man! (W.F.R. Macartney, *Walls Have Mouths*, 1936, pp. 162–3) *Blue and green*

The prisoner was sentenced to thirty-six strokes with the cat o'nine tails, a punishment which was not new to him as he had been lashed during a previous sentence. After his trial he was sent to the hospital. He had pneumonia, a fact which was duly reported to the Home Secretary, who was in a quandary as there was public pressure for revenge against the prisoner. After days of deliberation the order came that as soon as the inmate had recovered he was to receive fourteen strokes with the birch rod, the rationale being no doubt that his buttocks were sufficiently remote from his lungs. On the appointed day I accompanied him from the hospital to the place where the flogging was to be carried out. He was a man of about 40 and made no sound, not even a whimper. Very different from many whose cries remain as a haunting memory. Having dressed the raw areas on his buttocks I had him returned to the hospital. *'They'd have flogged my dead body.'*

The fact that such a punishment was inflicted on a man who had been so sick was abhorrent – the inflexible attitude of authority – the pound of flesh.

When I got back to the hospital I went along to Fred's cell. He was lying on his bed face down.

'Fred,' I asked, 'What has this done for you?'

'What d'you mean, done for me? You mean done to me, don't you?'

'Yes, I suppose so. Would you do the same thing again?'

'Course I would. I got flogged before; that didn't stop me, did it? I hate the fucking screws and the fucking governor. I'll do a better job next time.'

'Did you expect a reprieve when you got sick?'

'Sure I didn't. They'd have flogged my dead body.'

I felt ashamed and guilty at being an accomplice in such a deed – counter-violence which brought out nothing but the worst in all concerned. But, 'Abandon Hope?' No, not yet. (Dr Guy Richmond, *Prison Doctor*, 1975, pp. 28–9)

Gritted my teeth

I gritted my teeth, waiting for the excoriating first lash of the nine tails that would break my skin open. But I was anticipating things. First there had to be a bit of ritual so beloved by the British when condign punishment is to be inflicted.

The Governor read out the charge and sentence. Then he asked me if I had anything to say why the punishment should not be carried out. What did he expect me to say? Would it have added zest to the macabre grisly scene if I had begged for mercy? I contented myself by shouting a defiant: 'Bollocks!'

Then the first lash fell across my back as if nine cut-throat razors had been drawn simultaneously across my skin.

I braced myself for the next blow but again I was premature. Again there was a bit of ritual. The Chief Medical Officer had to play out his role. I felt the cold rim of his stethoscope pressed against my burning flesh to ascertain whether I was fit enough to continue receiving the punishment and in no danger of dying.

While this man of healing was carrying out this cursory check, the flogging screw was probably drawing the nine strands of the 'cat' through his left hand to remove particles of my flesh and skin adhering to them.

The Chief called out: 'Two!'

And so it went on, with the Chief Medical Officer pressing his stethoscope against my torn flesh after every blow. (Robert Sykes, *Who's Been Eating My Porridge?* 1967, pp. 98–100)

Not easy

At the present time in England, every prison officer knows that if he is assaulted the charge against the prisoner will be investigated by an impartial body of visiting justices, and they will, if satisfied of the prisoner's guilt, recommend to the Secretary of State that he receive corporal punishment. Under these circumstances the prison officer is ready to leave the prisoner to the arbitrament of the magistrates and the Home Secretary. It is, however, only reasonable to suppose that if the power of the Secretary of State to authorize corporal punishment were removed, the officers

The men in blue

concerned would be sorely tempted to resort to indiscriminate punishment, which was the outcome of temper rather than justice. (S.K. Ruck (ed), *Paterson on Prisons*, 1951, pp. 137–8)

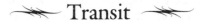 Transit

I'd been in Wandsworth twelve weeks when I was told I was being transferred to Parkhurst, on the Isle of Wight. I was classified an 'intermediary', due to my record. I joined a group of other intermediaries going to the same place. 'Face the wall,' an officer told us. A party of recidivists (prisoners who regularly return to jail) was passing. We weren't supposed to see them, so that we would not be 'contaminated'. That was part of the penal code in those days.

In the morning I was given an old, dirty-grey overcoat with white arrows and a cap to match. At the prison foundry a heavy, steel shackle was forged on to my right wrist. On it was a ring. One of the guards passed a long, steel chain through and joined me to the others. We could all move up and down the chain, but not off it. Like that, we travelled to Waterloo station in a roomy, old, horse-drawn wagon.

I could feel eyes boring into us as we shambled along on our chain; curious, condemning eyes. The chain and the arrows had turned us into social lepers. We soon ceased to care what people thought. We ducked and wove at the ground whenever we saw a sizeable 'fag-end', picking it up and pocketing it as though it was gold. The crowd probably thought we were a bunch of dangerous lunatics on our way to the asylum. (Wally Thompson, *Time Off My Life*, 1956, pp. 43–4)

The new prisoner could be glad that he did not want to go to the lavatory on the train because this involved quite a procedure.

Off the main chain

When such a request was made on the train, an officer slipped a shorter chain through the prisoner's handcuff and took him off the main chain. The prisoner and his guard would then proceed to the lavatory and the prisoner went inside with the officer remaining on the outside holding the other end of the length of chain. It was an underlining of the prisoner's loss of liberty that degraded him more than a lot of other experiences in custody. (Gerald Fancourt Clayton, *The Wall is Strong*, 1958, p. 44)

At Pompey we walked to the ordinary passenger boat in those days. To-day, a specially chartered tug takes the convict across the Solent to the Isle of Wight.

Pretty girls

We went on the lower deck. It was a magnificent day in late April. The ship was full of people, who walked past us curiously. Two pretty girls offered us chocolates. We thanked them, and they lingered to talk. They were kind creatures, but we were too shy, so perhaps they thought us sullen and went away with the idea that criminals are dull folk, not half as exciting as Edgar Wallace made 'em out to be. (W.F.R. Macartney, *Walls Have Mouths*, 1936, pp. 62–3)

One hand free   A Principal Officer who happens to be a 'villain' can work it with the coach driver so that it arrives at the train just a minute or so before it pulls out at 9.5 a.m. This trick is done to put the 'block' on prisoners having relatives or friends who come up to the train windows to see them off with parcels and food.

Usually the wives are allowed to say goodbye through the window – a heartbreaking sight when children are lifted up to kiss a father, him having only one hand free, and a small carriage window to put his head out of.

The train pulls out and the prisoners settle down in their seats for the long ride to Dartmoor Prison, or actually to the station called Tavistock. The train gets there at about 3 p.m. and the men step out and walk to the coach that is parked outside the station, prison officers all around. It is noticeable that although the prisoners laugh and chat all the way on the train ride they usually go dead quiet on the final stage in the coach from the station to the prison, especially if it happens when the mist is heavy and wet. (Tom Tullet, *Inside Dartmoor*, 1966, p. 191)

Cowering   Just prior to our arrival at Princetown we passed through a thick wood, but even this held that dead-alive atmosphere that invades and claims for its own every animate or inanimate thing within its reach. Suddenly we were through the vampire-like wood, and had our first glimpse of the dreaded Dartmoor prison as it lay cowering like some loathsome animal in the pallid cloak of mist, which hung like a winding sheet about its brow.

A few minutes later we were approaching the outer gates which were surmounted by a stone plaque upon which is inscribed the two Latin words '*Parcere subjectis*' – be forebearing to the subjected – but although I looked everywhere for the famous legend, 'abandon hope all ye who enter here!' my search was in vain. Then the inner gates clanged-to behind us and we were now inmates of the dreaded 'Moor'. (Peter Jenkins, *Mayfair Boy*, nd, pp. 165–6)

The men in blue

⫸ Escape ⫷

While we went through the usual formalities in the adjudication hall, and our manacles were removed, I remember hearing a clank of a chain behind me. I turned round and almost burst out laughing at the apparition standing dolefully on the cold stone floor. He looked like a pantomime clown, although the expression on his face was melancholy in the extreme.

His dress was dazzling, half drab, half vivid yellow. The right side of his suit was drab, the left canary. One of his legs was a flaming yellow, and the other a dull orange. His cap was quartered and, with a kind of diabolical stereotype, the broad arrow of Government service traced a sinister pattern on his motley. Round his waist was riveted a bright steel chain, two smaller pieces of chain were attached from the waist to each ankle, and I confess that I was disappointed at not seeing the cannon-ball between his feet – the cannon-ball that is so beloved of the Lyceum melodrama! (Charles George Gordon, *Crooks of the Underworld*, 1921, pp. 39–40)

A special set of clothes was issued to me, with three large contrasting patches of colour; one on my left breast, one on my left knee and one behind my right knee. This meant I was under 'Special Watch', known as SW, a treatment usually reserved for prisoners who have tried to escape. There I stood, branded like an animal. I know no instance of such a practice in any civilised country in our time except in Hitler's Germany, where I had seen Jews wearing the Star of David. (Gordon Lonsdale, *Spy*, 1966, p. 165)

Special watch

That night, the Chief Officer came along to my cell. 'Look here,' he said, rather officially, 'when you sleep, you're to face your bed towards the door, about a foot from the wall and keep your head and hands outside the blankets.'

The light gets in my eyes

'Whoever told you that?' I asked.

'Well,' he said, 'the Governor here's terrified of you and he says you've got to do it.'

'You go and tell the Governor I'm not going to do it,' I replied. 'I'm going to sleep exactly how I want to. If he doesn't like it he'll have to lump it.'

I wasn't being awkward because there was a forty-watt bulb by the door which was never switched off. I would never have been able to get to sleep. That night, just after I'd gone to bed, there was a kick on the door. I looked up and saw the night-watchman's eye staring through the spy-hole. 'What do you want?' I asked.

'Oh, it's all right,' he replied. 'As long as I see you moving.'

'What's the idea of that, then?'

'The Governor told me that if I couldn't see you moving, I was to kick on the door until I could. In case there's a dummy in your bed.'

'I'm not going along with that. Don't you keep kicking on my door.'

The next night, I deliberately faced my bed away towards the window and kept perfectly still under the blankets. When the night-watchman kicked on the door, I didn't budge an inch. He kicked again. He kicked a third time, even louder. I had arranged with the other prisoners on the landing to take this as the signal to break into an uproar, embarrassing to the authorities because there were a number of private houses near the prison. Everyone started shouting and banging. I kept motionless. About a quarter of an hour later, there was a sound of tramping along the corridor. A posse of warders halted outside my cell and the door was flung open. I looked up sleepily. 'What on earth's the matter?' I said. 'What's all the noise about?'

There was a sigh of relief that I was still there and the PO said: 'You know you're supposed to sleep round the other way.' 'I can't sleep round the other way,' I said. 'The light gets in my eyes. I'm sorry but you'll have to put me down chokey.' (Alfred Hinds, *Contempt of Court*, 1966, pp. 134–5)

'No thanks'   From the time when Bill carved his first bone up to the moment when he finished work on his last key, he had taken three years and six weeks. He kept the keys hidden in his cell for a further two weeks after they were completed because he was genuinely interested in finishing the crucifix. Only when he had completed this to his satisfaction did he use the keys. One night – or rather in the small hours of the morning – he unlocked his own cell door, then the door of a 'lifer', and finally my own. I was awakened from my sleep by the pair of them standing over me. One shook me gently while the other held his hand over my mouth so that I should not cry out. It was one of the biggest surprises I have ever had in my life, as I had no idea that Bill had been at work on the set of keys, but – in common with the other inmates – had come to believe that he had experienced a genuine change of heart. He gave me a whispered invitation to join him and his companion. I replied: 'No, thanks. I'll be going out of the front gate in three months' time, so it's not worth it. But I appreciate the thought.' It was just as well that I refused, for Bill's patient efforts took him and his companion only as far as the prison wall. They were seen as they attempted to climb it and recaptured without difficulty. (David Elias, *College Harry*, 1957, pp. 201–2)

The men in blue

The escape was now scheduled for Thursday 8 July, almost exactly a year after my arrival in Wandsworth. It was agreed that Paul would appear at the top of the prison perimeter wall at exactly ten-past three. Charmian, who had helped in the escape by providing money, established an alibi for herself by taking the children to Whipsnade Zoo so that she would be outside London and have a time-recorded ticket to correspond roughly with the time of our escape. Around nine minutes past three we went into the toilet to check our watches, and as the seconds ticked away we came out and started to walk towards the main wall. There were four prison officers at strategic points in the yard, but on the long section of the main wall there were only two screws, one standing at either end. A point between these two, right in the middle, was where we were going up. I pointed out to Brian and Jock the screws they would have to mind, and each knew which one to grab. As we walked towards the wall I stooped to do up my shoe to delay a little longer, and at that moment we heard the van pull up on the other side. A few seconds later I saw the top of Paul's stockinged head appear and almost immediately the first of the two rope ladders came snaking over the wall. We ran forward as the second one came down, then, suddenly, I froze, somehow unable to start climbing. I don't know why, I just froze on the spot for a split second until someone shouted, 'Get going, Biggsie,' and I started climbing fast. Paul was at the top of the wall sitting there with an axe in his hand ready to chop the ladders loose. He greeted me with: 'Hello, you big ugly bastard!' while below me I heard Brian shout, 'You're too late, he's gone. Biggsie's away.' He sounded highly elated. Later both Brian and Jock got twelve months for aiding the escape.

Once over the top of the wall we jumped on to the platform and then down into the van itself. Outside the wall was standing, much to my displeasure, the bloke with a shotgun; but he had done what was expected of him despite the gun, and when someone in the house opposite put his nose out to see what was happening he forced him into a shed while the escape took place.

After Eric and I had climbed the ladders, two other cons whom I barely knew decided to join us. This led to Paul and Ronnie Leslie being nicked later on. They had planned to set fire to the van as soon as we were over the wall, but when Patrick Doyle and Robert Anderson followed us over, there was not enough time to sprinkle the petrol to get a good fire going. This meant that the police were left with a nice set of fingerprints. Paul got four and a half years and Ronnie three and a half. (Ronnie Biggs, *His Own Story*, 1981, pp. 108–9)

Loud and clear 'This is Baker Charlie to Fox Michael, Baker Charlie to Fox Michael. Receiving you loud and clear. Over.'

We went quickly through the code.

'Well,' I said, 'this is it, then. This is the day. Everything is OK out here. How are things with you? Over.'

'Fine, my friend,' said Blake, 'fine. Everything is ready here for this evening. The conditions are perfect. Most of the others will be at the cinema, and there will be only two officers in the hall. And, by the way, I don't know if you can see it from where you are but our window has still not been fitted with a grid. Over.'

I looked across at the Gothic window. Blake was right. 'My God, Baker Charlie,' I exclaimed, unable to conceal my delight, 'I never thought the day would come when I would be grateful for the incompetence of those overalled layabouts. All those cold winters without proper central heating now seem worth it. Over.'

I heard Blake laugh.

'Yes, Fox Michael, I agree with you. It is quite incredible that this obstacle has not yet been put in our way. And it would indeed have been quite an obstacle. Over.'

It certainly would. Cutting a wire grid whose gauge was a quarter-inch would involve a lot of noise.

'Well, Baker Charlie,' I said, 'I had better go now. I will contact you at six o'clock precisely. Over.' (Sean Bourke, *The Springing of George Blake*, 1970, p. 151)

'Good old George' A growing murmur of sound breaks into my thoughts. I cock my head and listen. It is voices shouting from cell window to cell window. I cannot hear what is being said from where I sit, so I climb on to my bed and press my ear to the seven inch by five opening in the narrow, barred window. The men with radios are shouting the news to those without. The excitement in the voices I hear is unbelievable. There must have been nearer a hundred than fifty escapes in the years I have spent here, but I have never known a reaction like this. The shouts and cries go on and on. By concentrating, I can distinguish words and snatches of conversation.

'Blake ... Blake ... over the wall ... George ... had it away ... Good old George.' Cowboy yells of 'Yippee', only once or twice sheer savagery, directed against authority more than in support of Blake's escape. 'He's fucked 'em ...' And then, far away and faintly from the south end of the prison, singing, 'For he's a jolly good fellow.' (Zeno, *Life*, 1968, pp. 163–4)

Escape from Dartmoor For two hours no word of the chase came to the convicts who were watching and waiting at the windows. (James Spenser, *Limey Breaks In*, 1934, p. 290)

The men in blue

The Air is Filled with Whistles and Yells

My own cell window faced the main gates, and I could see the entrance drive distinctly. There were possibly 250 cell windows in this block facing the same way. Standing on my cell stool, I could just look out of my window.

From 2.30 p.m. until 9.30 p.m. that day I stood on my stool watching the entrance, and I knew that 250 men were doing the same. (Ex-Convict No:–, *Dartmoor From Within*, nd, p. 43)

Then, at about four o'clock in the afternoon, there was a commotion at the front gate and four warders came running through it frogmarching a man between them. Other warders ran alongside the frogmarched and helpless convict and hit at him with their truncheons. (Spenser, p. 290)

We almost cried when we saw his face twisted in agony as he ran the gauntlet of vicious kicks and blows. This is not imagination; many civilians and hundreds of convicts witnessed acts that day, and perpetrated on this man, that represent one of the blackest records in Dartmoor history.

One principal warder, when he thought he was unobserved by us at the windows, drove a thick hedge pole into 'The Bulldog's' stomach as the prisoner passed along B Hall passage-way. He did not fall because his hands were wedged up behind his shoulder-blades by warders – he could not moan – he had not the strength. (W.G. Davis, *Gentlemen of the Broad Arrows*, 1939, p. 43)

At once there came a terrific and terrible howl of rage from all the windows from which a view of the front gate could be got. Convicts cursed in the vilest language at the warders, and they shouted horrible encouragements to mutiny at one another. A wave of fierce and hysterical hatred swept the building from end to end, and the warders dropped their prisoner and stared dumbfounded up at the windows.

'Let me out!' yelled convict after convict. 'I'll kill the cowardly bastards!' (Spenser, p. 290)

FIRMLY ROOTED IN MY MIND IS THE BELIEF IT WAS THIS INCIDENT ON 7 AUGUST 1924, THAT SEEMED TO SET THE SEEDS OF REBELLION INTO GROWTH, ABOVE ANY OTHER.

The lags never forgot, and from that day an intense undercurrent of hatred was shown towards officialdom. (W.G. Davis, p. 44)

⟞ The Dartmoor mutiny ⟝

Shortly after my arrival at the Moor a Governor of the traditional school had been succeeded by one who had seen long service in the ranks of the army and prison service. He was a stern disciplinarian and was very familiar with staff and inmate practices and malpractices. He found it difficult to relate to both staff and inmates, but up to the end of 1931 there was no indication of any serious problem. (Dr Guy Richmond, *Prison Doctor*, 1975, p. 21)

Governor Roberts

It soon became apparent that Roberts had a tall order before him. Not only was Dartmoor going through difficult days, on account of the country's adverse economic conditions which were helping to breed more and more crime, but the new Governor was asked to reduce his staff, just when the number of prisoners he was accommodating was increasing. In November, 1931, we had one of the biggest batches in my time. Some forty men, mostly smash-and-grab gangsters, including the notorious Ruby Sparks, arrived, to add their quota of discontent to the atmosphere of unrest that was already fermenting, and all this at a time when, in the interest of national finance and to satisfy public demand, Government administration was forced to cut down expenses. (P.H. Baden Ball, *Prison Was My Parish*, 1956, p. 122)

Governor Clayton had organized night classes for good conduct lags, and teachers and welfare workers liked him enough to come up from Plymouth. It so happened I'd become a good conduct prisoner – just trying it on for size, and because with a man like Clayton you felt a bit silly if you weren't, somehow. I hadn't done much schooling, so at these classes I was learning English, French and arithmetic. *Pah!*

Two nights after Clayton had gone, I was at this evening class lark, and it was all quiet, just the instructor talking and the lags listening. No screws were in the room, as Clayton had said this wasn't necessary unless the screws wished to learn French or something, which they apparently didn't.

Suddenly the door flings open, and in rushes the screwdriver – the chief screw – and yells us all up to our feet. Behind him stalks the new Governor, flicking at his breeches leg with a riding-whip like a plantation overseer in *Uncle Tom's Cabin*.

He stared around the room, not saying a word to the teacher, who was a qualified geezer from a Plymouth school, volunteering his time. Then Roberts says: 'Pah! what rubbish is this?' And stalks out again. (Ruby Sparks, *Burglar to the Nobility*, 1961, pp. 84–5)

This atmosphere intensified when Speedle Davis, a psychopathic inmate, violently attacked an officer, ripping open his face with a chiv, a razor blade inserted in a stick. I sutured the wound which had penetrated the mouth. Speedle was of retarded intelligence but quite aware of the nature of his acts. He was later charged with inflicting grievous bodily harm on the officer. (Richmond, p. 22) *Speedle Davis*

FRIDAY, 22 JANUARY 1932

I went to see the prisoner in his cell in E Hall to which he had been taken after the assault. He made no attempt to explain his motive for what he had done. 'I suppose I shall be for it now,' was all he said. 'I've fairly put my foot in it.' I told him I would see him on the morrow, and would keep in touch with him each day in case there was anything I could do to help him. (Baden Ball, pp. 123–4)

SATURDAY, 23 JANUARY 1932

While I was in the vestry the Governor came in to say he wanted to have a word with the men, to tell them he had been to the cook-house and personally checked the porridge while it was being prepared for that morning's breakfast, and that it had appeared quite normal. So there was the implication that something happened to the porridge while it was being cooked. The chapel was packed as Roberts went into the pulpit. I was at the vestry door and S., the reprieved murderer, who was by my side, muttered in my ear: 'Now we're for it.' Before Roberts could say a word, there were murmurings of discontent from the prisoners. 'You're going to give me a hearing, surely?' he began, but there were shouts of 'Get down' and other more forthright observations. The prison officers realised that one false move on their part, and they would have trouble on their hands such as they had never before experienced. The tension was bowstring-taut. Roberts made another attempt to address the men, but his voice was drowned by their noisy disapproval. Now the language was growing more lurid, and he turned round to face me, his expression hopeless and utterly dejected. I followed him into the vestry, to the accompaniment of a jeeringly triumphant roar from the men. But still no one, prisoner or officer, moved. I asked the Governor what he wanted me to do. 'Carry on as usual,' was his reply. His face was ashen as he went off to his office. I looked at the vestry door, beyond which the roaring and shouting continued. My instructions were to carry on as usual even though it seemed to me the situation tended somewhat toward the unusual. (Baden Ball, pp. 124–5)

Solo hymn

The idea of turning my back on the situation found little appeal in my mind, and so without knowing what I was doing I opened my mouth and began to sing the hymn solo. I got through the first verse and the organ joined with me. Perhaps the prison officer playing it felt that my voice would sound better if it was drowned a little by the musical accompaniment. Ending the first verse, my impulse was to jump to the last verse, which I had done on occasions before when it was necessary to shorten a service. Then it occurred to me that if I did this now my understandable anxiety to get the thing over might appear too obvious. I ploughed through the five verses, and I must confess that each one seemed interminably long. However, by the grace of God alone I was guided to follow the right course. (Baden Ball, pp. 125–6)

SUNDAY, 24 JANUARY 1932

It was very important that there should be no more meddling with the food so it was arranged that the Deputy Governor and I

The men in blue

would visit the kitchen during the early hours of Sunday morning to satisfy ourselves that the porridge was not watered.

At about 10 p.m. the prisoners started shouting and the commotion increased throughout the night. There was pandemonium. We were in the kitchen at 4 a.m. and found the porridge of good consistency. I was due to hold a sick parade at 7 a.m. and it was decided to go ahead with it as usual. There was the customary line-up and it wasn't long before a fight started and one man was seriously hurt. (Richmond, p. 23)

I was told on my arrival how it was feared there might be trouble during chapel or just prior to it while my congregation were assembling. Governor Roberts now had the help and support of the Assistant Prison Commissioner, Colonel Turner, who had arrived overnight from London, and had posted all spare officers outside the prison to guard against escape attempts. Despite what was reported at the time, and has been stated subsequently, firearms were not brought into the prison. (Baden Ball, p. 128)

Colonel Turner

It wasn't until next day, when those of us who were left had come out into the exercise yard and were trudging around, that they started to sort us out. So I hit the screw nearest to me, knocking him cold, and then it occurred to me to put on his cap. I had just pulled it on to my head when I heard an uproar from the other yard, and about a dozen lags came running through to me, shouting: 'Ruby – we've started it!'

That was how the Dartmoor Mutiny actually started – both exercise yards just blew up at the same time, and all the screws went running to the gate and out of the prison. All that could get out. They left Dartmoor in charge of us lags. (Sparks, p. 91)

Uproar

While the Governors were seeking sanctuary the Assistant Commissioner left the office and walked towards the mob in an attempt to negotiate, but he was jostled and seized and someone poured porridge down his neck. Another inmate stole his watch and dropped it down a drain. Finally a friendly prisoner led him to one of the prison wings where he locked him up for safety. This convict was subsequently rewarded by having the remainder of his sentence remitted. (Richmond, pp. 23–4)

Stole his watch

Having vented their almost hysterical fury upon the Governor's office, smashing up all the furniture, then setting it on fire, together with records and documents, the mutineers turned next to the officers' mess, on the way raiding the fire-station and sending the fire-engine crashing against a prison wall. Breaking

Beer and lemonade

into the officers' mess, they smashed open cupboards and drawers, searching for alcohol and cigarettes. There were plenty of the latter, which they fell upon, but the only drink available was a few gallons of beer and lemonade. By now, as came out at the subsequent inquiry and trial, the mutiny was becoming to the majority engaged in it more in the nature of a schoolboy rag. Most prisoners could find nothing better to do with their new-found freedom than to dance together on the parade ground, or amuse themselves and their companions by dressing themselves up in prison officers' uniforms, or banging out tunes on the officers' mess piano, and graciously offering their looted cigarettes to all and sundry. (Baden Ball, pp. 130–1)

My much loved spaniel

I felt sure that most of the prisoners would scale the walls and terrify the families of the staff, raping the women, pillaging and destroying all they could. I was very anxious about my own home so close to the gate and the safety of my much-loved spaniel, my sole companion at that time. (Richmond, pp. 24–5)

Shot through the neck

A member of the Birmingham gang had climbed on to the twine-shed roof, from which he somewhat rashly sought a view of the officers on duty outside the prison wall. I heard the shots fired at him which knocked him down, shot through the neck. (Baden Ball, p. 132)

He screamed once as he toppled, and landed in a lumpy heap near to me.

He wasn't dead but that scream was the last sound he ever made. The bullet had hit him in his voice-box. I tried to plug the hole in his neck with my grey prison handkerchief, but the blood was coming out of his throat as if from a burst in a cistern. Afterwards, as a result of this single bullet and the fall, his arm withered and his leg shrank, for he had broken the main bones in them and it was a long time before he got attention. (Sparks, p. 95)

This incident fanned the wrath of those who set about the wholesale destruction which followed. The hospital windows were smashed in, the entire administrative block was set on fire and completely gutted. The records office presented an obvious chance for the rioters to destroy records concerning them, and they soon had a bonfire of documents blazing away, the flames from which caught the office itself afire. (Baden Ball, pp. 132–3)

The men in blue

Dartmoor Mutiny, Sunday 24 January 1932

Flames and smoke

I was a freelance journalist then which meant that I could write for whoever I wished but, of course, I had to find the news to write about. Dartmoor Jail was always a potential news source but it was not easy to break through the strict censorship and the Home Office's tight-lipped hush-hush policy. Nevertheless I had my 'contacts', friends inside and outside, who would drop the odd hint.

That night I knew that police and troops had been asked to stand by to help in any emergency and so on the Sunday I made another visit to Princetown. It was a pleasant winter day, ideal for a round of golf, I thought, as I cruised past the course at Yelverton, blissfully unaware that a mutiny was in full fury at the Prison with 440 convicts in complete control of an orgy of destruction, arson and looting.

Suddenly a black, blue-lined car flashed past me. I recognized it was that of Plymouth's Chief Constable, Archie Wilson. Off in pursuit I set, only to be overtaken again, this time by a 29-seater single-decker bus packed with police. As I drove up Devil's Elbow flames and smoke coming from the Prison could be plainly seen.

We reached the Prison gates together. I watched the thirty-odd policemen get out and form up while Archie Wilson had a quick discussion with warders in the outer offices between the massive iron-studded outer oak doors and the iron barred inner gates. No senior prison officers were available and so the Chief Constable took command. Through the iron bars he could see 100 or more convicts milling about with their improvised weapons completely in control for the warders had in accordance with standing orders fallen back to man the walls in pursuance of their main duty – to prevent escapes.

Archie Wilson spoke to his men. Most were in uniform but a few were in plain clothes. They were all equipped with truncheons and three had revolvers but with strict orders only to use them if essential and then to fire in the air. 'Remember it's them or us. Spare no mercy,' said Archie Wilson as he led the charge into the main avenue clad in plus fours and tweed cap and wielding his ash-plant walking stick. (Rufus Endle, *Dartmoor Prison*, 1979, pp. 34 and 36)

A sandwich

And now the main prison gates were flung dramatically open and in came about thirty policemen, led by the Chief Constable of Plymouth, carrying his stick, with which he let out left and right. One prisoner sitting on a wall munching a sandwich obtained from the cook-house was challenged by the police official: 'What are you doing up there?' 'Eating a sandwich,' came the reply. 'Well, here's something else to put in it,' and the police officer

The men in blue

felled the other to the ground with a blow from his stick. (Baden Ball, pp. 134–5)

Dirty coward

When those of us who could still stand were lined up for the second time, Governor Roberts came surging valiantly forward with a pick-shaft in his hand. This was the first time he had deigned to enter the conflict. He began delivering horrible clouts at the nearest man. I shouted to him: 'Roberts, you dirty coward – come here and I'll put that stick where you'll remember it!' His face went livid, but before he could reach me with his pick-handle a nearby policeman thumped me on the jaw and I went down. I was out for only a few blinks, but the screws were insisting upon beating up the chief ringleaders, and when they came along the line to me the fact that I was just staggering to my feet did not in any wise deter them. So I had a go at them, naturally, and was soon on the floor again, which felt very tranquil and comfortable. (Sparks, p. 97)

Scalps

It was not long before a convoy of wounded prisoners was escorted to the prison hospital. The Senior Medical Officer was safely back there. He had walked among the rioters trying to reason with them, and they treated him with respect. Between us we must have sutured the scalps of at least 70 victims. The Assistant Commissioner had been released from his cell and I saw him walking up the driveway dazed and in shock. By 1 p.m. all was over but the mopping up. Groups of resistive rioters were subdued and safely locked up; then darkness fell, except for the glow from the embers of the administration building. We were still apprehensive next day as there were rumours that leaders in the criminal world were on their way from London to free members of their gangs. (Richmond, p. 26)

Champagne

It took the Jury five hours to reach their verdicts. Five men were found guilty of riotous assembly, sixteen of malicious damage and nine were found not guilty. Some of these nine whose sentences had expired since the mutiny were released at once. The others received sentences ranging from twelve years to six months. Altogether Mr Justice Finlay passed sentences on the thirteenth day of May 1932 totalling a few months under a hundred years.

During the trial one of the defence solicitors, later to become Plymouth's first full-time magistrates' clerk, had promised the head of our team and myself a bottle of champagne for every one of his clients acquitted. There were four and we had a festive journey back to Plymouth, for naturally we two journalists had to return the honours. At one of the four pubs we stopped at, defence counsel, later to become, like his father, a High Court judge, mentioned that the tally might have been five. One of his clients had a cast-iron alibi but he decided not to use it. The penalty for homosexuality in those days was far more severe than for wilful damage. (Endle, p. 44)

Dragged him face downwards

The first mutineer to arrive came direct from Dartmoor and refused to stand on his feet the whole way from there to Parkhurst. When he arrived at the prison gate I found him lying on the ground and blaspheming all round him. I told him that if he would not walk he would be taken by the feet and dragged to the Reception Ward. He refused with another mouthful of invective and so two officers seized his feet and dragged him face downwards over the gravel of the prison path. It did the trick. He sat up, still cursing, rubbed his face and walked. (Gerald Fancourt Clayton, *The Wall is Strong*, 1958, pp. 140–1)

Davis would not submit

Davis, on his arrival at Parkhurst, was immediately placed upon the 'observation' or the 'barmy landing', and here began a fight between the English prison system and one convict. Davis would not submit. Punishment followed punishment. Bread and water or a restricted diet extended over weeks. Strait jackets, padded cells, and physical beatings were employed by an administration accustomed to win. And Davis would come up, ready for a fight, cheeky, smiling, and shrill. His history in the punishment cells would make a book by itself. Some nights he wedged himself in his cell and smashed everything to pieces keeping the whole prison in an uproar, whilst prison engineers tried to smash the door in with crowbars. Davis fought the jailors hand to hand. They left nothing out of punishment; he left out no device to cheat them. Excrement smeared all over himself and his cell would sometimes render him immune for a time from rough handling. His insults and jeers, his marvellous gift of rasping repartee, his ability to wound the delicate susceptibilities of the jailors by reference to their female relations, made him detested and feared.

At last officialdom gave in. Clayton took Davis up from the punishment cells into the ordinary prison and put him on his honour not to do this and not to do that. Davis, who is an intelligent fellow, now does what he feels like, in reason. He does not actually meet the gaol-house administration half way, but he admits that there has to be some give and take. But Tom does most of the taking. I have seen him make a warder sweep his cell out, which is stained mahogany in spite of Standing Orders. He is now the jobber in the prison, and goes round the married quarters fixing up things like stoves and baths. He has been in prison five years, and has about twelve to go. He is one of the gamest men who ever walked through a prison gate, and I am proud to call him my friend. (W.F.R. Macartney, *Walls Have Mouths*, 1936, pp. 24–5)

⤛ The edge of the volcano ⤜

Prisoners react quickly to any break in their normal routine. One evening I set out to visit a man in the prison hospital, and I was feeling rather pleased. I am a somewhat heavy walker and my footsteps made a considerable noise on the slate balconies of the prison. As I made my way to the hospital, I was whistling softly. All was very quiet otherwise, as it usually is when inmates are in their cells. Someone did not like my disturbance and swore vigorously his disapproval. Almost at once, the whole prison broke into the most appalling row, and all or most of the men beat their metal cups and plates against the floor or the bars. It was some time before this ceased. This form of mass hysteria occasionally takes place, and it is an alarming affair. On my future visits, I wore shoes with rubber soles. (Alfred Salt, *Jottings of a JP*, 1955, pp. 22–3)

The wing officer explained that the men were upset about the dress order and refused to go to their cells. I hadn't a clue as to what to do. I happened, however, to have in my mind my small bunch of car keys. I saw this mob of, say, 200 men in front of me just waiting to see what I'd make of it. It was the first time they had been, as you might say, face to face with me. It must have been an interesting situation for them, all agog with expectation to weigh me up. Little did they know how I felt, but with my little bunch of keys (I never carried prison keys), I walked through the lot of them to the end of the wing and back again, throwing my keys up and down and catching them again many times. All eyes were upon me all the time and there was a deadly hush. Cross and sullen men are not the most prepossessing sight. I am certain I said a silent prayer for guidance and then I finally turned round towards them and called them towards me and said with all the composure that I could muster: 'Well, what's to do?'

A silent prayer

One of their spokesmen told me about the order the Chief Officer had given and that they thought it was a liberty and that they should be allowed to dress as they pleased for their spare time recreation. He had told them not to wear their working clothes but to wear their best clothing and ties for association, and this was just provocation, and they were not bloody well going to.

I said to them 'Do you think that just because a mob like you refuse to do what the Chief Officer orders that I am going to reverse the order – you need your heads seen to', or some such words. I added that I would look into what they complained of but that was *all* I would do. I would consult the Chief Officer and if they didn't want to dress as he had said, then they couldn't go on association and that was their affair.

One man whose name escapes me, but who was very content working in my garden and did not look underfed, said 'All we want is peace and no aggro, Gov.' Then they all went back to their cells. (Alastair Miller, *Inside, Outside*, 1976, pp. 101–2)

⤐ Hull prison 1976 ⤐

Things came to a head when it was discovered that one inmate had been beaten up by screws in the segregation unit and word went round the prison that inmates would meet on the centre of D wing for the purpose of seeing the governor (No. 1) to see what he would do about the beating up of the inmate. The Deputy Governor was told that we wished to see the inmate in order to find out if it was true that he had been beaten up. He assured us that no inmate in the seg. unit had been touched. We then asked for the inmate to be brought so that everyone present could be satisfied that that was the truth. He said 'I do not have the authority.' As requested he phoned the No. 1 Governor and he came back with a refusal to the request to see the inmate. That was when it was decided to stage a sit down. (Peter Ra-Jah, in PROP, *Don't Mark His Face*, nd, p. 67)

Things started getting smashed

After a few minutes of murmuring among us a fire bucket full of water was thrown down and the screws and Manning ran out locking gate and door, then things started getting smashed and it carried on from there. (Michael Davis, in PROP, *Don't Mark His Face*, nd, p. 9)

Shout out our anger

They were great times and were good for everyone. The prisoners couldn't believe the number and the joyous noise of the kids! Very early on some of us began making banners. And what we did was shout out to everybody around asking them what we ought to put on them, and after much ribaldry and some crazy suggestions like 'What's happening?', 'Send largactil urgent', 'We

The men in blue

demand transfers to Holloway' etc. etc., the ones which appeared were the agreed upon ones in the end. 'Four screws beat up one prisoner', etc. Someone was pushed to the front of the roof to talk to the media, that was one of the best things – just to stand there, all of us with our arms around each other's shoulders and to shout out our anger and our contempt and our hopes and our strength and for everyone to endorse by whispered 'Yeahs' and 'Go ons' and raised fists and people saying 'say this, say that' and to stop, ignore the TV, radio etc., and have a quick round of everyone to see that everything was fair. We said we were here because of brutality, that they could read some of the details on the banners, that this was just the tip of the iceberg, that the brutality was in every aspect of the system, in the control units, both the ones which were well known and the ones which operate in every prison under the names of segregation units and rule 43. (Like the fact that 90% of the men in Wakefield control unit had been sent from Hull prison.) That right below our feet there was the control unit of Hull where a prisoner was beaten up by 4 screws, where they had just installed 8 cells which had the glass brick windows and the blank walls which are a feature of control units. We went on about the finding of the files, the language of them, the rampant lies, the hysterical paranoia, the completely inhuman marking down of every prisoner's past, present and future in terms of ABSOLUTE HOPELESS EXISTENCE FOR LIFE, that they clearly showed what we all knew – that the prison system was an industry trading in our lives, that we were here to tell people we would never be relegated to being passive 'products' on the conveyor belt in order to let screws, police, judges, politicians, bureaucrats get fat off us, that we would protest and demonstrate and take action again and again and until the last prison in Britain is shut forever. Also we mentioned about the work we were forced to do for a few pence a week, making furniture for prisons in Iran, and asked the media and people standing there, is this what we've come to?, supplying everything to kill, torture and imprison people all over the world. We all screamed for a while:

'FUCK THE SHAH OF IRAN, FUCK THE SHAH OF IRAN.'

How the end was reached was so kind of natural, most people felt there was little point in staying, many of the guys who had been let out of their cells had wanted to give themselves up (they outnumbered the original 80 or so people). We didn't want to let them go and many of the original lot too, leaving only a few to face what might come. There was a general feeling 'we've done it anyway', 'for this time', virtually put the jail out of action, so we got everyone together by general consent, a vote was taken, it was a vast majority for an end but not a surrender. (Jake Prescott, in PROP, *Don't Mark His Face*, nd, pp. 62–3)

Totally helpless   'The beatings' – not a feeling of fear as such, but a feeling of despair knowing each of us were totally helpless, I heard the screws work their way along my landing one at a time, cons were battered to breakfast and battered back again, when they got to me I was opened up, grabbed by the hair and dragged along the landing. I was kicked and punched about the body the whole way up the landing by screws who screamed and yelled as if they hated me more than anything in this world. I was in a ball to protect my face, head and privates so they lifted me by the hair and dipped my face in a tray of jam, I was then beaten back down to my cell and dumped on the floor, a few mins later they came back again and said bye byes. (Paul Michael Hill, in PROP, *Don't Mark His Face*, nd, p. 21)

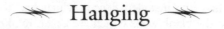

Hanging

Knowing very well that however men juggle statistics, there is no proved relationship between the amount of crime in any community and the amount of capital punishment, I went to live in a prison house. And then suddenly, one day, I learned that one of the men on the other side of our dining-room wall was to be killed.

A hush fell over the house. A sort of darkness came over the neighbourhood. Not darkness, literally. I will not exaggerate. But a light had gone from the world. It was not only night. It was nightmare. No one would discuss it with me. 'You musn't mind' they said. 'Don't think about it. The man doesn't mind. He is an idiot. He doesn't realize what his death is to be, any more than he realized what his victim's death was.' I said to my husband, 'Resign and let us go away. We never counted on this when you joined the service. We don't have to earn our living by shedding blood.' 'That would be like resigning a commission when war broke out,' he said. I argued that that would be the best time in the world to resign a commission. But he would not agree. He hadn't himself to do the deed, he said. He had only to arrange for it. (Margaret Wilson, *The Crime of Punishment*, 1931, pp. 134–5)

The right
thing to say   I then visited another condemned cell, where I saw another young fellow who was condemned to be hanged for murdering a girl in a butcher's shop. The only thing this man required was something

better for dinner. I advised him to ask the medical officer to change his diet.

It always makes me very sad after leaving these condemned cells, and I find it very difficult to know just the right thing to say to the men in them. (Sir Sidney J. Pocock, *The Prisoner and the Prison*, 1930, p. 78)

'I'm the prison commissioner.'

One day I had a visit from a very smart looking gentleman in a nice grey lounge suit and a homburg hat. He came to my cell and sat on the bed, stinking of whisky.

'Who the fucking hell are you?' I asked.

'Me, laddie? I'm the Prison Commissioner.'

'You look drunk to me. You smell of whisky. What's your name, guv'nor?'

'My name is Alexander Patterson.' The late Sir Alexander Patterson was a good man. 'Laddie,' he said, 'I must tell you. I couldn't come into this cell to visit you unless I had one or two large scotches.' (Jimmy O'Connor, *The Eleventh Commandment*, 1976, p. 82)

An ordinary interest

The door in the living room of the condemned cell was an ever present reminder of my rendezvous with death. This door of course, was kept locked until the last minute and it was the one spot in the whole place which we tried to avoid looking at.

But eventually I became curious, and soon was consumed with a desire to see what was on the other side. At length I bluntly asked Terry to tell me what it was like out there.

He looked at me in confusion, 'Ah, don't talk about it. Read your book. Forget about it.'

'But I want to know what it looks like,' I pleaded.

'How should I know,' he shouted angrily. 'You're too morbid. Forget it.'

I got up and walked over to the door and tried to open it. Both Terry and Ted leaped to their feet and pulled me back.

'Are you mad?' Terry snarled 'You'll find out soon enough what it's like in there.'

Then suddenly I felt angry. I might have lost my temper but I was swept by a feeling of utter lassitude and sank back into my chair.

The incident was, of course, reported to the Governor and he came to see me in the afternoon.

'What's all this about?' he demanded.

'It's simple,' I explained. 'I'm going to be hung in there. I shall have a mask over my head. I shan't see any of it when I go in, so I'm curious to see what it looks like now. It was just an ordinary interest, I can't understand why everyone is making so much fuss.'

That was my genuine feeling. I had just wanted to look at the scaffold. Apart from food, it was the only interest I had shown in anything since the trial, and I was angry at the attitude of my guards.

The three of them just stared at me open-mouthed. Then the Governor left. (John Edward Allen, *Inside Broadmoor*, 1952, p. 36)

The hangman with him

The most I could hope for was a fight. They would club me or shoot me or stupefy me with drugs, and then hang me after all. But they would have to do those things. Empty propaganda phrases would not suffice as an alternative.

But everything turned on the first few seconds. After those seconds there was no chance for even a fight. But during them, while there were momentarily only the usual two warders, making their last hour of 'duty', a powerful and agile man, with courage and with a weapon of some kind, could front an army, make them show and use their force.

The printed forms dealt with the removal of everything that might be used as a weapon. The warders' chairs, their table, my own table and chair – all would be sneaked away during the last night, to leave only an iron bedstead, fastened to the ground.

Nevertheless, I would have a weapon. Nothing much – nothing more than would fit in a man's sleeve, the kind of thing I had often used in Dublin during the Constabulary attacks. Nothing much, but enough to serve me for those first few seconds, make the brute-force behind the nice phrases show itself.

Wherefore I was glad my young ex-sailorman would not be on duty that last morning, and that it seemed likely the grizzled chap would be absent. Jim Phelan was going down – but he was taking the hangman with him if possible. Thus were my thoughts. (Jim Phelan, *The Name's Phelan*, 1948, pp. 294–5)

Opportunity for travel

The first attraction was the individual social status that might make me something more of a person than the scores of thousands of anonymous worker-ant millhands who toiled or idled alongside me in grey industrial Lancashire. I am sure that many of them had their ambitions, and some of them achieved their aim, to be an individual, in politics or the Buffaloes or football. I had another target.

The second attraction was the opportunity for travel that would come to me. Travel today seems to imply only long journeys – to South Africa or the Mediterranean or the Riviera –

The men in blue

and I have made all these trips in my time. But people forget today how much of *our own country* was a romantic faraway dream when I was a young man. Many parts of it a chap like me could only afford to see if he was paid to take the journey. There was no run-of-the-mill car jaunt out to interesting countryside, because no one in my circle ever had a car in the 1920s. You could only get away by train, only do it frequently if your expenses were paid. There was still an enormous glamour in the idea of travel within the home country, and in travel by the railway. That and the prestige were the 'perks' of the job which my father appreciated most, and I could read it in his narratives time and time again. (Albert Pierrepoint, *Executioner Pierrepoint*, 1974, p. 79)

At midnight on the Monday the Governor – brought from bed to meet the London messenger – came into my cell and read a long paper to me. I was respited, would go to penal servitude for life. (Jim Phelan, *The Name's Phelan*, 1948, p. 298)

Respited

The important thing was to try to keep from him the realization that his time was drawing near. I tried to keep his mind occupied right up to the last minute before he was to be taken to the gallows. He was due to be hanged at nine o'clock. I wanted to look at my wrist watch to see what time it was so that I would be ready to go down with him, but I didn't want to put my cassock on too early for fear of upsetting him. I bent down as if looking for something on the floor, and as my arm was outstretched I managed to steal a glance at my watch. It was ten to nine. He must have noticed because he said: 'Not long to go now, is there, Father?' Just to keep his mind occupied I asked him if he would help me into my cassock. I also made some excuse about it being creased so that he could spend another few minutes helping me to smoothe the creases out of it with his hands. Then they came for him, but they had no trouble in getting him to the gallows. He walked there quite properly and he was in good form right up to the very end. He bowed beautifully to each of those who were present – the doctor, the Governor, the Assistant Governor, the Sheriff of Leeds, the chief officer, the second chief officer and myself. He bowed to each of us separately as he was going out to the gallows. He had murdered a girl in Barnsley. (Peter Crookston, *Villain*, 1967, pp. 104–5)

Bowed beautifully

I remember trying to concentrate thoughts on Derek in his cell. But my mind wandered to and fro between his childhood and the last interview with him in Wandsworth Prison a few hours before

The radio

– between the Blackfriars and Edgware days to the time when he left the house for the last time.

It is all a blur now, except for the last half an hour before nine o'clock. At eight-thirty I got up from my chair and walked to the front door. It was a damp, raw morning; the sky was livid. The crowd of the previous night had dispersed. A postman came along and handed me a packet of letters without speaking. A few people passed by on their way to work; they glanced in my direction and hurried on.

My watch said it was eight-forty when I returned to the sitting-room. I put the packet of letters on a chair and kissed my wife and children. Then I turned on the radio and switched it to the Light Programme which began at nine o'clock. In a few seconds the mains hum could be heard.

I prayed silently and I am sure my family did.

The tune of 'Oranges and Lemons' burst out of the loud-speaker. I turned the knob to mute it. Then we all stood up. Suddenly Big Ben gave out its chimes. The stroke of the first hour crashed and filled the room, leaving a shuddering silence until the second stroke.

I saw it all.

We clung together. My wife and Iris and the little boy wept.

I turned off the radio. My wife left the sitting-room and went upstairs. Half an hour later I found her lying across Derek's bed, her face buried in his pillow. She did not answer when I asked her to come downstairs. So I left her. We had to bear our own load in our own way. (W.G. Bentley, *My Son's Execution*, 1957, pp. 161–2)

Except love   All the emotions except love filled the screams which rang through the prison long after the condemned man was dead, and perhaps even love – love of life – was there somewhere beneath the rage and the fury. And the rage and the fury, what – who – was that directed against? The police? The impersonal law? the judge? society? themselves? Or was it against the man himself, the already dead man, who by his act and his death had brought them all one step closer to the grave. I did not know as I sat on the bed he had slept in. I do not know now, and I do not think I shall ever know. I do not believe I want to know. Because although I sat and smoked through it all, there was one moment when I was nearly caught up like thistledown in the howling wind of their cries, the sheer animal intensity of their voices infecting some part of me, so that in another kind of life I should have leapt to my feet and run with the pack. (Zeno, *Life*, 1968, pp. 14–15)

The men in blue

The silence that descends on a prison after a hanging is the most fearful thing I have ever experienced. But for some enlightened legislation, although I could not know it then, such a silence would have been my own epitaph. For make no mistake, but for the abolition of capital punishment, I would have joined the ranks of Timothy Evans and possibly James Hanratty, dying at the end of a rope for a murder I did not commit. (Patrick Meehan, *Innocent Villain*, 1978, pp. 35–6)

The silence that descends

Wade had fixed the tackle above. I passed a rope under the armpits of my charge, and the body was hauled up a few feet. Standing on the scaffold, with the body now drooping, I removed the noose and the cap, and took his head between my hands, inclining it from side to side to assure myself that the break had been clean. Then I went below, and Wade lowered the rope. A dead man, being taken down from execution, is a uniquely broken body whether he is a criminal or Christ, and I received this flesh, leaning helplessly into my arms, with the linen round the loins, gently with the reverence I thought due to the shell of any man who has sinned and suffered. (Albert Pierrepoint, *Executioner Pierrepoint*, 1974, p. 133)

Between my hands

The modern execution in this country is wonderfully efficient and merciful. Everything is arranged to make matters go silently, smoothly, efficiently, and swiftly, and the frequent reports which one reads in the Press that the sound of the trap falling can be heard by the other prisoners with a consequent demoralizing effect is just pure rubbish.

The coroner's verdict

The condemned man has only to walk across a corridor into what looks like and is, indeed, another cell. The floor of this room is really the scaffold and the man finds himself standing on the trap without knowing it. Indeed, before he has time to realize where he is, he is dead. Actually, only some twenty or thirty seconds pass between the time the executioner enters the condemned cell and the time when the man is hanging by the neck dead.

Nothing could be less brutal or more merciful than this modern method of carrying out the dread sentence of death. The scenes which used to take place at executions less than a hundred years ago were dreadful and degrading, and must have added greatly to the misery and torture of the victim. Everything now is, of course, done in strict privacy, apart from the necessary presence of certain officials; and I can state that death is quick, merciful, painless, and instantaneous. (Dr Samuel Ingleby Oddie, *Inquest*, 1941, pp. 143–4)

A flutter

I assisted Oddie to write his autobiography, 'Fifty Years a Coroner,' and he told me, although he refused to allow me to include it in his book, that on one occasion, two hours after the body of an executed man had been cut down, and he viewed it . . . *the man opened his eyes*. His neck was broken but there was still a flutter of life.

'I tried to revive him,' he said. 'My whole instinct was to try and revive him, but I am glad I failed.' He added that he could never forget the horror of that ghastly experience. (Allan K. Taylor, *From a Glasgow Slum to Fleet Street*, 1949, pp. 162–3)

Dignity

At this stage in my life I had no particularly strong opinions on the efficacy of capital punishment as a deterrent. I suppose I conventionally accepted the line that it worked. But, much later, when I came to reflect on the problem in depth, my mind often went back to the details of this my first execution in England. For it seemed to show that a prisoner could be to all outward appearances unshaken by the prospect of his death. Put it down to his courage, his fatalism, lack of sensitivity, or, as some people far from the actual scene have often said, the brutal stupidity of the man about to die: the fact remained that this man met his death jauntily. And he was by no means unique. I came to experience much the same attitude in many other condemned men. The thought that kept occurring to me later was that the existence of the death sentence had not deterred them, and the immediate prospect of death had not consumed them with terror. Possibly the thought of the noose which hanged *them* deterred *others*, but the actual execution inspired respect for the man rather than revulsion. And if such an execution had been held in public, witnesses would have felt sympathy for the man's dignity rather than satisfied recognition of society's vengeance – which is not what the theory of capital punishment preaches. (Albert Pierrepoint, *Executioner Pierrepoint*, 1974, pp. 113–14)

 Ghosts

My first experience of yard patrol occurred when I was undergoing training at Hull Prison and I shall never forget it. In the course of the patrol I had to pass near the burial ground where executed murderers were buried. On the nearby wall, at the head of each grave, there was a slate slab on which were the initials of the murderer and date of execution. The moon was at the full; there was not a breath of wind, and the silence was deathly. As I

The men in blue

drew near the burial ground, a shaft of moonlight struck across the graves. Suddenly cold dread gripped me as I saw rising from the graves wraith-like forms of perfectly terrifying aspect.

I stood rooted to the spot. Seconds passed, and then the moon went behind a cloud and the spectres vanished in the blackness of the night. It was, of course, pure fancy on my part – the product of a fevered imagination. While slowly pacing a prison yard, many thoughts come unbidden to the mind of a brand new 'rookey' whose nerves are on edge. (L. Merrow-Smith and J. Harris, *Prison Screw*, 1962, p. 32)

Officer No. 1 'They always began with an icy coldness at the back of my neck. I've been in some creepy places – even slept in a mortuary – but these were harrowing experiences.' *By the neck*

Officer No. 2 'Sometimes when I tried to lock the door I had the feeling somebody was pushing from the outside although nobody could have been there.'

Officer No. 3 'One night I felt I was being pinned down by the neck. I haven't been in that room since.'

Officer No. 4 'I had a paralysed feeling that didn't go off until dawn.' Said Mr. Wigginton, 'The night I was in the room I found nothing unusual.'

Prebendary White also discounted the ghost stories. 'I was forced to the conclusion that the men's fears were groundless,' he said. 'I don't believe in ghosts anyway.' Father Patrick Ryan, Roman Catholic Priest, was also sceptical. 'I spoke to one or two Roman Catholic prisoners,' he said, 'but I'm afraid I laughed it off.'

But in the jail many people were talking of a local fable that the 'White Lady' haunts the 360-year-old prison during autumn and winter! (Francis Disney, *Heritage of a Prison*, 1985, p. 108)

About one o'clock in the morning I was at the window, and just after the church clock had struck I heard footsteps going round the exercise yard. Naturally enough I presumed that it was the night watchman and fully expected to see him come into sight from round the toilet in the yard. There was no doubt about it being the heavy footsteps of a man, but though it was nearly bright as day in the beautiful moonlight, he did not appear. What was so strange was that I could not see him. It was a physical impossibility for anyone to walk out without my being able to see him as it was a very small yard with nothing, other than the toilet, on it. In one corner there were the graves of those who had been hanged there; there were no names, just numbers, which were cut into the wall in Roman figures that you would not even notice *Footsteps* unless you had to walk round it all day. After a bit I got curious and shouted out, 'Getting some night air?' But there was not even a pause in the pacing footsteps as they continued to go on and on around the yard. By now I was getting a bit uneasy so I rang the bell to summon the night screw. 'You want to tell that night watchman to get his exercise elsewhere,' I said.

He said there was no one on the yard, and the only two doors leading to it were locked up at nights. 'For Christ's sake,' I said, 'I can hear him when I get up at the window.' I think what convinced me that he was telling the truth was the fact that he looked a bit scared. Now you can draw your own conclusions about what it was in the yard that night. I do not believe in ghosts, but it definitely was not a screw and those footsteps were not my imagination, and to this day I cannot understand it. (Andrew Keith Munro, *Autobiography of a Thief*, 1972, pp. 87–8)

Cold all over   I had a funny experience while I was in Wandsworth. It sounds ridiculous, but it's true. One evening I felt someone or something clutch hold of my shoulder. I went cold all over, I was dead scared. Broad daylight, a fine bright summer's evening, I thought to myself, It's so stupid, I must be imagining things. I lifted the bed board up and I searched the cell thoroughly, but I couldn't find nothing. But I swear I felt something or someone clutch my shoulder.

Anyway, about three days after that I was called up before the Governor. My boy Bonar had fell in the canal and a man had dived in and saved him from drowning just around about the time I felt that hand clutching at my shoulder. That's true. I don't believe in tales like that but this genuinely happened. I even rung the bell, got on the bell and told the screw, There's something bloody peculiar going on in this cell, I said. (Henry Ward, *Buller*, 1974, pp. 76–7)

Old lady   Periodically a band of Americans still visit the graveyard to pay homage to their men who died so long ago. The graveyard is well kept by the convicts of to-day.

I myself was employed in the American graveyard for several weeks, cutting the grass and weeding the paths. One day I saw an old grey-haired lady – a very old lady she seemed – kneeling before the stone.

I looked round for the officer, thinking he might speak to her. He was outside on the road. I went to tell him, and he came back with me, but the old lady had gone.

We looked in every direction. Then he recommended me to report sick when we returned to prison.

I went back to the stone, and there on the ground we saw a bunch of red roses – roses but freshly cut. I wonder if anyone else has ever seen the Old Lady of the American Graveyard. (Ex-convict No:–, *Dartmoor From Within*, nd, p. 62)

BOOK FIVE

The Prison Experience

Strangeways Prison

I wanted an inquiry into the running of the prison, so I decided to swallow some articles. I thought I would be sent to hospital to have them removed, and some high-up would say, 'There's something wrong here, he's never done this before', then I could tell him all about what was going on in the prison.

So one day, in the cell, I broke the mouth-piece off a spoon, and swallowed the handle. Then I broke some pieces of wire from the bed-spring and swallowed those; then some fittings from an electric bell and part of an electric light bulb.

As you swallow each article you have a drink of water. You're sick, perhaps a dozen times, and it may be half an hour or more before you can get it down, but I always seemed to have the perseverance to keep at it. I never felt any pain, except once when I swallowed the chain from a sink-plug in the bathroom. It was about eighteen inches long, and seemed to wrap itself round my spine. I was terribly sick but it went down. Another time I swallowed a lavatory chain. It was a flat one, like a lot of little cuff-links joined together, and I could taste the green mould on it. (Ronald Lloyd and Stanley Williamson, *Born to Trouble*, 1968, pp. 155–6)

We'll get it into you

When no attempt was made to bring me before a magistrate, no doubt because the authorities didn't want me up on my hind legs in court arguing the toss about lawful custody, I decided to continue with my hunger strike. . . .

For the first two days of my hunger strike, I hardly felt a thing. The third morning, when I was called up to see Malone again, my eyes went misty and the whole prison began to spin round. . . .

After ten days had gone by, Mason came in to see me. 'We've weighed you and you've lost two stone,' he said. 'We've got to forcibly feed you.'

'What's the procedure?' I asked.

'We'll get it into you. You can do what you like.' (Alfred Hinds, *Contempt of Court*, 1966, pp. 129–30)

Rammed down

The gag was forced into my mouth while I was held down. This was to get my teeth apart so that the tube could be thrust down my throat. I was rather handicapped in the matter of the gag because I had some teeth missing on one side of my jaw and I had taken out the denture which I customarily wore. This made it easier for the gag to be inserted. Once it was between my gums it could be twisted so that it caused me violent pain and compelled me to open my mouth.

When the gag was firmly fixed the doctor forced the tube down my throat. This tube was a rubber one, about two feet in length and very flexible. The bottom of the tube was sealed and rounded off, and there were holes on both sides of the tube near the bottom of it. After the tube had been rammed down my throat the food was poured into the funnel to which the tube was attached, and the job was done. (De Witt Mackenzie, *Hell's Kitchen*, 1930, pp. 283–4)

One morning when they opened up he was standing in his corner facing the wall. Nothing the screws could do would make him turn round and face the other way. Eventually, of course, they got him by dint of three of them pulling and tugging. Well, two days later this man took his razor blade and ran it across both his eyeballs. Pieces of his eyes were found on the table when the screws went and found him sitting there with the blood streaming down his cheeks. (Brian Behan, *With Breast Expanded*, 1964, p. 166) *Both his eyeballs*

When I first came in I got that down with it beccause I was doing 2½ year. I thort I will never do this. I cant read much beccause of my eyes. I got depresion just sitting there on my own with nothing to ocypy my mind. I was going mad with it. So at night I cut my arms open. When the night patrol man come he seen all the blood on the floor. They had me out and in the hospital for five week and they put me back. Then I had a do with them and they put me in the paded cell. When I was right they put me back. Soon after I cut me again. I done it four times in about twelve months. In the hospital all you get is sleeping drafts and ijections. They dont have no consideration and no symphaty. One screw says to me the last time, you want to make a propper job of it, you do. I am not making a propper job of it just to soot them. (Robert Roberts, *Imprisoned Tongues*, 1968, pp. 191–2) *Cut my arms*

When my cell door was unlocked, first thing in the morning, I followed the other convicts to the recesses where slops were emptied down large black lavatories and water drawn from pressure taps over large flat sinks. As I returned I noticed that the fellow next door was bringing his narrow, rickety-legged cell table out into the landing; his name was Spiers, a pleasant fellow, good-looking and kindly. He wedged the table up against the steel rails running round the landing, climbed awkwardly on to the table, poised swaying for a second or so, bent his head down, threw his shoulders and weight forward; his legs straightened out, his heels flashed and he dived face first on to the cement *Vomited* passageway 15 feet below. The impact was sickening. Blood and flesh from a squashed face and a splintered skull spread out in an irregular and ugly pattern. Amid the shouting and excitement I turned away and vomited at my cell door, nearly spattering poor Hatry who also had been a witness to one way out.

Spiers was to have been flogged for robbery with violence and besides that fearsome punishment was to serve a sentence of ten years' imprisonment. He avoided both. (Red Collar Man, *Chokey*, 1938, pp. 50–1)

A bit stiff

An inquest was held later of course, and then there was a chance for people to learn the truth. In the first place, the sentence could not have been carried out for ten days at least, that being the period allowed in which to appeal. Moreover, the man's wife gave evidence that when she saw him before he left the court after sentence he said, 'I can manage the flogging, but I'm not going to do the ten years,' or something to that effect. And when I myself saw him that night he remarked that the ten years was a bit stiff, but made no reference to the flogging. So the matter whittled down, evidently, to its being the long sentence that he funked, not the 'cat'. (Lieut. Col. C.E.F. Rich, *Recollections of a Prison Governor*, 1932, pp. 218–19)

 Medicine

The dispensary was really two cells converted into one. The men, belonging to all three classes, filed in one door and passed out the other, like a football mob pouring through the turnstiles. We doped and dosed a hundred in less than fifteen minutes.

A long counter running the length of the two cells divided the dispenser and myself from our 'customers'. The dispenser stood opposite the entrance door behind the counter on which was arranged an assortment of bottles and pills. The counter was just far enough back to allow a foot of space for the convicts to pass along it on their side between the two doors. I stood behind the counter opposite the exit door. My stock consisted of only two bottles and *one* medicine glass – two enormous bottles, one of white mixture, a laxative (*mist. Alb*) and one a chocolate-coloured concoction, a cough mixture.

The dispenser was a man of few words. He merely looked at his patient questioningly. No doctor was present. The first man entered. The dispenser peered at him enquiringly.

'Cough,' said the convict, banging his chest. 'Cough,' said the

The prison experience

dispenser to me. 'Cough,' I repeated, and handed him a dollop of the brown stuff – and out he went.

'Constipated,' said the next man. 'Constipated,' said the dispenser. 'Constipated,' I repeated – out. And so on. We had only one medicine glass – and we didn't wash it often. (Allan K. Taylor, *From a Glasgow Slum to Fleet Street*, 1949, p. 153)

Then one day about the middle of November the 'flu hits the Scrubs and being as I have no luck worth shouting about I am one of the first to catch it and as the day wears on I am feeling more and more under the arm till I reach the apex after supper and collapse without warning on the bedboard white as a ghost. There I am shut up by myself and next to dying with the walls of the cell going round and round and the ceiling feeling as though it is slowly coming down on top of me and squeezing all the air out. You can see I am not kidding you one little bit when I say I am in a fine old predicament. In the end I muster all my strength in sheer desperation and go over to the door and ring the bell.

Ring the bell

Well, I have just got back onto the scratcher when I hear footsteps coming along the landing and the indicator outside gets slammed up while the door rocks back on its hinges and the screw storms in and plants his No. Eleven right bang in my ribs. Well, well, now, that is service for you. And who is it of course but my old friend Monkeyface.

'What the fughin' hell's up with you then?'

'I'm sick,' I gasp and if I had half the chance I would get up and rap him across the nut with the table.

'Oh, so you're sick, are you?' he says.

'Yes, sir. Dying sick.'

'Well, that's your bleedin' hard luck! And if I hear you ring that bell again I'll come up and trample you into a dirty mark on the floor! All right?' (Patrick O'Hara, *I Got no Brother*, 1967, p. 110)

I done six months out of the nine and came out with a broken leg. I got it messing around inside, me and another chap shaping up for fun, whilst we was slopping out, and I wind up breaking my leg. And when I broke my leg, they made me walk over the hospital. It was towards the end of that first sentence and I spent the last six weeks of the six months in the prison hospital. Anyway, I'm saying to this screw, I've broke me leg, I'd better go over the hospital. And he's saying, Well if you want to go over the hospital, you got to walk over there, don't you? And I say, It's broke, I can't walk on it. And he says, You've got to walk. Otherwise you won't never get over there, will you? So in the end I have to walk over the hospital and when I get there, this doctor

You've got to walk

he says, Here, this man didn't ought to've walked over here with his leg all broke like that, and give the screw a terrible coating. (Henry Ward, *Buller*, 1974, p. 50)

Take him away!

Am flanked by prison warders. The doctor sits at his desk some distance away also flanked.

'Are you suicidal?'

'You tell me ... you're the overpaid expert.'

'I am a doctor and you must answer my question!'

'Are you a real doctor?'

'If you do not co-operate ... I will place you on a charge.'

'You're probably more experienced at doing that than practising medicine!'

'Take him away!'

I am placed on a charge to see the Governor Monday morning. (Toby, *A Bristol Tramp Tells His Story*, 1979)

Malingering

One day a man, almost on the eve of his release, went into hospital suffering from what appeared to be a stroke of paralysis, which affected one leg. The medical officer had finished his visits and the man was temporarily accommodated in one of the separate cells. These cells are used in connexion with dietary punishment, but one is specially equipped, temporarily, to house sick men who may subsequently be admitted to hospital. Into this cell the man went, the officer admitting him expressing the opinion that it was a case of malingering. Later the man was taken into one of the hospital cells and put to bed. As soon as he was in bed a covered metal bottle filled with boiling water was wedged between his feet and the bed rail and left there until the day following. The unparalysed foot was not burned because the man could feel the heat and get the foot away, but the other foot was damaged to a dreadful extent. The fact that the leg was paralysed was proved beyond any question, but six weeks after the man should have been released he was still lying in the hospital. I remember lifting him out of bed one day and helping to put him on the scales, and thinking how little of the man remained. (Adam John Loughborough Ball, *Trial and Error*, 1936, pp. 139–40)

Died

Then there was a man named Bachelor who was confined to his cell a week or two before I left Wormwood Scrubs. He had a medical case history from outside, which was well-known to the authorities, yet he was persistently treated as a malingerer. I had to take him certain medicines and other necessities to his cell, and, before I first visited him, I was given specific orders to ignore his complaints and to do nothing to assist him. In fact, I did the little

The prison experience

I could to comfort him and to make him more comfortable. After a gradual decline, he died. It was shown that his death was accelerated by the withholding of drugs found necessary for his condition by the outside doctors, and by the use of certain treatment which his case history showed to be detrimental to the action of his heart. (Peter Baker, *Time Out of Life*, 1961, p. 152)

Religion in the city of cells

There was a chaplain at Parkhurst in 1926. I have forgotten his name. (Jim Phelan, *Jail Journey*, 1940, p. 204)

One man in particular I have in mind. How he came to be offered the job, whether it was the case of influence or to get rid of him, I do not know. What I do know is that of all the parsons in the world he must have been the most unsuitable. I saw this man at work every day. I spoke to him daily and spent many hours a week in his company while he carried on the work of prison chaplain and chief of the librarian staff. I knew his difficulties, and I knew that he knew within one month that he was totally unfitted for the work. (Anonymous by necessity, *Five Years for Fraud*, 1936, p. 215)

Unfitted

'You're going to run straight?' he next queried.

'Possibly, if I get a chance,' I fenced.

'Ah, my lad,' said the divine, 'there are opportunities for every man in this life. You will find your niche if you only look for it. The DPA (Discharged Prisoners' Aid Society) will only be too ready to assist you in finding a job, and I, too, will use my influence. I don't want to see you back here.'

'Nor do I want to come back,' I said, speaking truthfully.

'Then take my advice, lad, run the straight course,' he urged.

It is so easy for these parsons to give advice to men in prison, to tell them how to go on when they get out, but I have often wondered what do the Chaplains know of life in the raw as lived by the majority of men and women who form the prison population of this country? (Eddie Browne, *Road Pirate*, 1934, pp. 63–4)

Take my advice, lad

I used to attend the prison chapel regularly. It broke the monotony, and there was a bit of a concert at the end of it. One week-end, a prisoner sentenced to death was brought to Wandsworth. He was appealing on the Monday against the

The wages of sin . . .

sentence before the Central Appeal Court, so the Chaplain soothed his fears by preaching from the text, 'The wages of sin is death.' (Harry Pollitt, *Serving My Time*, 1940, p. 251)

Got rid of him

Whenever the Church Army captain read the lessons there would arise a carefully organised humming noise, perfectly punctuated. Every man kept his mouth tight shut, but practically every man was making a humming sound, which rose and fell like waves of sound. Every officer was on the alert to catch one single man. The chaplain was appalled, the Governor furious, but nothing could be done.

As soon as any section was approached that section ceased. The end was that the Church Army captain was replaced by another. There was a perfectly understandable reason for that. This good man had a most unfortunate manner. He would refer too frequently to asses and fools in his sermons. He had a loathing of the Labour Party and all its works, and he never missed an occasion when he read the news – supposed to be entirely unprejudiced – of making some contemptuous comment about Mr Cook or Mr MacDonald. The convicts were helpless to take direct action, but they got rid of him in their own way. (Warden, *His Majesty's Guests: Secrets of the Cells*, 1929, pp. 149–50)

The communicants

Presently the door at the far end of the Hall was opened, and in trooped the communicants, the majority of whom were men who had been sentenced for sexual offences.

An elderly man hobbling along on two sticks brought up the rear of the procession. He had been convicted for assault on a young girl of fourteen, a brutal act in which he had been assisted by the child's mother, who had pinned her to the bed while the old satyr had his way.

Late breakfast stood ready for them at a special table, and they took their seats at once. But no sooner were they ensconced at the table than a howl of rage and dismay arose.

It appears that the orderly detailed to carry the bucket of porridge from the cookhouse had fallen down and spilt the whole of the contents on the ground, and on this occasion, at least, replacement was impossible.

I have heard a variety of curses in all sorts of places and in all sorts of circumstances, but never in my life have I listened to such a sustained flood of filthy and uncanonical language as on that Sunday morning, and from men who had just returned from taking part in communion.

The officer turned to me in despair. 'I have been in this prison five years,' he said, 'but I will never understand the mentality of

The prison experience

these fellows. They are all professing Christians, and have just celebrated the most solemn rite of their religion. And yet look at their behaviour now.' (Richmond Harvey, *Prison From Within*, 1937, pp. 266–7)

This brings me to what must be the ultimate aim of the chaplain's work – to bring men to God. In my opinion, the position of some men in prison is so devoid of hope or so ingrained in a criminal way of life that the only hope for them is quite literally a new relationship with God. What else is going to change a man who has been in ten times except a real conversion experience? What real hope outside the Christian Gospel can there be for a man who has been given a stipulated period of thirty-five years in jail? For most people change is never something which comes easily, and some men in prison are looking for such a complete trans-formation that I believe for most of them it is only God who can provide the answer. For this reason when I visit a man who is interested in the faith or who has a particular need at that time I always ask him before I go if he would like me to pray. The prison chaplain must be a man who prays with prisoners on the right occasion, and also for them when he goes home at night. (David Jardine, *In Jail with Jesus*, 1978, pp. 113–14)

A new relationship with God

My confirmation was a tremendous day for me. The Catholic priest had made the many preparations that had to be put in train. I was exceedingly fortunate in witnessing the confirmation service entirely in Latin, which I should have desired in any case. When one is confirmed, one chooses the name of a saint – I chose St Raphael, one of the archangels who accompanied Tobias on his journey, as his protector. The church was packed for the service and there were several other Catholics being confirmed at the same time. As Archbishop of Westminster, Cardinal Heenan told us that he was no stranger to prisons as he had held retreats in them many times, and indeed he asked us to pray for his mother. After the service he asked the organist, Miss Hughes from the Brompton Oratory, how long she was serving; she said life but did not want any remission. The fact that she was allowed to come in at all was a privilege for us all. The Cardinal spoke to each confirmation candidate privately. Afterwards, one of the men in the prison blocks, who did not attend, asked if he might see him. The Cardinal went straight away to one of the gaunt buildings and asked for his cell; it must have caught the staff by surprise. A prince of the Roman Church going to see a prisoner in the lowliest place invented by man. What I thought so admirable about this gesture was that Cardinal Heenan thought his visit to

St Raphael

us and to this prisoner just as important as going to see royalty. (John Vassall, *Vassall – The Autobiography of a Spy*, 1975, p. 159)

Just part of the gloom

To the prisoner religion in prison is just part of the business of serving a sentence, one of the many extraordinary things that comprise the prison system. It is not a light in the darkness, but just part of the gloom. He feels that the place of religion in prison is one of compulsion, not of glad free service. In some mysterious way it is mixed up with his punishment and he accepts it in common with the rest of his experience. It enables him to leave his cell for ninety minutes every Sunday and for that he is grateful, but otherwise he is in no way affected. If he gives the matter any thought at all he leaves prison convinced that Christianity has no message big enough to meet his desperate need. (H. J. Woods, *Congregational Quarterly*, Vol. IV, No. 3, July 1926, p. 289)

⟫⟫ The causes of crime ⟫⟫

I encountered a youngish-looking man, athletic and intelligent, who had followed an artistic career until he fell into criminal habits. We spoke freely and easily for a few moments, and then I asked him, as sympathetically as possible, what had brought him to his present condition.

'Oh, the same thing,' he replied, rather sadly, 'that has brought nearly all the others to this place, just simple vanity.'

I told him that his answer interested me, because I have long thought that the root of nearly all the evil and stupidity in the world is, as he said, just simple vanity.

He said, 'We are like children, or savages, and want to show off. We want more money in order to cut a dash in the world. We feel that we are entitled to fine clothes, luxurious meals, and an easy idle life with leisured people. What we earn with our little talents is not enough for this purpose, and so we begin to look out for short cuts to our desires, gambling first of all, and bit by bit we slip into bad habits, and at last find ourselves parasitical and criminal.' (Harold Begbie, *Punishment and Personality*, 1927, p. 86)

Pregnant half-wit

It is known that there are 300,000 mental defectives in this island home of ours, most of them without restraint of any sort, male and female, in a position to beget children. What is the result?

It is almost inevitable that a mentally defective liaison, even if one of the sex be perfectly sane, will produce a mentally defective child.

In the name of humanity should this thing be allowed?

Do you know of a pregnant, half-wit woman in your town, my reader? Take her to a doctor, and persuade him, for pity's sake to think of the future of the still-lifeless thing in her womb. If he listens to you, you may find yourself one of the jury who will sit in judgment upon him and it will be your duty as a good citizen to send him to take my place between half-witted Jerry and Irish Charlie in the dreaded stone-sheds of Dartmoor. (Jock of Dartmoor, *Human Stories of Prison Life*, nd, pp. 64–5)

To One in Prison

To-day we have remembered sacrifice and glory
And the Cenotaph with flowers is overstocked:
A single gun to soundlessness has clocked
And unified King, Communist, and Tory. ...
I have listened to your broken stumbling story,
And trespassed in your mind, slum-built and
    shoddy.
You too have shared the Silence; you have knelt
In the cheerless Prison chapel; you have felt
Armistice Day emotion brim your body.

Six years, you say, you've worked at baking
    bread
(A none-too-wholesome task that must be done
By those whom God appoints). You are twenty-
    one
(Though I'd have guessed you less). Your
    father's dead
(Run over by a lorry, I think you said,
In the Great War, while coming home on leave).
Your brother got in trouble and spent three years
In Borstal (all these facts I can believe
Without the reinforcement of your tears).

Your brother failed completely to 'make good';
Your brother died; committed suicide
By turning on the gas, a twelve-month since.
Now you're in prison for stealing what you
    could:
Mother's in prison for the same offence:
And I've no reason to suspect you lied
When you informed me that you 'only tried

To stick to mother.' I was touched. You stood
So young, so friendless, so remorseful-eyed.

Therefore I find myself compelled to add
A footnote on your candour and humility.
You seem to me a not insensitive lad
Of average emotional ability.
You've 'been upset to-day.' 'By what?' I query.
'By the two-minute silence.' Then your weeping...
And then your face, so woebegone and weary.
And now – what use, the pity that I am heaping
Upon your head? What use – to wish you well
And slam the door? Who knows? ... My heart,
    not yours, can tell.

(Siegfried Sassoon, *Collected Poems, 1908–1956*, 1984, pp. 185–6)

Distracted
father

The particular observation I would offer relates to the subsequent history of the three-months'-old baby who was in his mother's arms when she was killed. The distracted father, when I saw him in prison awaiting trial, extracted from me a promise that I would adopt the child. Being only twenty-one I felt incompetent to assume direct care of the baby and sent him to most excellent foster-parents in the country where he enjoyed for the next twenty years an ideal home-life. His father's family were drunkards, his mother's family were prostitutes. Would so ill-favoured a heredity or so healthy an environment have greater weight in the growth of character and body? There were indeed clear physical signs of a predisposition to tubercle, but these were successfully countered by the diligent care of his foster-parents and the influence of country air and regular habits. Of his character and ability there was never any question. He attended the village school, won a scholarship to the county secondary school, and is now at the age of twenty-five settled in a permanent job of sound prospects and about to marry a steady girl of some education. It is a striking instance of environment proving itself a stronger influence than heredity. (S.K. Ruck (ed), *Paterson on Prisons*, 1951, p. 32)

Ceased to be
boss

I remember Sir Alexander Paterson saying that the persistent law-breakers in Borstal and Dartmoor were likely to have bowed legs, the result of malnutrition and rickets. Perhaps it is fair to say that the modern delinquent is likely to be knock-kneed and cowardly, and to carry some kind of weapon to defend himself, and to work in gangs.

There was a change at the end of the 'thirties, and I used to think that trade unionism, in itself a great movement, had something to do with this. If I went to some of the homes in the East End from which the Borstal lads had come, it was common to find that the father was continually complaining of his bosses and saying that the unions would put them in their place. The father appeared to his children to stand for a negative principle, and in the end ceased to be boss of his own family. In other words, his family grew up to respect no one. Later on, the boss was the Government itself. At the same time there was a lack of religious instruction, and Sunday School ceased to be universal. (John Vidler, *If Freedom Fail*, 1964, pp. 146–7)

The sleeping princess of psychology found her deliverer in Sigmund Freud, and now stands prepared to assist society in all its problems. The influence of the Freudian hypothesis has been enormous in every branch of sociology, but in none has it been more marked than in our conception of crime, in none will it be greater than in our future treatment of the criminal. Freud's psychology, and that of those who once followed but have now parted from Freud, is a normal and not, as is sometimes supposed, a pathological psychology. The reactions of neurotic patients are but exaggerations of the reactions found in each one of us. The actions of the criminal are but examples of the operation of normal human impulses. Acquisitiveness prompts the actions of the financier, and indeed of everyone else, just as it prompts the actions of the burglar; only the mode of outward operation is altered. The topic of the influence of the Freudian psychology upon our conception of crime is of fascinating interest, and I have endeavoured to illustrate it more fully elsewhere. Suffice it to say here that we are all under bondage to our personal complexes. When we say that it is necessary to punish an offender we are influenced, to a large extent, by our personal 'sense of guilt' and the demand of that sense of guilt for punishment. (M. Hamblin-Smith, *Prisons*, 1934, pp. 60–1)

The sleeping princess

It is significant that among the many hundreds of people I visited in prison and Borstal, almost none were loved as children. Early deprivation of affection and understanding tends to embitter to an extent which is liable to produce an anti-social type, but even when they are not embittered, it is difficult for the people deprived in this way to become socially adapted human beings, since they have not been able to abandon the 'pleasure principle' through the normal process of wishing to retain their mother's love. (Dr Kate Friedlander expresses this most clearly in her book 'The Psycho-Analytical Approach to Juvenile Delinquency.') Also, they endeavour to compensate themselves for having been deprived of what they sub-consciously feel to have been their natural right by every possible means, however likely these are to

Insecurity and inferiority

involve them in trouble. Their craving for luxuries and for extravagances of all kinds should be ascribed not only to the operation of the 'pleasure principle', but also to a deep conviction that in some way they are 'owed' these things. The conscious and unconscious feeling of insecurity and inferiority which this lack of early love has induced, may make it so imperative for these people to obtain affection and admiration that they will stop at nothing to get it. For this group of offenders, prison is usually a cruel punishment, but punishment does not cure or even deter these types. (Honor Earl, *Prison Once a Week*, 1948, p. 5)

 Reform

From 1918 onwards every prison in England was a centre of speculation with regard to the reforms which were believed to be on the eve of introduction, and, naturally at a large prison where men were allowed a certain freedom of speech during working-hours outside the walls, the changes in internal administration which were hinted at or foreshadowed during 1918 – 1920 became almost the sole topic of discussion. Excitement reached fever point when it was rumoured that the Home Office had definitely resolved to give some tentative expression to the increasing demands of the public, or at least a small section of it, for prison reform, and had called a consultation with the governors of every prison in England.

Towards the end of 1920, therefore, our governor set forth for Whitehall in full regalia – topper and morning dress – to confer with the august arbiters of our destiny. On his return, the ancient brotherhood of lags was convened in full convocation in the chapel of their Order to hear the result of his journey. There we all were, therefore, one bright morning in October, all gathered together to hear the momentous news that, from that time forward, our prisons were to be, not places of punishment, but schools of constructive citizenship. From the hospital came the halt and the lame, from the hall of the weak-minded came the vacantly giggling or sullenly scowling troupe to whom reform could mean little or nothing, and finally came the toothless veterans of Chatham and Portsmouth to whom it came too late. Here and there, as if to point the moral and adorn a tale, came the metallic clash of chains as the men wearing them fidgeted uneasily in their seats. When the Governor, the Deputy and their attendant satellites in brass-hats entered there was a thunderous burst of handclapping and shouts of 'Good old governor!'

The prison experience

The hand-clapping died away and, amidst a silence that could be felt, he began to outline the new policy. 'Men,' he began, 'I have great news for you. On and after the 1st of January next year many new and, I hope, far-reaching reforms will come into operation – reforms which will make a great difference in your lives here and, I trust, long after you have gone from this place to resume the responsibilities of freedom.' (Stuart Wood, *Shades of the Prison House*, 1932, pp. 315–16)

It is fitting that, before passing to examination of the present system, something should be said of Alexander Paterson, to whom especially it owes what merit it may have. After his death in 1947 Sir Alexander Maxwell wrote:

Alexander Paterson

'Alexander Paterson will be affectionately remembered in the Home Office and the Prison Service as an honoured leader who won loyalty and devotion not only by his intellectual gifts, his zest and driving energy, his humanity and sympathetic under-standing of men and women of all types, his wisdom, wit and humour, but by his ever-present sense of life's high ends. The many activities of his crowded official career were lifted above the common level by the intensity of his faith and vision. A practical idealist, whose grasp of reality was as firm as his aspirations were lofty, he was as fertile of constructive ideas as he was powerful to kindle enthusiasm. To his imagination and inventive force we owe almost all the schemes of penal reform which have been developed in this country in the last twenty-five years.'

Out of all his rich contribution to the revolution in the spirit of our prison and Borstal systems, perhaps that part which above all bore the stamp of Paterson's personality was his insistence that it is through men and not through buildings or regulations that this work must be done; his flair for finding the right men to do it; and his ability to inspire them with his own faith. (Sir Lionel Fox, *The English Prison and Borstal Systems*, 1952, pp. 72–3)

Prison visitors

Whilst I was at Pentonville the first batch of male Prison Visitors ever to be appointed took over their duties. In the first place the Governor submitted a list of names to the Prison Commissioners who duly approved them.

Major Blake was a member of the Garrick Club and the

majority of the first volunteers came from there. Unfortunately I am not sure that they were quite the right type, although they were all most charming and distinguished people. (Gerald Fancourt Clayton, *The Wall is Strong*, 1958, p. 10)

Futile little history

10TH AUGUST 1922
W.B. Age 21. 6 months Hard Labour. Stealing a cashbox

This young man had also asked to see me. When I entered he was lying asleep on his mattress with his blankets almost over his head. The noise of my shooting the safety bolt wakened him with a jump. He seemed dazed and took some time to scramble to his feet. I then saw what a fine-looking youth he was. Tall, rather heavily but well built, with fair hair, blue eyes, and good features, he was thoroughly attractive save for something weak – not to say silly – about his red-lipped boyish mouth. His manners were excellent, but more like those of a docile, very miserable child than of a fellow of twenty-one. I found him positively ill with unhappiness and brooding, and on my asking if he had wished to see me for any special reason his eyes darkened and filled with tears. Could I get in touch with his wife? That was what he wanted terribly to know. He had received no answer to his letters, nor had she come to see him, and he was tortured by the thought that he was losing not only her but his child. For his own sake I had to speak to him firmly, telling him to get on with his story like a man. My orderly room tone had a good effect, and although his eyes, which he never removed from my face for a moment, remained piteous he got through his tale fairly composedly. And what a miserable, futile little history of immature human relationship and folly it is! ...

There was nothing for it but to talk to him frankly. It was easy enough to do it kindly, for in spite of his foolishness he is as attractive and biddable as a puppy. He took his lecture with a docility that made me feel a brute, promised to give up lying on his bed brooding, to do his work and eat properly, and, in the evenings, read and study like other men round him. I promised him a book on physical exercises to keep himself fit and to come as often as I could. But I announced for his own good, that if he didn't brace up I hadn't the time to waste on him while there were so many others who were willing to be helped. Of course I added a kindly word as I was leaving; whereupon he gulped down his sobs and made every sort of promise to start afresh from that moment and show he was worth any trouble I could spare. I left him looking almost happy; but as I reached the corridor outside his door I glanced with dismay at the apparently endless vista of yet unvisited cells lining the galleries of the great dim Hall. How

The prison experience

was one to find the hours to do this sort of thing properly? (Gordon Gardiner, *Notes of a Prison Visitor*, 1938, pp. 15–17)

A man whom I call 'Number 12' set me a formidable conundrum to solve. Against all the traditional prison loyalties and, I suppose, because he hoped to curry favour with me, he informed me that a robbery was planned to take place at a certain house at a specified time. It may, or may not, have been the truth. My difficulty was that, had I passed this information on, and it had become known to the prisoners that I had done so, their belief that Visitors were used to obtain such information would entirely destroy any chance of Prison Visitors having any further influence. The value of their extremely useful services would be gone in this jail. I decided not to say anything, and, because I preferred the type which still held on to their misguided loyalties, I visited him no more. I never knew if the robbery took place, but if it did, I hope that the unfortunate victims will have the understanding to forgive me. (Alfred Salt, *Jottings of a JP*, 1955, pp. 19–20) *Forgive me*

≈ Education ≈

I became a teacher by mistake. One morning in the autumn of 1922, I was examining my correspondence in the Board of Education, and I came across a curious letter, bearing the Manchester postmark. 'Why is there no education in prisons?' ran the letter. I was nonplussed. I had no idea. But the Chairman of the Prison Commissioners lived but a few yards away. It was not even necessary to go outside. There was a bridge. I wandered into the Home Office. The door of the Chairman's room opened. I entered and was lost ...

Maurice Waller showed me to a chair. Already rather embarrassed, I asked my question. Why was there no education in prisons? Maurice Waller did not know. Had I any ideas to sell him on the subject? I had not. Would I like to do something about it? For very shame I could not say no, and although I had entered the room without any attention of occupying my spare time in prison education, I left in a chastened spirit and in the enjoyment of the dignified title of Educational Adviser to Wormwood Scrubs Prison. I held the title for five years. (Charles Douie, *Beyond the Sunset*, 1935, pp. 201–3)

After a time I persuaded Dorothy Massingham to give readings of Shakespeare plays, with her friends, on Sunday afternoons in *A girl pianist*

Wormwood Scrubs. She was succeeded by Jean Cadell, Sybil Thorndike, and Margaret Yarde, and for a period of years some of the greatest actors and actresses on the West End stage gave readings of plays (often contemporary plays) in the prison. This added to the interest taken in the classes in dramatic literature, but it created problems. On the afternoon of Christmas Day, Margaret Yarde arrived with her company to find that all the prisoners had been assembled in a hall; these included the prisoners in a wing of the prison reserved for men whose record was so bad that they were classified as irreclaimable. The noise was terrific, and a wave of mass hysteria broke over the prisoners, creating an ugly situation. At this point a girl pianist, showing remarkable courage, went to the piano and invited the prisoners to sing. She played for a quarter of an hour all the most popular music hall songs, and the prisoners, singing lustily, calmed down. I apologized to Margaret Yarde afterwards, but she had remained unperturbed. 'When I was younger,' she said, I used to act in a Glasgow music hall on a Saturday night. This evening was child's play.' (Charles Douie, *So Long to Learn*, 1951, pp. 92–3)

Dartmoor Hippodrome

The lights went up.

'Look at the Kissing Burglar, Val,' said Jimmy Jason. The convict he mentioned was one of the most hardened habituals ever to don the 'broad arrows', a Bill Sykes fear-nothing specimen, with a face that only a mother could love. But at that moment he sat with bowed head and the tears coursed down his cheeks.

We passed out of the chapel somewhat subdued, living in the recent memory of civilization shown upon a canvas. *Mighty Like a Rose* left such sentimental unrest generally that days elapsed before Dartmoor reverted to its hard and callous tone.

I expected every convict to express a desire to see another film performance, but the first man I approached on the subject had other views.

'How did you like the picture?' I inquired of a 'lifer', who was undergoing the maximum term in connection with a famous murder case.

'I never want to see another one in prison, Val,' he surprised me by replying.

'Why not?'

'I can't bear to see the outside world, even if it is only a screen glimpse of it – when I have twenty years to complete before I am back in it,' he answered brokenly.

'Sorry, old chap, I know how you feel.'

I did, indeed. My own punishment was heavy enough to appreciate the position of men undergoing the major sentence.

The Press reports of the film shown at Dartmoor probably alarmed the Home Office authorities. Cartoons showed close-cropped lags of 'Charlie Peace' philosophy reclining ungracefully in cushioned seats at the 'Dartmoor Hippodrome'. Pugnacious jaws held cigars, with bands on, warders were depicted as cinema attendants ushering in their patrons, the lags, while others carried loaded trays of cigarettes, chocolates, etc., for the consideration of their charges. (W.G. Davis, *Gentlemen of the Broad Arrows*, 1939, p. 53)

... there was one experiment which I introduced at Parkhurst which I think was an unqualified success and to which any knavery on the part of the lags was completely absent. I had noticed that some of the Special Stagemen took chess quite seriously and often applied to have books sent in on the subject. One of the leaders of this little group is now a well known author, and as a prisoner more trustworthy and intelligent than most. I decided to convert this group into a club limited to thirty.... There is no doubt that chess materially helped the good discipline of the prison and assisted the Dartmoor mutineers to settle down after a series of events which caused the Chief Officer and myself many anxious moments. (Gerald Fancourt Clayton, *The Wall is Strong*, 1958, pp. 153–4)

Chess

An application for admission to the Debating Society was refused on the grounds that the membership was already exceeded. The men in charge were nearly all young LCC teachers, and competent enough according to the book. What struck me about them – and I joined other classes at a later period – was their almost unanimous belief that the present social system had outlived its usefulness, and was fast approaching dissolution.

Sentimentalism

There was a very strong sympathy for the Russian experiment, and what appeared to me to be a great deal of muddled sentimentalism about the brotherhood and equality of mankind. There was also a tendency, I thought, to question the motives, and belittle the past performances, of the British Empire, and I often wondered what their influence must be on the formative minds of the rising generation. On the prisoners they had no effect at all. The classes were regarded more as a form of entertainment than as a school of serious instruction. (Richmond Harvey, *Prison From Within*, 1937, p. 97)

The debate class was extremely valuable in giving men something to think and talk about all the week. While the debate itself finished at eight o'clock it really continued all the following week.

The 'right' nearly always won

My job was to find the speakers for each week's debate and sometimes help them to 'swot' up the case they were to present. I found prisoners with 'left' tendencies in politics always ready to take the floor, but speakers for the right wing were not so easy to find, yet when it came to voting on the motion the 'right' nearly always won. Many members of the class were of course impervious to ideas and had made up their minds which way they would vote before the debate began. (H.W. Wicks, *The Prisoner Speaks*, 1938, pp. 181–2)

Election at Dartmoor

On February 12, 1950, a mock election was organized by Father Reece, the Anglican Chaplain attached to the prison, and Mr Taylor, the Deputy Governor, and was held with the Governor's permission in the prison chapel. The results were Conservative 150, Liberals 106, Labour 63 and Communists 52. Quite frankly this result surprised me for I had expected the majority of the chaps to be roaring red. It seemed, however, that they were possessed of more good sense than their confrères in the real election. (Peter Jenkins, *Mayfair Boy*, nd, p. 175)

Copybook

Owing to the kindness of my friend, Mr Alfred Rose, who made a special application on my behalf to the Home Office, I was allowed a school copybook and a pencil while I was in the hospital. I wrote my poem in this book, and the Home Office, for reasons best known to itself, refused me permission to bring it out with me when I left prison. (Lord Alfred Douglas, *In Excelsis* 1924, p. 9)

Not ... for sensational stories

The prisoner can now write what he likes in his book, provided it is not indecent or subversive of discipline, and he can take it out provided it contains nothing against the security or good order of the prison, and no autobiographical writing or other 'crime stuff' or descriptions of prison life. These note-books are not issued for the preparation of sensational stories for such newspapers as might be disposed to publish them; on the contrary they are intended, as part of the process of training, to divert the prisoner's mind from his criminal activities and his real or alleged grievances to more constructive attitudes.

In future, therefore, there need be no fear that any work of art conceived in a prison cell will never see the light. If it be retorted that under these restrictions 'De Profundis' would have remained buried, there are several answers. First, that 'De Profundis' did in fact emerge. Second, that Oscar Wildes do not come into prison with any frequency: since 'De Profundis' only one man of letters is known to have written anything of note in a prison – oddly enough, Lord Alfred Douglas. Third, it has long been the rule that if any prisoner claimed that his notebook contained matter worthy of preservation it should be kept for ten years. What was to happen at the end of the ten years was not, at the time, decided; and it may be fortunate that under present practice the question is unlikely to arise. The Advisory Council examined all the notebooks retained in the prisons over a long period of years, and found in them nothing of the slightest literary or artistic value. (Sir Lionel Fox, *The English Prison and Borstal Systems*, 1952, pp. 216–17)

In Excelsis

I

Torment of body, torment of the mind,
Pain, hunger, insult, stark ingratitude
Of those for whom we fought, detraction rude
But sanctimonious, cruel to be kind,
(Truly for bread a stone): all these we find
In this our self-appointed hell whose food
Is our own flesh. To what imagined good
Have we thus panted, beaten, bound and blind?

God knows, God knows. And since He knows indeed,
Why there's the answer: who would stay outside
When God's in prison? Who would rather choose
To warm himself with Peter than to bleed
With Dismas penitent and crucified,
Facing with Christ the fury of the Jews?
(Lord Alfred Douglas, *In Excelsis*, 1924, p. 13)

Corrective Training

You will, if you ever bother to read the reports of the Prison Commission, see a great deal written about Corrective Training. You will read in the papers that judges and magistrates often send men to Corrective Training, 'and not to prison'. But I can assure you that most of what you read is absolute nonsense!

Not long ago I read a case in the paper where a learned judge, sentencing a man to prison, said: 'I had considered sentencing you to three years' Corrective Training, but, having reviewed your case, I consider it to be of such a serious nature that I have changed my mind. I am now sending you to prison for two years.'

Now whatever the judge meant to do to this man it was obviously his intention to punish him more severely after having reviewed his case. No doubt all those who heard the sentence passed in court went away thinking the prisoner was paying a higher price for his crime as the result of the judge's change of mind. But what, in fact, the learned judge had done was to send the man to prison for eighteen months instead of two years. If that man had been sentenced to three years' Corrective Training, he would have served two years in prison and one year on licence. Moreover, had he been sent for Corrective Training he would, in all probability, have been sent to the *same* prison. That case is concrete proof of how little some of our judges know of the machinations of the Acts of Parliament under which they dispense the law. And, of course, the public, the taxpayers who foot the bill of approximately £6 per week for the 25,000 odd men and women and boys and girls who are in prison at this moment, know very much less!

The CT prisoners in Maidstone lived almost exactly the same life as I did myself. The only difference was that *once* a week they were supposed to attend a special class provided for them, when various speakers talked to them on such social problems as child welfare, income tax and birth control! But they were not even obliged to attend. Apart from that, there was no special training for them whatsoever. And that is a *fact*. (Anthony Heckstall-Smith, *Eighteen Months*, 1954, pp. 62–3)

The Norwich System

The Norwich System was devised by the Prison Commissioners in 1956 as a means of improving the relationship between prison officer and prisoner. Mr J.J. Beisty, Governor of Norwich, was charged with carrying it out. Its success was such that later on it was adopted in numerous other prisons including Shrewsbury, Swansea and Oxford, and indeed it has had a profound effect on prisons – both men's and women's – throughout the country.

The two most serious weaknesses of the prison system have been the long periods the prisoner spent locked in his cell and the shortness of the working day.

The scheme, to a great extent, remedied these shortcomings. Under this new plan ten to eighteen prisoners were allotted to two designated officers. These officers were required to get to know their men personally and to be fully informed about them: instead of being discouraged from speaking to their charges, officers were now at liberty to talk freely to them. It was their duty to prepare a written memorandum about each prisoner under

The prison experience

their care within a week of his reception at prison, and to make a final report on him before discharge. Apart from the two reports, paper work was to be eliminated to the greatest possible extent. (Xenia Field, *Under Lock and Key*, 1963, pp. 139–40)

The difference which this approach has made in just over two years is very striking. Almost as soon as one gets inside the gate at Norwich one realises that the atmosphere there is very different from the atmosphere in Strangeways, for example. In fact it is difficult to believe they are both parts of the same penal system. The officers joke with the prisoners, and the prisoners joke back. As a visitor is shown round, the prisoners quietly barrack him – a more unnerving reaction, but a healthier one, than the sullen apathy with which one is faced in most prisons. (Michael Frayn, *The Guardian*, 24 April 1959)

To me, this whole idea of trying to reform people's character by friendliness is rubbish. The grandly titled 'Norwich Experiment', for instance, where the screws are encouraged to act as friends and counsellors – it's complete balls. The men don't want to be friends with the screws any more than the screws want to be with the men. All the money spent on training prison personnel along these lines is money poured down a drain. For the simple reason that the whole scheme is based on talk, on good advice – which prisoners don't want, don't understand, and, a lot of them, heartily resent. They've been having it all their lives ever since they were kids whenever they were in trouble. If they could pay any attention to it, if they were the sort of people who could benefit from good advice, they wouldn't be in prison in the first place. On top of that, it's impossible for jailors to sit on both sides of the fence. When they try, it simply leads to confusion in their own minds and everyone else's. Whatever a screw says to a prisoner, there's always bound to be the feeling of an order behind it. How can screws reform men's characters like that? Most men in prison, they're way beyond the help of top-class psychiatrists, let alone dim-witted screws. (Tony Parker and Robert Allerton, *The Courage of His Convictions*, 1962, pp. 170–1)

Complete balls

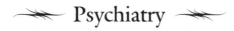 Psychiatry

He asked me how many times did I like to go with a woman. I said, 'As many times as I can.'
  'How many times do you go in a night?'

'What's that got to do with you?'

'I'm trying to judge your character.'

'Well,' I said, 'you can't judge my character by asking me how many times I go with women. How many times do you go with your wife?' (Ronald Lloyd and Stanley Williamson, *Born to Trouble*, 1968, p. 72)

Respect

RLM: The problem that faces us, Frank, is that unless somehow or other a man comes to see himself in a different kind of way, all the psychiatry, all the psychology, all the so-called treatment in the world won't make him change, because basically he doesn't want to change. Now I think the solution lies in respect for the individual. One must patiently, and for a long time, be prepared not to lecture, not to moralise, but to accept a person as he is and for what he is, to keep on giving him the opportunity to take a look at himself, to re-examine himself in his own time and in his own way. It seems to me it's this respect for the prisoner as an individual that's the most helpful thing that one can show either in a prison setting or in any other kind of setting. Any other approach, in terms of moralising or lecturing or telling somebody how they ought to behave or how they must behave or how they'll be punished if they don't behave, is worse than useless. (R.L. Morrison talking to Frank Norman, *Lock 'em Up and Count 'em*, 1970, p. 43)

Therapeutic community

A psychiatric unit exists in the prison hospital which is manned by four doctors and a psychiatric social worker. There is a full-time chaplain assisted by a Church Army Captain to see to the spiritual needs of the men. There are two pychologists, a tutor organiser, and two welfare officers with links to the probation service, concerned with the men's preparation for release. With the services of those specialists and the intimate knowledge that the officers gain of the prisoners in their day-to-day contacts over a long period, it is possible to gain a comprehensive picture of the prisoner, his past difficulties and his future prospects.

This, however, should be more than just an information-getting process. It should add up to a body of people able to create a secure atmosphere for the prisoner in which he can feel that, though he has been rejected by society outside, he counts as a person inside: an atmosphere in which he can form a web of understanding relationships that will help him to become a more mature person able to face himself realistically.

The problem, par excellence, facing the prison administrator today is to transform the ordinary body of men and women that constitute the staff into people able to foster this type of

The prison experience

therapeutic community: to guide and train them towards this new kind of understanding: and to maintain and support them in it throughout the frustrations and rebuffs that inevitably arise when dealing with some of the most complex personalities in the country. This requires from everybody a high level of understanding, extreme sensitivity and enormous patience and tolerance. (Nicholas Tyndall, *Prison People*, 1967, pp. 111–13)

⟞ Grendon Underwood ⟝

That evening, when the notice had appeared about Grendon, I stayed in my cell as I wanted to be alone to collect my thoughts, and if possible, analyse my feelings about being transferred to a hospital. It would mean acceptance on my part that I was in need of psychiatric treatment, and this was something I had battled against in the past. Geordie was right when he told me I lied to myself, except I wasn't so much lying as putting on an act, trying to convince myself that all I said and did was how I wanted to be. What the real me was, even I didn't know. All I did know was that I wanted to be a normal person, at any rate in the opinion of people of my own age. The sort of people I would like to have had as friends would no longer have anything to do with me; the labels I had gathered for myself might just as well have said, 'Beware of the bull. He's dangerous.' Two of my labels would be prefixed 'ex' when I was released from prison, they were, nevertheless, labels: ex-Borstal boy and ex-prisoner. Could I, I wondered, become an ex-psychopath? For psychopath was my psychiatric label, and one which I particularly disliked as it was used against me in an abusive way. If I were accepted for a transfer to Grendon, would that label be replaced by another? (Frances Finlay, *Boy in Prison*, 1971, p. 56)

Life to me in Grendon was very strange. I first went in there and I was full of mad ideas. I didn't really want to be cured of taking drugs, I went to Grendon because it seemed to be a nice easy place to spend my term of imprisonment. But when I got there I was very shocked because you had to do certain things in order to stay there, so at first I wouldn't try, you know, I wouldn't conform, I was a bit of a rebel. But you go on an induction course to get used to Grendon, Grendon's ways. It's called an induction group, and this lasts for about four weeks until you're allocated to one of four groups. I was allocated to group one. They thought I wouldn't stay there because I was so anti-social.

An ex-prisoner recently released from Grendon Prison

So anyway after about two months, and getting into bother and all sorts of things, I suddenly thought, well, if I don't start soon I'll never get out of here. So I really conned my way through, but even if you con your way through, just being at the place affects you, no matter what. You're just living as a community and there's the intense therapy that is required and something's bound to happen to your personality. And I changed and I suddenly got very involved with the place, you know, and I was agreeing to all their rules and trying to make something of it, not just for myself but other people I started helping other people.

This was very strange to me because I'm very selfish – I was terribly, terribly selfish but after a while I began to think more of others and this was very strange indeed. You sit in a group and people tell you various things about their lives and their problems, and all they're trying to do is get a little bit more insight into themselves, but the way it usually works is on a reflection basis. You use the group as a mirror, where you can see other people, the similarities of character and you start to recognise this and you point it out to other people, you suggest all the time. (Frank Norman, *Lock 'em Up and Count 'em*, 1970, p. 27)

Shocking

The Wing Meetings are shocking, all they are is slagging sessions, with everybody working-off their own personal scores on people: and it's not just the prisoners that work them off on the staff, either. I've seen and heard some members of the staff tear a bloke apart, in front of everyone else: they say things about him which ought to be kept confidential, and I've known blokes lying on their beds crying after it's been done to them. It's always the ones who can't talk, who can't defend themselves and turn the argument on to something else, they're the ones who really suffer. I think it ought to be recognised that some people can't say what they ought to say in their own defence, they just don't know the right words. And I think this is cruelty; it's as cruel as in other prisons where a bunch of screws will go into someone's cell and do him over physically – only here it's done verbally in front of everyone else. (Tony Parker, *The Frying Pan*, 1970, pp. 20–1)

Neither approval nor co-operation

Almost without exception the doctors and medical staff of Grendon disagreed with my being given permission by the Home Office to go there. The idea of a writer staying day after day, week after week and month after month, and talking to whom he liked about what he wished, was not acceptable; and before my arrival they agreed among themselves they were going to give me neither

The prison experience

approval nor co-operation. (Tony Parker, *The Frying Pan*, 1970, p. 212).

⊱— Barlinnie Special Unit —⊰

The screws were very friendly towards me, calling me Jimmy, but I wasn't being taken in by that. I did find it very hard to accept but through keeping up my façade I managed to pull through this first stage without causing any bad feelings. I felt like someone lost in a wilderness. Ben made me a coffee and took me aside to whisper in my ear that the place might be bugged. He explained to me how the screws were very friendly but they had to be watched – he didn't have to tell me. He also told me that there were a couple of screws who had reputations for brutalising prisoners in the place but that there were one or two others who seemed okay. I was then *asked* by the screw if I would come round and sort out my personal property with him. I went, and while we opened the parcels containing old clothing he did something that to him was so natural but to me was something that had never been done before. He turned to me and handed me a pair of scissors and asked me to cut open some of them. He then went about his business. I was absolutely stunned. That was the first thing that made me begin to feel human again. It was the completely natural way that it was done. This simple gesture made me think. In my other world, the penal system in general, such a thing would never happen. (Jimmy Boyle, *A Sense of Freedom*, 1977, pp. 229–30)

It was sheer coincidence that the Special Unit was conceived at a time when I was struggling with my own identity. In having a vague notion of where we were both going and what needed to be done I had to handle these realities even at this early stage. Ben and Larry were so full of hate and mistrust for the authorities that their behaviour constantly bordered on physical violence both to each other and to the staff. Being the recognised leader, I soon found my position was to support, and prevent them.

Hate

An example of this took place within a month of my arrival. I happened to be in one part of the Unit with Ben and some staff when Rab came running in, excited, saying that Larry was in trouble. We all ran through to the cell area to find Larry standing with a pair of scissors at the throat of a member of staff. I walked in and across to Larry and told him to give me the scissors. The atmosphere was very tense. The staff who had been following Ben and me stood there and let me do the talking. Larry reluctantly gave me the scissors and Ben moved in to separate Larry from the staff member. There was a whole series of on-the-spot decisions taken here that resolved the matter without physical injury. On seeing Larry threatening a colleague, the staff didn't go for their batons and rush in, but stopped, and allowed Ben and me to handle it. Had they drawn their batons then we would have turned on them as a group. (Jimmy Boyle, *The Pain of Confinement*, 1984, p. 9)

Wary of art

Joyce Laing, the art therapist, was coming in from time to time and though we were very wary of art and the therapy bit, we liked her coming as she was a pretty good looking bird. So we had to compromise and pretend to have an interest in art in order to keep her coming back. One day she brought in a 7lb bag of clay for us to mess around with and the five of us sat there humouring her and having a good laugh till such time as she had to leave. Although I had been joking along with the others I felt as though I had an affinity with the clay, almost as though I had known it before. That may sound like a cliché but it's what I felt and I did mention it to one of the others. When Joyce left, the clay was abandoned by the others but I kept on with it. The day was hot and we sat in the prison yard and I sat messing around with the material doing a portrait of one of the guys. I liked it and that was what mattered. Then I did another straight off, without a model and this pleased me. I felt excited as did some of the others when they saw them. I made arrangements to get hold of more clay and I did some more pieces, so that when Joyce returned a couple of weeks later she was surprised to see the results. I felt great pleasure in creating the sculptures and knew that I had stumbled onto something within myself. (Jimmy Boyle, *A Sense of Freedom*, 1977, p. 250)

People, goodwill

Out of everything that makes up this Unit, the thing that costs nothing in terms of money is staff and prisoners getting together and talking; it is the one thing that has brought about results. The emphasis is placed on seeing the individual as a person in his own right without relying on labelling or categorisation in order to identify. It is unique in the sense that two opposing factions have come together and worked towards building a Community with a remarkable degree of success. An important lesson is that no professional psychiatric or psychological experience was needed to make it so. Our basic ingredients have been some people, goodwill from all sides and with those we became the architects of a model that could be used anywhere. (Jimmy Boyle, *A Sense of Freedom*, 1977, pp. 263–4)

The prison experience

⟫⟫ Visits and letters ⟪⟪

On my first visit to an English prison, it was the 'visiting box' which left the deepest impression on my mind, for it brought home to me the way in which a prison sentence cuts a man off from his fellow humans. The visiting box was one of a row of small cubicles in which the prisoner was allowed to receive his wife or family on their occasional visits. It was separated from the cubicle in which they sat by a sheet of plate glass with a perforated metal grill on each side, so that the prisoner could speak to his visitors and see them – but he could not touch them. And all the while prison officers stood watch, on each side of the grill. The object of this arrangement was to prevent trafficking, and for some prisoners precautions are always certainly necessary. But this was a depressingly inhuman arrangement. (Sir Harold Scott, *Your Obedient Servant*, 1959, pp. 71–2)

Whisky

The visiting boxes are stall-like affairs, convicts and their outside friends face each other through close-wire meshing and glass partitions, while warders patrol behind.

There are two sets of wire meshing in each box, placed twelve inches apart, the glass section extending to within four inches of the sides.

This leaves a space without glass, but no instrument thicker than the average knitting needle can penetrate the small-gauge wire meshing. Nevertheless, at every visit, I manage to obtain a drink of whisky, by the simple method of having a knitting needle thrust through with eighteen inches of cycle-tyre valve rubber fixed on the end. The rubber tubing is taken off the needle, placed in my mouth, and the whisky, held by my visitors and carefully concealed, sucked through it. (W.G. Davis, *Gentlemen of the Broad Arrows*, 1939, pp. 18–19)

The 'flash'

... at Pentonville there existed (on good authority) a more concrete device known as the 'flash', or 'flash up'. A wife or girl friend when she sits in the visiting box is screened by a wooden partition on either side, as is the prisoner, and at a suitable moment she will briefly expose her breasts or raise her skirts to expose her genitals, having come to the prison without the relevant items of underclothing. In January 1959 two informants reported a new racket. Two ponces in the prison were alleged to have made arrangements whereby in return for ¼-oz of tobacco per week prostitutes would visit men and provide them with a 'flash'. Both informants felt that it was unlikely that officers would be suspicious of the same girls reappearing on the scene to visit different men and claimed that 'flashes' between husbands and wives were quite common and that officers ignored them. (Terence Morris and Pauline Morris, *Pentonville: A Sociological Study of an English Prison*, 1963, p. 186)

A hard case That night I lay awake as I always did when I had had a visit from Billie, would she really wait for me all that time twenty months, twenty more long months before I would be free again, she'll wait I know she'll wait, she told me she would, that should be good enough for me. I'll write a letter next week and tell her how much I love her, I don't know though if you keep telling a woman how much you love her it's usually the best way to loose her, be a hard case and don't bother to write for a few weeks; that always gets them at it. No I can't do that I'll write next week I'm due for a letter. I'll tell. ... (Frank Norman, *Bang to Rights*, 1958, p. 43)

Dear Frank So one day I was walking around the exersize by myself which I quite often did, stareing at the deck deep in thought when a geezer came up to me and said something about cheering up or something. I'd seen this geezer around but hadn't spoke to him before as he was a bit of a flash mug, and I didn't recon him nothing.

'How long you got to do now?' He asked.

'About a streatch.' I answered.

'I've got eighteen moon to do yet; but I'm doing four,'

So what, I wish you'd piss off, what do you think it's clever to get a four. You think your a real hard case don't you?

'That's tough still it will soon go, and then you'll be out and get back to graft puting the cane about' I replied.

'Too true I'll be again as soon as I get home. My old woman's still out on the hoist now and she's a bleeding good earner. She's got a nice few quid saved up for when I get out, so I can get a jamjar and a new whistle.'

Yer Yer yer.

'Thats nice my bird's gone bent.'

'Never mind there's plenty more fish in the sea.'

'Yes.'

'When did you get the belt?'

'Last week.'

'What happened, did you get a letter?'

Why don't you drop dead.

'Yes she went case with some geezer now she's liveing with him.'

'She must be a right slag, my old woman wouldn'nt do anything like that.'

'Listen you c… if you don't shut your trap I'll put my hand in it.'

At this a look of serprize apeared on his boat.

'I didn't do nothing mate,'

'Forget it,' I said and walk away leaving him standing there looking very bewildered.

It had happened as I have said the week before, I got a letter from Billie. Dear Frank and that's all it said. (Frank Norman, *Bang to Rights*, 1958, pp. 72–3)

"Dear Bella,   *Dear Bella*

"I don't want nothing more to do with you seeing as you have been going to the pictures with Jim and Alf and Bert. You are nothing but a rag and bone girl with swanky hair.

"Your ever loving,
"Sammy."

Here followed several crosses.

(Wallace Blake, *QUOD*, 1927, p. 199)

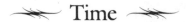

Time

It is the moment at the end of the day, the moment I love best; when the turmoil of the association hour is over, when the last bell has sounded, and busy tongues are hushed; when we are locked in alone. The night watchman has just switched on the light in my cell, but it is the late twilight hour of summer-time, and night is not yet. Over the high wall opposite my window sycamore trees display the leafy fullness of June; the voice of a child, calling to its playmates in the street, rings clearly in the still air; a tiny train moves slowly along the valley, its engine throwing out little burls of steam as it mounts the long incline. Immediately facing me over the wall is a long straight street up the hill, looking precipitous from my angle of vision. At the crest is the home of a senior member of the staff, hidden by tall trees; but he has pointed out the spot to me. At this hour he will be busy there in his garden, on whose quiet beauty he loves to dwell, unmindful in his enthusiasm of the nostalgia he invokes. On the skyline, blending with the cumulus clouds, are upland pastures and the wide downs. (James Leigh, *My Prison House*, 1941, pp. 55–6)

I have been standing on top of a chair gazing out of my window   *A different*
for half an hour or so. I can see over the wall from my cell, but   *world*

more importantly I can hear the kids from some local school nearby screaming, shouting and having a pleasant time generally. Occasionally one can hear a lorry go past – it's amazing how such sounds can lift up the soul. Sounds from a different world. (Andrzy Jakubczyk, letter to Una Padel, personal communication, 1987)

Night in prison   Night in prison brings to a man a false sense of privacy; it holds out balm to bodys weary of watching and being watched, sick with wearing the day's cloak of toughness. It is time to relax, to weep, to pray. How good it is to cry softly, how consoling to pray – 'Oh, God, help me do my time!' (Robert Roberts, *Imprisoned Tongues*, 1968, pp. 194–5)

The blackest day   Sunday was the blackest day of the week, for there was no work to do, and apart from the church service or Bible class (I always wonder if the visiting clergy really believe that prisoners are such ardent worshippers as the packed chapel suggests) the boredom was interminable. My cell window was high above the floor, but by piling the books I had on my stool I could just see out and listen to somebody playing an instrument in the Canongate on Sunday afternoons. (Emmanuel Shinwell, *Conflict Without Malice*, 1955, p. 72)

Precious   Monday morning came as a relief to an intolerable monotony for many of the lags. Personally, at the beginning of the sentence, I liked the week-end, even although I was without books. I knew no one in the prison when I arrived there, and I was glad to be alone, away from the nagging and the general air of intimidation. At least in our cells we were not shouted at. The halls were so quiet. In fact their silence became precious to me. A convict in those days came to love the deadly silence of the hall. (W.F.R. Macartney, *Walls Have Mouths*, 1936, p. 93)

Re-visiting   When I was in solitary confinement I could spend hours revisiting in my mind the various outstanding museums I had visited and the plays, operas and ballets I had seen. A review in *The Times* mentioning various actors and singers would immediately make me visualise in the flesh and I would dream of the time when I would be able to see them again. (Gordon Lonsdale, *Spy*, 1966, p. 119)

Amused myself   When it was dark I amused myself by tearing pieces of paper out of the Bible, rolling them up into little balls, and then scattering them about the cell and finding them again. This is an old trick

Blundeston Prison

with men who are undergoing punishment and who are not allowed to have the cell light lit, and if you resolutely refuse to stop searching for the balls of paper until you have got back all you scattered, the time simply flies. (James Spenser, *Limey Breaks In*, 1934, p. 160)

I wish I could think of nothing a lot of the time, but it's hard because you've got too much time. You sit there and work yourself into a depression. Then I read a book or listen to a tape or something. You have to push yourself to do things. Even like some days I don't feel like going to the gym but I always push myself because you have to have something to occupy yourself. I feel that everyone has to have a bit of discipline in prison. But sometimes I feel that if I discipline myself so much that I can stop worrying – about my wife, for example – it'll be like letting go. I

I wish I could think of nothing

remember when I first came in, I was on the cleaners and the work is just about an hour a day, so the rest of the time I used to lie there and think about things and write letters. At that stage I was feeling as close to my wife as if I was still out there. And then when I went to Reception to work, I was so busy all the time that I was too busy to think about it, and it felt like I was being taken away from her. (James Campbell, *Gate Fever: Voices From a Prison*, 1986, p. 26)

A day is not a day

By this time, I was realy gone, my mind had become dead and if it was not for my painting and reading I am certain that, I would be a bit potty now. When I think back to the time it took for that year to pass it seem's unbeleiveable that time could go so slow. It is just like so much nothingness, nothing happend and nothing much was likely to happen. A day is not a day a day is just a nothing in which you don't do anything at least you dont seem to do anything. You wake up in the morning and you stay awake for a few hours then you go to sleep again and that's how it goes day in day out never vareing never changeing, just a wast. To stick a man in the nick is not a punishment in the sence of being punished. It's just a wast. (Frank Norman, *Bang to Rights*, 1958, p. 104)

Castles to ashes

Can you imagine what it is like being a prisoner for life, your dreams turn into nightmares and your castles to ashes, all you think about is fantasy and in the end you turn your back on reality and live in a contorted world of make-believe, you refuse to accept the rules of fellow mortals and make ones that will fit in with your own little world, there is no daylight in this world of the 'lifer', it is all darkness, and it is in this darkness that we find peace and the ability to live in a world of our own, a world of make-believe. (Stanley Cohen and Laurie Taylor, *Psychological Survival*, 1972, p. 110)

Time

Snout is about the only real consolation in prison. Being locked up in a damp, dull prison cell for fourteen, and sometimes eighteen, hours out of twenty-four is enough to drive one round the bend. Some blokes did go crazy. But I had long ago acquired the faculty of being able to mentally transport myself out of that nick and to some place where life was pleasant and rosy. I still can do that, so that I don't suffer from neurosis. Why, many a long night from 8 p.m. until 6 a.m. I've had the time of my life living in a wild fantasy of dreams. My prison surroundings have been completely a life apart, something so far away that at times it was my real circumstances which seemed so fantastic. In between I

The prison experience

went over jobs which I had pulled off and mentally surveyed them to see how they could be improved upon. Then I went over my mistakes again, and learned how they had occurred and let me down. So you see there was always plenty for me to do when I lay on that board with no occupation but thinking. And plan future jobs. Oh yes, if a survey could be taken it would be proved that most of the big criminal jobs, and thousands of small ones, are planned in gaol. Planned to the last detail because there is not sufficient alternative interest to occupy prisoners' minds. Naturally one tends to get philosophical as well. Don't think it didn't hurt, that lagging I got then. It did. And I smarted a bit for it. But I was not complaining. When you're in my job you soon get to realise that there are several ways of doing bird. But the only sensible way is to do it the easy way. That is, to take all they can give you and swallow it. Yes, it's a shattering life. It does tend to break you. But when you know that's what it's for, you don't let it achieve that objective. Do your bird and make the most of it, I always said. So I did just that, and I thought up more jobs in stir than I did out. I also thought about getting married. (Billy Hill, *Boss of Britain's Underworld*, 1955, p. 39)

Reflecting now, after a further three years' experience of solitary *A broken vase* confinement, on my mental states of that time, I find myself more decided about the value of the considered opinions of the Great Minds. I utterly fail to see any privilege in sitting in solitude. My experience has been that it is more pleasant, and more reformative, to share the company of the worst cut-throat unhung than to live for twenty-fours hours a day with yourself. No doubt there are exalted beings for whom it is a privilege to be alone. But the unexalted rest of us, until we actually do find ourselves solitary, do not realize the tremendous debt we owe to the press of near obstructions.

For solitude has the effect of forcing one's acquaintance upon oneself; and in the narrow scrutiny of self that follows, faults are much more manifest than virtues, even as the brokenness of a broken vase is more manifest than its vaseness. One comes to see the inner life as the bloody battlefield it really is, as the tragedy where strengths are frittered in self-conflict and achieve only a tithe of their potentialities nor arrive at any peace. One is surprised to find that this self of ours, this seeming entity we designate so assuredly with an individual name, is really an unreconciled aggregate of many selves and anti-selves, much too divided to merit a single epithet. (Mark Benney, *Low Company*, 1936, p. 283)

*So the
months …*

So the months rolled on. Winter turned to spring and then summer – that beautiful summer of 1932. The agony which we poor captives endured every night after four in the afternoon can easily be imagined. Our cells were like Turkish baths, for there was very little ventilation. As a matter of fact, most of us stripped and laid on our bed-boards naked, almost gasping for breath. I used to sit up at my cell window, stark naked, looking into the green distance and thinking of all those who were in freedom and able to enjoy that gorgeous weather. (Netley Lucas, *Crooks: Confessions*, 1925, p. 349)

*Anger has
replaced
despair*

I have completed two years of my sentence. I know this, and the passing of time is all that I am sure about. It is a frightening thought to realise that of twenty-four months in my life my knowledge of anything certain is limited to an isolated fact. I have been imprisoned for two years; I have spent two Christmases and three Easters behind bars; on each of over seven hundred days I have felt myself subjected to minor humiliations and petty indignities, and each new one smarts: I am not yet hardened – my skin is still too thin.

A recurring anger has replaced despair, and perhaps a Catholic priest would say that this was good, for is not despair the greatest sin? I do not resent being imprisoned. Were they to crop my head, dress me in broad-arrowed canvas, manacle my legs, and set me to work breaking stones with a sledge, I should not resent it: I believe I should welcome it, for it would reduce my sentence to two dimensions – retribution for me and a deterrent to others. Retribution means vengeance, society's vengeance for the crime I have committed against its laws. Recompense. And the recompense demanded is an indeterminate number of years from my life. I can accept this without necessarily agreeing that it serves a useful purpose, for it is part of the law and one of the proclaimed intentions behind imprisonment. The second intention is that imprisonment should act as a deterrrent to others. I am convinced that the threat of imprisonment keeps a great many on the straight and narrow path who, without such a threat, might well commit a crime. But there is a third intention. It is laid down quite clearly that prisoners should be rehabilitated; that they should be taught to lead an 'honest and industrious life'. (Zeno, *Life*, 1968, p. 81)

*Eats your
insides out*

The fact is that prison eats your insides out, and ties your stomach in knots, leaving your heart very heavy. All of this takes place when you are alone, but it wouldn't be the done thing to let this be seen by other people. At nights I would get up to my window

The prison experience

and look out from the top flat and could see the cars and buses and people walking in the streets and, though this hurt me, I never said that I wouldn't be back because by this time I was fully involved in being a criminal, and I only knew that I wanted to be out and be big in crime. I felt all the feelings but could never get it all together to see what I was doing to myself. Instead I took these feelings as signs of personal weakness and would never dare let anyone see them. What the fuck is it all about? (Jimmy Boyle, *A Sense of Freedom*, 1977, p. 107)

Summer had come, invincible like a tide, even into our prison. I cannot tell fully with what feeling I watched the sky turn a deeper blue and saw the deepening of the green of the trees – especially those the tops of which peeped over the prison walls. Summer was in the air and in the earth. It came up every crevice where there was soil. Like a tide it had entered our prison in a myriad ways and it had welled up in our blood. The hollyhocks near the main gate were ten feet high and deep flushed flowers had bloomed low down, under the leaves. Poppies of another variety had come out in that narrow bed in the exercise yard. To see them come out was a great delight. First opened broad green leaves, revealing rich green buds already developed, with slender stems, the buds and stems a delicate very pale green. The plump buds new born, fresh and pure in the sunlight, lay at first on the opened leaves like babes, the stems feeding, but too weak to lift, the buds. They seemed to be asleep. Then, almost as one looked at them, the stems filled up, strengthened, and the buds rose up, cracked and burst and, shaking out from a million tiny folds, behold! delicate paper-like petals, like wings in the sunlight, some pink, some white, some red. (William Holt, *I Was a Prisoner*, 1934, p. 57)

Summer had come

So the years went by at Winchester, one day much the same as the next except that once a week there was a bath. Officially there were twenty minutes allowed for this from the time of leaving the workshop to time of resuming work. A clean shirt, vest, shorts, socks, handkerchief and a huckaback towel were issued on emerging from the bath. These articles, plus a pair of trousers, a jacket, one pair of shoes, a bib and brace overall and a spare shirt to be used as a nightshirt, were all the kit issued in local prisons. The clean underwear, socks and handkerchief came from a communal kitty: if anything fitted, you were fortunate. A woollen pullover was issued in cold weather. I never had a hat on my head for more than nine years, irrespective of the weather. (Harry Houghton, *Operation Portland*, 1972, p. 137)

So the years ...

Male company   Also do you know any woman about my age or younger who would care to visit on one occasion that would fill up my visits at Bristol. After twenty two years in jail I'm a little sick of male company. There's a little garden outside my cell and I fed the birds during the cold spell. I found out that blackbirds, wagtails will eat bread. I thought they only ate live worms etc. There's also two robins I see regularly. They are the first I've ever seen in my life. (Frank Marritt, letter to Jim Little, personal communication, 1986)

Nonchalance   The need for nonchalance, in the face of small accidents which might have serious consequences, was very great. Nowhere more than in a jail is the penalty for losing one's head so severe. Thousands of times, in an ordinary sentence, the convict has to display a stoicism beside which the fiction-Indian calm is as the excitement of a dancing dervish. Again and again I have seen men lose their most treasured possessions, under the eyes of a watching warder, without even a side-glance. (Jim Phelan, *Jail Journey*, 1940, p. 280)

We should be proud   The first quality noticeable in the long-sentence men was their courage. We like to think that courage is a national characteristic and are proud of exhibitions of it in war, exploration, pioneer flying and in such emergencies as flood and fire. We should be proud, then, of our criminals. Whatever they have done, or have not done, to offend society, their behaviour when subjected to the cold-blooded inhumanity of a long sentence is beyond praise. There will be no credit given for it, no rewards, no medals – indeed the medals they earned by more spectacular courage in another sphere will have been snatched from them. They have none of the consolations of the soldier undergoing privation or imprisonment by the enemy, they are allowed to feel no pride and know that they can never rebuild their lives. There is no 'civvy street' waiting round the corner for even if they survive their sentences it will be to face a mistrustful and hostile world in which all ties have been broken by time. They know that for three, five, seven years, for eternity in fact, they will follow the same deadly routine, eat the same food, do the same dreary tasks, sleep in identical cells. They have nothing to live for, and they are made to remember it hourly. Their will to rise, their self-respect, their pride – all these have been broken, not by any overt act of cruelty, not by any physical punishment or individual show of malice, but by an inexorably grinding system which, while hypocritically proclaiming its good intentions, continues to confine men in a grey limbo, without relief, or hope, or variety. Yet these long-sentence men are among the most cheerful in prison. Resolved to

The prison experience

survive and remain sane, they know that they can only do this by fighting against self-pity and despair all day and each day. Whatever they may be in their cells, here in this doleful chasm between cell doors they must somehow achieve geniality, for their own sakes and for the sake of their fellows. They do it, and put to shame the melancholy antics of short-sentence men who are sorry for themselves. I have never found human nature more admirable, I have never been more conscious of the essential goodness and great-heartedness of mankind. (Rupert Croft-Cooke, *The Verdict of You All*, 1955, pp. 112–13)

⟫⟫ Self-realisation ⟫⟫

You come to prison, you submit to the disciplines of the place, you act and react like a prisoner; but there is a part of the mind that rejects these things as false and insubstantial. Always you are waiting, waiting, though you know not for what. Footsteps approaching along the landing towards your cell quicken the pulse of expectancy in you; they are bringing a letter to say that your case had been reconsidered . . . they are going to let you out. The faintest rattle of keys starts a thousand fantasies in your brain, and although the rattle always dies away in silence, although the footsteps always pass your door, yet you cannot be reconciled to the fact of imprisonment, its tediums and constraints. Like some untameable brute in a cage, this megalomaniac nucleus of your mind defies the evidence of the senses and hurls itself against the bars of reality. Once in a while it roars out a passionate denial of the squalor and brutality of life, then sinks back exhausted but unconquered. Later it loses some of its confidence, skulking in the dark and listening. At night a chance phrase of music blown into the cell will set it palpitating, so that it starts up in triumphant affirmation of a beauty that passes even with the moment. Such resistance is long, it may outlast many prison sentences, and while it still obtains there is no place for reason in that mind; all social values must be impressed from without, not impelled from within. But at last the resistance flags and ceases, and for the first time you *realize* imprisonment, the unrelenting hardness of the walls, the implacable aggression of the bars. (Mark Benney, *Low Company*, 1936, pp. 339–41)

All the railway platforms and the other carriages of this train I was on were packed with sailors bound for Bristol and Plymouth. Faces like kids, and yet you knew what some of them must have

Mad animal

seen. And most of them all joking and eager. I couldn't help thinking: 'Ruby, this is a shabby mess you're in, boy. Chained up and going back to prison.' It was the first time it dawned on me that all I'd done with my life was qualify to be treated like a mad animal. I didn't like it. (Ruby Sparks, *Burglar to the Nobility*, 1961, p. 142)

Learned to write

Have all the nine years been wasted? No, it wouldn't be true to say that, for during my time here I have learned to write, at least well enough to have had a book published which is selling well, and is to be published in America and translated into several European languages. Is it to the credit of the prison system that I have been able to do this? My instinctive reaction is to give them no credit at all, for Arthur Koestler instituted and financed the award scheme under which prisoners may write literary and musical compositions, paint, and construct models and works of art which can be sold on the prisoner's behalf if they win an award. But the Home Office have permitted this, and therefore some credit must be due to them, although whenever they have had to play a part it has appeared ineffective and incompetent. One year the closing date for entries was 31 August; the following year it was 30 May, but we were not informed by the Home Office that the date had been brought forward until six weeks before the new closing date. When an appeal was immediately made to the agents for the Koestler Award we were told that they had informed the Home Office of the new date in October of the previous year. It hadn't occurred to the person responsible to pass the information on to the men most concerned, the prisoners.

How many other men have I known who have been fortunate enough to be able to spend the otherwise wasted years doing something that is constructive? Hardly any. There is so little opportunity, and time alone is not enough. Most of them are here because they could not cope without help, and there is no help.

I have been able to do something, but I am by no means convinced that what I may have gained in character and ability in any way outweighs what I have lost. I know that the years have made me *unsocial*: I can only hope that they have not made me anti-social. At this moment, I am reasonably sure that they have not. (Zeno, *Life*, 1968, pp. 183–4)

Balance the past

I want to prove myself, not by doing useless jobs such as mailbags year in, year out, but by giving something tangible and worthwhile. I mean, not so long ago, after the previous hunger-strike, at the risk of making a fool of myself, I seriously considered the

The prison experience

possibility of inquiring about donating a kidney to some hospital, for the satisfaction of knowing I'd done something *real* to balance the past. But I eventually decided that such a gesture would be perhaps too ostentatious and that my motives would be misinterpreted or construed as the passing fad of a mental defective. (Ian Brady, letter to Lord Longford, *The Grain of Wheat*, 1974, p. 145)

Meanwhile I was still giving thought to the past and the life I had lived. All the older guys that I had looked up to when I was a kid were either dead, alcoholics, or serving long prison sentences. The Gorbals had changed physically with all the new buildings and different people moving in and out but the problems were still very much the same and possibly worse. Parts of me had changed and for the first time in my life I was thinking not as a victim but as a person who had been responsible for doing things that I shouldn't have. I qualify this by pointing out that whenever I was sentenced in the past for something and came into prison, the humiliation and degradation I met with there made me think of myself as the victim. I hadn't given a shit for the person or deed I was in for, or had any sympathy, as I had been too concerned with my own miseries and misfortunes. The reason for this was that the unit was allowing me to function responsibly and in order to achieve this one had to think responsibly. As a person I was growing and developing, seeing things through new eyes, and a clear mind. The visitors coming into the unit played a big part in my becoming more socially aware, and my relationships with the Unit Staff were still strengthening. (Jimmy Boyle, *A Sense of Freedom*, 1977, p. 251)

The life I had lived

The critical influence was my son. I was deeply ashamed of the way my criminal activities had affected his life, and might do so again, depriving him of a father as completely as I had been deprived. I was re-creating in his life many of the conditions which led to my own indoctrination into crime. I knew that my own relationship with my son could never be anything like that between my father and me; but I started thinking about my father for the first time since he died. I started to read books on child psychology; at first, I suppose, to try and understand the development of my own son, but it quickly grew into a passion to try to relive and understand my own childhood.

Critical influence

My effort left me with some understanding of, and insight into, my upbringing, but with very little grasp of how and why my criminality had emerged and developed. Remember that I had lived by crime and had known hundreds of professional criminals.

I knew that by and large they were not actuated by the simple motivations of lust, greed and hate; those that are are often ostracized by the criminal community as ruthlessly as the criminal is by society. I also knew that all the penal measures adopted in this country are, as a means of reformation, a joke (e.g. remissions of sentence are fortuitous and unpredictable). But this was all knowledge which had been learned intuitively from my own experience and I could not articulate it for myself. One element in this store of acquired knowledge was the criminological fatuity of my prison dossier, which was an added stimulus to me to try and achieve the means of understanding which I needed. For myself, I found them in the sociology of roles and values, and tried to explain my criminality by the concepts it provided.

I have tried to summarize this explanation in this document. I said at the beginning that I wanted it most of all to be the truth. I could have failed to achieve this in two ways. I might have failed to communicate properly and/or I could have misinterpreted my own experience. I have been very conscious of both these dangers. I have been trying to communicate something which is at the very limit of my own understanding, and I have only a smattering of psychology, criminology and sociology to work with. But however much I may have failed in both respects, this account remains true for me. It describes what was a genuine advance in self-awareness, and its validity is that it has changed me. (John McVicar, *McVicar by Himself*, 1974, pp. 195–6)

～ Release ～

Around this time, January 1936, George V died and the reactions amongst the prisoners were interesting. The majority expressed themselves in one of two ways. Either it was 'a bloody good thing the old man had died for he had been responsible for shutting everyone within the walls of the flaming prison'; or it was an equally good thing because every prisoner would be granted an amnesty when Edward was crowned. The latter rumour fled like fire around the whole prison and to such an extent that the Governor had to make a special announcement one Church Parade, informing everyone that the days of granting such an amnesty by a Sovereign no longer existed. Thereupon Edward's stock slumped as low as his father's amongst the less thoughtful of the prison population. (*Personal Column*, 1952, p. 230)

The prison experience

In February 1974, without any warning, I was called before the governor, who was obviously overjoyed to inform me that I had been granted parole and would be leaving his prison in three weeks. I was apparently expected to leap with joy, but instead I felt a cold anger. They had destroyed everything significant in my life. During five previous parole reviews, they had destroyed the goodwill that existed for me in the outside world. On the five previous occasions, I had the promise of employment. I had all the favourable criteria that could have ensured my success on parole. Yet now, when I had no job to go to and now I had lost the support of people who felt the authorities had destroyed my good intentions, they decided to release me. Having done everything they could to prepare me for failure, they released me. (Wally Probyn, *Angel Face*, 1977, p. 225)

Without any warning

The lights are out, my cell is in darkness, but still I pace the narrow floor up and down, up and down.

No illusions

What have the years of prison done for me? Physically I am perfect. My muscles are like iron. My face and arms are tanned. My senses – the sense of smell and hearing particularly – have developed at least 80 per cent. I have no illusions now of life. I know men as I know myself.

It is over five years since I held a woman's hand. To-morrow I shall be free.

I grow weary at last, and I lie down fully clad. (Ex-convict No.:–, *Dartmoor From Within*, nd, p. 231)

'Cheer ho! Frankie!'

Cheer ho!

'Be seeing ya around.'

I did'nt look back but kept on walking towards the gate.

'Send us a card at Christmas.'

'Have a drink for me Frankie.'

The voices grew faint as I reached the gate. I heard one faint voice in the distance.

'All the best Frankie.'

I went through the first gate, this was the same gate I went through every morning but this time it was different this was the last time the very last time.

No more worries about getting nicked.

No more worries about not haveing a smoke.

No more worries about rotten grub.

No more worries about being caged up.

All I had to worry about now was how I was going to stay out. Where was I going to live?

How was I going to get the rent every week, when I had got some where to live?

Where was I going to sleep tonight?

What was I going to eat tomorrow if anything?

Had I still got any friends?

Would I have to go screwing today the very first day that I got out?

What was I going to do, No where to go, and dead skint.

Never mind that, now I was getting out and that was the only thing that matter now. (Frank Norman, *Bang to Rights*, 1958, p. 191)

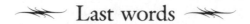 Last words

The Victorian penal reformers were emphatically men of Christian principle, and into the complicated fabric of their theories and practices they wove a strong purpose to reform their victims. Fortunately their views on this subject fitted snugly into the general pattern. Criminal behaviour was the result of ungodly living and associations. But when sequestered from bad influences, alone in his separate cell, subdued to a receptive frame of mind by the stern, salutary discipline of the establishment, the criminal cannot help but meditate on his past mistakes. By reading the Bible and conversing with the chaplain he will prepare himself to lead a sober, honest, and frugal life.

That was the Victorian theory. It was wrong; it never worked. Gradually the theory was laughed out of court.

Since then the oppressive discipline has been much relaxed. Cranks and treadmills have disappeared and been replaced by useful industries. The food has been improved and a few little amenities introduced. But although the Victorian theory of reformation has been abandoned, no other of equal courage has been introduced into its place. For the timid innovations of the past score of years – the occasional 'approved' prison visitor, the occasional evening class, the monthly concert, the permitted notebook – these cannot by any stretch of the imagination be construed as an applied science of criminal reform. Theories, successful and unsuccessful, there have been aplenty; and energetic application too. But their fruits are to be found in the newly developed alternatives to imprisonment – Borstal Institutions, Probation Service, etc. So far as constructive efforts at reform are concerned, the prisons of to-day receive less attention than those of the eighteen-forties.

To sum up this analysis of penal aims; Our prison system is designed to incapacitate, separate, punish, deter, and reform offenders. Of these original intentions, all but the function of incapacitation has been greatly modified in the past half-century. But in general these modifications have been such, in comparison with changes in the world beyond the prison, as to emphasize the purely punitive elements of the system. (Mark Benney, *Gaol Delivery*, 1948, pp. 9–10)

I remember an old Bolshevik, who spent six months in a Scottish *Old Bolshevik* prison, telling me that our Scottish prison system was more revolting and barbarous than the conditions of a Czarist prison. He spoke of the awful silence; the isolation; the useless labour in cells; the barbarous practice of making prisoners stand with their face to the wall while inspection was being made, and so forth, and the poor quality of the food. (Thomas Bell, *Pioneering Days*, 1941, p. 287)

Prison is terrible beyond belief. It makes me indignant to read *Beyond belief* letters and articles from people who talk about 'coddling' prisoners. I would like to give such people (and also most of the judges on the Bench) just what I had in the Second Division – six months, which, with remission marks, is really only five months. It is unrelieved misery all the time. I was better off in the hospital, because I had enough to eat, and was allowed as many books as I wanted. But, on the other hand, I was soon ill from want of air and exercises. You are not obliged to do any work in hospital, but many do it to kill time. It is awful to be locked up for twenty-two hours (sometimes twenty-three hours) out of every twenty-four in a tiny cell. Each day is like a month. Time passed much quicker before I went to the hospital. If I could have had the food I had in hospital, combined with the fresh air and exercise I got in the garden, I would not have complained. But it was a choice between starving on the one hand and claustration in a kennel on the other. (In a ward you may be worse off than in a cell.) (Lord Alfred Douglas, *Autobiography*, 1929, p. 315)

Nothing could give it you unless you had the actual experience. *On being dead* Reading all the books there've ever been about prisons won't bring you anywhere near it, because they're mostly written by people who haven't been inside. Even those who have would only be writing about how it was to them anyway. I mean if you write a book or paint a picture or compose a piece of music what you're doing is recreating a personal experience and it'd be different to someone else. I've never read anything that made me feel whoever'd written it had got near to what it's like to me. I suppose all I could say would be that when I die I might – I just might, though I doubt it – know what it's like to be dead. But I couldn't have any idea beforehand what it might be like because no one's written a book on being dead from personal experience. Those people that have written on prison from personal experience are different from most prisoners anyway because at least they can write even if it's badly, I mean put down on paper what they feel. But the majority of prisoners couldn't do that, so how does anyone know what they're feeling or suffering, or not feeling and not suffering. All you know is they can't put it down on paper, but it wouldn't be safe to take it for granted therefore that nothing was going on inside them.

Roy S. (48)
Offence: murder.
Sentence: life.

(Tony Parker, *The Man Inside*, 1973, p. 17)

A simple moral issue

A colleague had spent a lot of time helping him mend his marital problems and he was grateful for this. He told us that he would be going back to his wife and children and that he was determined to settle down for their sakes. He had bought a shop with this in mind.

As a parting question one of us asked how he found the money for the shop. 'That's what I've done my bird for', he said, as if the question were asked by a fool. The prison had thus held this man for two thirds of four years; had paid social workers to sort out the domestic consequences of his behaviour, had respected his intelligence by giving him a key job in the prison; and yet had failed to attend to the one matter that most people would have expected it to be peculiarly concerned with, which was a simple moral issue of right and wrong. He would, like so many prisoners, admit to having been foolish, or to having done a silly thing, but it would not have been borne upon him by prison that he had been wicked. (Michael Sorenson, *Working on Self-Respect*, 1986, p. 88)

Cannot have both

Imprisonment cannot be curative or redemptive in some parts, and, in other parts punitive or retributive. If there is to be training in prison, the whole system must be invested with rightly conceived principles of training; if there is to be education in prison, the whole system must be consonant with educative work; if there is to be the practice of religion in prison, the whole system must itself be, at the least, not irreligious; and, if there is to be a

The prison experience

psychological treatment in prison, the whole system must itself be firmly rested on sound psychological principles. Given these conditions, instructors and teachers, priests and ministers, psychologists and psychiatrists would be enabled to work together in a powerful team of mighty redemption. That is what a prison could be, and what a number of people even think it to be. In reality, it is a place of punishment wherein a few reformative elements have been incongruously and unprofitably planted. The public must take its choice between the two. It cannot have both. (Norman Howarth Hignett, *Portrait in Grey*, 1956, p. 201)

My friends said: 'In a few weeks you will have forgotten it all. It *It will fade* will fade from your mind like a bad dream. It's over and done with now, and nobody wants to remember it.' They meant to be kind, but I knew that they were wrong. I could never forget. I would always carry with me, like a hidden scar, the memory of what I had seen. From now on, perhaps, I could never be wholly happy; but at the same time I could never be wholly selfish or consumed with pity for myself, because wherever I went I should be haunted by the faces, savage or resigned or drained of hope, of those hundreds of men so much less fortunate than myself. Society might have succeeded in forgetting them, but I never could. I knew what it was like to be a criminal, to know that everything you did would be misunderstood or used as evidence against you, so that you just drifted, hopelessly, from one prison sentence to the next. I knew something of the bitter rage which wells up in a man's mind during the long cold nights, when he thinks of the punishment which Society, with icy impartiality, is exacting from his wife and children. I knew the dreadful isolation of the prisoner, meticulously deprived of every contact with the world into which, one day, he will be released. I knew how it felt to be a member of a minority, under-privileged even in gaol because of the shape of one's nose or the colour of one's skin. (Peter Wildeblood, *Against the Law*, 1955, p. 173)

Life in a prison is the most abject form of slavery which could be *Slavery* devised. It is strange, is it not, that we abolished slavery for our negroes 120 years ago, because we knew it to be degrading alike for the slaves and the slave-owners, while for our fellow-countrymen who have offended against our rules of conduct we maintain it still, if not for life, at least for a period, and often enough for time after time, practically for life.

Life in prison is far more degrading than the slavery of the negroes, because it is far more complete, and it is just as degrading for our State to hold its army of slaves as it was to the landowners of Jamaica. We persuade ourselves that it is good for them and necessary for Society, just as the slave-owners, when they struggled against the emancipation of their slaves, argued that slavery was necessary for them and good for the slaves. (A. Mitchell-Innes, *Martyrdom in Our Times*, 1932, pp. 37–8)

Irreparable   After what seemed an interminable length of time my sentence expired and I went free never, I hope, to return to prison again. I know far too much of the vicissitudes of life – especially the vicissitudes that beset the ex-convict – to have the presumption to assert that I will never, under any circumstances, return; but having kept out for five years I hope that that chapter of my life bears the inscription 'Finis'. I am still in much the same circumstances as when I lost grip and rushed blindly into the abyss, but several people have been so kind to me that I do not think I could ever hurt them by reverting to the old life or shatter their faith in me. And, apart from personal considerations such as these, I am conscious that prison life has wrought such irreparable mental injury to me that I can only consider prison as the high-road that leads to despair, ruin of mind, enervation of body, and spiritual negation. (Stuart Wood, *Shades of the Prison House*, 1932, p. 402)

THE PRISON SYSTEM CAN BE ABOLISHED

The object of penal reformers should be not to reform the prison system, but to abolish it. So long as we maintain the present unscientific system of taking all types of law-breakers – thief, drunkard, debtor, prostitute, political offender, sexual offender, physical assaulter, murderer – and shutting them up under identical conditions without any consideration of the personal and environmental factors which led to the offence, or of the individual remedial action necessary, good results can never be expected. It would be just as sensible to treat every hospital case by operating on the appendix. You may sing to this varied collection of human beings, you may teach them to read and write and sew, you may allow them to discuss safe subjects; but all this does nothing to change either the personal or social causes of crime. Indeed, the unnatural conditions of prison existence, the long hours of cellular confinement, the punitive discipline, the suppression of personality, and the artificial segregation do more positive harm in most cases than any palliatives can do good.

To demand the abolition of the prison system is not to use merely a rhetorical phrase. It is a practical policy. Thirty years ago the prison population was 30,000. Before the war it was 16,000. To-day it is 10,000. The figure has fallen because alternative methods to imprisonment have been adopted. There is no reason why these methods should not be extended until necessity for prisons disappears.

I am compelled again to emphasise the fact, however, that so long as the existing conditions of poverty and social injustice continue, not only will 'criminals' be created, but the saving of offenders from a life of crime will remain difficult. It is like the stupidity of taking a tubercular case from a slum to a sanatorium and then returning him to a slum. Unless a change in our social system accompanies the change in our penal system, we may rehabilitate an individual by appropriate treatment only to see him ruined again by his environment and the absence of opportunity to live a healthy and honest life. (Fenner Brockway, *Socialist Review*, December 1926, p. 26)

EPILOGUE

~

The Twentieth Century

Long Lartin Prison

～ A good and useful life – and beyond ～

Alexander Paterson was appointed to the Prison Commission in 1922 – the year that *English Prisons Today* was published by Stephen Hobhouse and Fenner Brockway.[1] In his upper-middle class origins and education there was little to distinguish him from his fellow commissioners, but in his experience of social work after leaving Oxford, and in serving as an NCO with his East End lads at the beginning of the First World War, he was distinct from both his contemporaries and his predecessors in prison administration.[2] Even so, Paterson represents the end of a line of 'heroic' figures whose influence on the English penal system was both far-reaching and personal. Where Jebb had been systematic rather than charismatic in his leadership style, and Du Cane had combined both of these qualities in making concrete his personal vision of discipline, Paterson propounded and lived out in his own life a doctrine of human perfectibility. It was one that could be achieved only through personal influence deployed in an environment designed to resemble the Arnoldian ideal of the public school; and in its pursuit, Paterson possessed, according to C.A. Joyce, 'infinite vision – extraordinary ability– boundless enthusiasm – unquenchable faith'.[3]

He never became chairman of the Commissioners but, by example and the force of his personality, Alexander Paterson attracted into the prison service a whole generation of idealistic young men to run the Borstal system. Their individual successes flourished like flowers in the desert – isolated and exotic blooms in an infinite vista of infertility. Eventually they withered and died – metaphors for the eventual demise of the whole 'treatment and training' philosophy that Paterson embodied.

But to begin with, his ideas made some headway into the adult establishments for which he had responsibility. After the end of the First World War, prompted in part by the findings of the Hobhouse–Brockway book, the Prison Commissioners slowly relaxed the most restrictive features of the Du Cane discipline that had somehow survived more than two decades of supposed reform. The silence rule was in theory abolished, association with other prisoners allowed, education – entertainments even – were permitted. Some Governors began to take a personal interest in some of the men they held captive, and they encouraged the subordinate or uniformed prison officers to follow their example. The spirit of all these changes was eventually enshrined in Rule 1 of the Prison Rules:

> The purpose of the training and treatment of convicted prisoners shall be to encourage and assist them to lead a good and useful life.[4]

CLASSES AND STAGES

The conductors of the Borstal initiative had sought to mitigate the corruption of the innocent through the creation of an ethos devoted entirely to personal reform. The adult prisons relied on more mechanical devices to divide the sheep from the goats – and to keep both of them from the clutches of the wolves. Classification was not an invention of the new century but it was applied with vigour, and with an apparent faith in its effectiveness. The most fundamental division of prisoners that it made was between those who were 'Stars' and those who were 'Ordinaries'. The 'Star' was a convicted offender who had not previously served a sentence of imprisonment. The 'Ordinary' was one who had. Keeping them apart on prison premises was an elementary measure of moral housekeeping.[5]

Evelyn Ruggles-Brise, when urged by Churchill to extend the system of classification in prisons, calculated that there were not less than twenty-one categories of prisoners already in use.[6] Even so, twenty-one classes were scarcely sufficient to exhaust the complex and deviant humanity committed to prison by the processes of justice. Truly innocent young men continued to serve sentences alongside Stars whose previous offences had simply not been detected, and some offenders with a previous minor conviction found themselves hauled off to Dartmoor to consort with the worst criminals that the then existing system could muster in one place.

'Classes' divided prisoners from each other in terms of their pre-prison behaviour: 'stages' distinguished them according to how long they had spent in the prison and how well they had behaved whilst there. The stage system of discipline was first devised by Alexander Maconochie in the Australian penal colony.[7] Later it was assumed wholesale into the home-grown system of penal servitude that took the place of transportation. The scheme made it possible for the individual prisoner to earn by unremitting good behaviour, tiny but incremental privileges of association, visits, and food, as well as rather more substantial rewards in the shape of early release. But by themselves the classes and stages did hardly anything to combat the corrosive effects of long-term incarceration on the minds of prisoners, and equally little to prevent the corruption of the 'innocent'.

THE MOVEMENT OF CRIME

Alongside these continuities in the English penal tradition of the early twentieth century, two opposed influences were at work on the nature of life inside. On the one hand far fewer people were being committed to prison for minor offences. This was mostly, but not entirely, due to the Criminal Justice Administration Act of 1914, which made it possible for the poor to pay their fines over a period of time. In 1913 there were 74,461 committals for non-payment; in 1918 there were 5,264.[8]

Convictions for criminal offences remained remarkably stable throughout the inter-war years of economic depression – precisely the conditions under which theories of crime causation linked to social factors would have predicted a great increase in the commission of offences, and particularly property ones. The failure of the figures to oblige this theoretical requirement, and a co-incidental decline in the proportionate use of imprisonment, forced the Prison Commissioners to abandon a number of their smaller establishments. But any quantitative losses at the lower end of the tariff were soon matched by qualitative changes that affected the longer-term departments of the prison empire. For officials these were changes for the worse; for the prisoner class they represented the reverse since they brought into their company a class of committed and daring robbers, some of them rejoicing in the newly minted title of 'motor bandits'.[9]

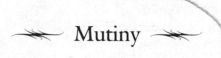

Mutiny

It was an influx of the latter into the punitive climate of Dartmoor, then the country's most notorious prison and reserved for the most desperate and violent of convicted men that led, in January 1932, to an outbreak of serious disorder in the prison. The Dartmoor Mutiny, in what appears with hindsight to have been a rehearsal for later *émeutes*, followed an attempt to reintroduce an older notion of discipline after the relatively liberal governorship of Gerald Fancourt Clayton.[10] Nothing like this scale of violence had been known in an English prison since the upheaval at Chatham convict station in 1861.

For a brief period the whole of Dartmoor was left in the hands of the mutineers. Shots were fired at prisoners who got up on the walls and order had to be restored by squads of policemen brought in from Plymouth. The fact that it had happened at all was a considerable shock to a system that had hitherto thought of itself in more or less reformist terms. Long prison sentences were subsequently handed out to the ring-leaders of the mutiny and many of them were transferred to Parkhurst to serve their additional years. It is from the Dartmoor and the Parkhurst of the 1930s that there first emerge in the published biographies of prisoners and ex-prisoners signs of a truly articulated inmate society, one that speaks in the authentic tones of the criminal classes.

PARLIAMENT

The Second World War cut across Parliamentary moves to introduce a Criminal Justice Bill widely advertised in advance as a progressive penal measure. It eventually passed – much reworked – onto the Statute Book in 1948, and was intended to consolidate and give fresh expression to the reformist tendencies that had been at work in the system – albeit on a tentative and geographically piecemeal basis – since the publication of the Gladstone Report in 1895. Its main formal novelty lay in the introduction of Corrective Training, a slightly longer sentence intended for offenders at a critical stage in their criminal development; and designed to fill their days with improving training and the benign influences of kindly warders.[11] It proved to be a popular sentence with judges, but convicts counted it as just one more amongst the many failures of prison administrations to deliver in practice what Parliament had decreed in theory. Otherwise the reformist drift continued much as it had before the war, but without much conviction. Open prisons were opened, for men at Wakefield and Maidstone, and for women at Askham Grange near York. Here and there, forceful governors like John Vidler[12] at Maidstone or Gilbert Hair[13] at Wormwood Scrubs tried, without much success, to do what Paterson had tried and failed to achieve a generation previously.

Group therapy, then the fashion in California under the guidance of Norman Fenton, was imported into the English prison after the end of the Second World War.[14] Its most impressive manifestation was to be seen in what was called the Norwich scheme (after the prison where it was first implemented).[15] Selected prison officers were given groups of inmates with whom they met on a weekly basis. The idea was that these meetings should operate as therapeutic groups along Californian lines. But since group therapy is a highly specialised, not to say esoteric, application of psycho-dynamic or psycho-analytic theory, it seems unlikely, looking back on the experiment, that basic-grade prison officers without specialist training would ever have been able to do much more than go through the motions. And all the evidence is that this is what in fact happened, although it may have served some tension-easing functions in permitting prisoners a forum for some of their grievances. The scheme spread to other prisons, but like most penal fashions it lasted for a brief season only, was highly commended in the annual reports, and then quietly buried without ceremony in an unmarked grave of the kind then reserved for hanged murderers.

A more permanent monument to the psychological approach to crime and its 'treatment' was created with the opening in 1962 of Grendon Underwood, a psychiatrically oriented prison for long-term men. Originally planned before the Second World War – when it was known as the East-Hubert Institute after the two psychiatrists whose idea it was – Grendon has run since its inception as a 'therapeutic community'.[16] Within a generally permissive regime men are required to attend daily or weekly group meetings in which 'therapeutic' exchanges are manipulated by a psychotherapist and volunteer prison officers. The theory underlying this activity has never been precisely articulated, and evidence about its effectiveness is, understandably enough, ambiguous.

The development of more 'therapeutic' methods, although it only affected a minority of all prisoners, was accompanied by a progressive relaxation of the remnants of the silent, punitive regime of the nineteenth century: the abolition of flogging for prison disciplinary offences, the eventual disappearance of bread and water punishments, and the coincidental ending of judicial hanging for murder. But unlike the changes of the 1930s, those of the post-war period were taking place against a background of unprecedented growth in rates of crime. From 1953 onwards increases in known crime and recorded convictions began a precipitous ascent that continues into the present. Despite this growth in business the courts continued throughout the 1950s and 1960s to send proportionately fewer people to prison. Even so they were unable to prevent the beginnings of physical overcrowding, especially in local prisons where remanded cases and newly sentenced prisoners are first received. Meanwhile it came to the notice of the newspapers that men were escaping in numbers from the prisons before duly completing the sentences passed on them by the criminal courts. From 29 escapes in 1955, the figure had risen to 114 in 1961 – and this was from secure conditions.[17] A hue and cry was started that culminated in the controversy surrounding the escape in 1966 of convicted Soviet agent George Blake from Wormwood Scrubs, where he had begun to serve his 42-year sentence. Lord Louis

Mountbatten of Burma was appointed to look into the whole issue of escapes and lapses of security, and his subsequent report represents a watershed in the history of the modern English prison.[17]

MOUNTBATTEN

The importance of Mountbatten's labours lay not so much in the detail of what he proposed – a lot of it was rejected as a basis for keeping long-sentence prisoners locked up – as in the spirit of security-consciousness it engendered. His report represented a psychological turning point for a system that had spent the previous seventy years paying at least lip-service to its reformist pretensions, and it fundamentally altered the ways the prison system both saw and spoke of itself. Security was to be the new watchword; vague sentiments of reform were replaced with a tough-sounding managerialism that somehow managed to talk of efficiency without ever defining towards what precise ends this should be directed. The prevention of escapes was, however, high on the list of priorities, special secure units were built in a number of older prisons (Durham, Leicester), and some of the new prisons such as Gartree and Long Lartin were thought secure enough in their original designs to serve the same purposes. An 'A' list of men who should not be allowed to escape at any cost was drawn up; some two hundred names appeared on it and these were the candidates for the secure units.

This shift in emphasis away from an overt reformism, albeit one that masked an entrenched conservatism, was reflected in a parallel reversal of sentencing trends. Whereas magistrates had been sending a declining proportion of offenders to prison up to 1972, in 1973 the proportion began to increase. These changes in the system were accompanied in the early 1970s by a resurgence of criticism from outside pressure groups on the subject of overcrowding in prisons. There were even more fundamental calls from organizations such as Radical Alternatives to Prison for the virtual abolition of penal establishments.[18]

It would not be entirely accurate to say that the increasingly repressive atmosphere of security and control led directly to the formation of Preservation of the Rights of Prisoners (PROP), but it almost certainly contributed to it.[19] PROP was a pressure group for serving prisoners, and although there were pre-existing models for the organisation in Scandinavia and North America, its emergence in English prisons intensified a process of polarisation between staff and prisoners that was soon to be expressed in a number of destructive and sometimes bloody riots at Parkhurst, Albany, Hull, Durham, and Wormwood Scrubs. More use began to be made of segregation under the provisions of Rule 43 of the Prison Rules, and at Wakefield a control unit was built to a design that incorporated features of sensory deprivation. The increased use of tranquillising drugs also became a feature of life inside.

During this period, major changes were also taking place in the administration of the prison service. The independent Commissioners of Prisons were abolished in 1966 and absorbed into the Home Office administrative structure, thus reducing the freedom of manoeuvre of the department and placing it directly under the control of the Home Secretary and his officials. There was also a move to industrialise prisons. Coldingley prison in Surrey was opened in 1969 to act as a laundry and manufacturing prison on commercially viable lines, and a special section of the Prison Department was set up to promote and co-ordinate the industrial activity of the whole system. It was named PRINDUS – which has the sound of an unfortunate medical condition – and it did not prosper in any material sense.[20]

Perhaps because of, but at any rate, contemporaneously with these management changes there began to be seen a much more militant assertion of the interests of the uniformed staff of the prison service through the machinery of the Prison Officers Association. Using the strains of overcrowding and undermanning to maximum advantage the union has sought since the end of the 1960s to exercise a degree of control over basic policy: it has refused to admit remand cases to already over-full local prisons, refused to do overtime to service association periods for prisoners, and contributed to a climate in which massive disciplinary disorders have taken place throughout the system.

DUAL POLICY

From the mid-1970s there can also be dated what is best described as a dual official policy in response to the pressures and strains facing the English penal system. On the one hand it has signalled the beginnings of a programme of prison building that has grown in time to become the biggest such undertaking since the mania of the 1840s; on the other hand there has been an emphasis on measures such as those incorporated in the 1972 Criminal Justice Act for diverting offenders away from custody. More diversion/more custody is still the policy that is being pursued by the Home Office. It is one solution to the perennial dilemma of penal politics – the one embraced in the conclusions of the Gladstone Committee proceedings, namely, how to reconcile punitive with reformative elements. Both elements are actively and persuasively promoted by vocal and persistent lobbies in the penumbra of pressures and influences that are constantly exerted on policy makers in areas of public concern. The current answer to this long standing question – and it is not a new one – is to face in both directions at once.

A century will soon have elapsed since Gladstone re-articulated the reformist agenda for the prison service – a hundred years in which prison administrators have struggled to give coherent expression to the contradictory demands of deterrence and reform. They have failed in practice, and the politicians continue to voice the irreconcilable elements of the rhetoric without any sense of inconsistency.

The prospects for more rational corrections in the twenty-first century are not good.

NOTES

1 Stephen Hobhouse and Fenner Brockway (1922) *English Prisons Today*, London: Longman.

2 S.K. Ruck (ed.) (1951) *Paterson on Prisons*, London: Frederick Muller.
3 C.A. Joyce (1955) *By Courtesy of the Criminal*, London: Harrap.
4 *The Prison Rules* (1964) Statutory Instrument 388.
5 Lionel W. Fox (1952) *The English Prison and Borstal Systems*, London: Routledge & Kegan Paul.
6 Shane Leslie (1938) *Sir Evelyn Ruggles-Brise*, London: John Murray.
7 Alexander Maconochie (1846) *Crime and Punishment, The Mark System*, London: Hatchard.
8 Andrew Rutherford (1986) *Prisons and the Process of Justice*, Oxford: Oxford University Press.
9 Eddie Browne (1934) *Road Pirate*, London: John Long.
10 Gerald Fancourt Clayton (1958) *The Wall is Strong*, London: John Long.
11 Lionel W. Fox, op cit.
12 John Vidler and Michael Wolff (1964) *If Freedom Fail*, London: Macmillan.
13 Peter Wildeblood (1955) *Against the Law*, London: Weidenfeld & Nicolson.
14 Norman Fenton (1961) *Group Counseling*, Sacramento: California Institute for the Study of Crime and Delinquency.
15 See *Report of the Commissioners of Prisons* for the Year 1956, London: HMSO.
16 W.N. East and W.H. de B. Hubert (1939) *The Psychological Treatment of Crime*, London: HMSO.
17 *Report of the Inquiry into Prison Escapes and Security* (1966), London: HMSO.
18 *The Abolitionist* no.1, January 1979, London: Radical Alternatives to Prison.
19 Mike Fitzgerald (1977) *Prisoners in Revolt*, Harmondsworth: Penguin.
20 *Prisons and the Prisoner* (1977) London: HMSO, p.57.

Epilogue: the twentieth century

BIBLIOGRAPHY

John Edward Allen (1952) *Inside Broadmoor*, London: W.H. Allen.

Trevor Allen (1932) *Underworld. The Biography of Charles Brooks – Criminal*, London: Newnes.

Anonymous by necessity (1936) *Five Years for Fraud*, London: Sampson Low, Marston.

L. Atthill (1937) 'The British prison', *Spectator*, 8 October.

Peter Baker (1961) *Time Out of Life*, London: Heinemann.

Adam John Loughborough Ball (1936) *Trial and Error: The Fire Conspiracy and After*, London: Faber.

The Rev. Baden P.H. Ball (1956) *Prison Was My Parish*, London: Heinemann.

Charlotte Banks (1958) *Teach Them to Live*, London: Max Parrish.

Harold Begbie (1927) *Punishment and Personality*, London: Mills & Boon.

Brendan Behan (1958) *Borstal Boy*, London: Hutchinson.

Brian Behan (1964) *With Breast Expanded* London: MacGibbon & Kee.

Thomas Bell (1941) *Pioneering Days*, London: Lawrence & Wishart.

Mark Benney (1936) *Low Company*, London: Peter Davies.

Mark Benney (1948) *Gaol Delivery*, London: Longmans Green.

W.G. Bentley (1957) *My Son's Execution*, London: W.H. Allen.

Ronnie Biggs (1981) *His Own Story*, London: Michael Joseph.

Raymond Blackburn (1959) *I Am an Alcoholic*, London: Alan Wingate.

Wallace Blake (1927) *QUOD*, London: Hodder & Stoughton.

Sean Bourke (1970) *The Springing of George Blake*, London: Cassell.

Jimmy Boyle (1977) *A Sense of Freedom*, Edinburgh: Canongate.

Jimmy Boyle (1984) *The Pain of Confinement. Prison Diaries*, Edinburgh: Canongate.

Fenner Brockway (1926) 'The prison system can be abolished', *Socialist Review*, December.

Eddie Browne (1934) *Road Pirate*, London: John Long.

Shifty Burke (1966) *Peterman*, London: Arthur Barker.

Jane Buxton and Margaret Turner (1962) *Gate Fever*, London: Cresset Press.

James Campbell (1986) *Gate Fever: Voices From a Prison*, London: Weidenfeld & Nicolson.

Victor Carasov (1971) *Two Gentlemen to See You, Sir*, London: Gollancz.

Pat Carlen, ed. (1985) *Criminal Women*, Oxford: Polity Press.

Roy Catchpole (1974) *Key to Freedom*, London: Lutterworth.

Gerald Fancourt Clayton (1958) *The Wall is Strong*, London: John Long.

Stanley Cohen and Laurie Taylor (1972) *Psychological Survival*, Harmondsworth: Penguin.

Rupert Croft-Cooke (1955) *The Verdict of You All*, London: Secker & Warburg.

Harley Cronin (1967) *The Screw Turns*, London: Longman.

Peter Crookston (1967) *Villain: The Biography of a Criminal*, London: Jonathan Cape.

L.J. Cunliffe (1965) *Having It Away*, London: Duckworth.

Douglas Curtis (1973) *Dartmoor to Cambridge*, London: Hodder & Stoughton.

W.G. Davis (1939) *Gentlemen of the Broad Arrows*, London: Selwyn & Blount.

George Dendrickson and Frederick Thomas (1954) *The Truth about Dartmoor*, London: Gollancz.

Francis Disney (1985) *Heritage of a Prison*, Shepton Mallet.

Lord Alfred Douglas (1924) *In Excelsis*, London: Martin Secker.

Lord Alfred Douglas (1929) *The Autobiography of Lord Alfred Douglas,* London: Martin Secker.

Charles Douie (1935) *Beyond the Sunset*, London: John Murray.

Charles Douie (1951) *So Long to Learn*, Oxford: George Ronald.

Honor Earl (1948) *Prison Once a Week*, London: Psychological and Social Services.

David Elias (1957) *College Harry*, London: Longmans Green.

Rufus Endle (1979) *Dartmoor Prison*, Bodmin: Bossiney Books.

Ex-convict No:– (nd) *Dartmoor From Within*, London: Newnes.

Xenia Field (1963) *Under Lock and Key*, London: Max Parrish.

Frances Finlay (1969) *A Boy in Blue Jeans*, London: Robert Hale.

Frances Finlay (1971) *Boy in Prison*, London: Robert Hale.

Mike Fitzgerald (1977) *Prisoners in Revolt*, Harmondsworth: Penguin.

John William Fletcher (1972) *A Menace to Society*, London: Elek.

Sir Lionel Fox (1952) *The English Prison and Borstal Systems*, London: Routledge & Kegan Paul.

Michael Frayn (1959) 'Overcrowded local prisons', *The Guardian*, 22 April.

William Gallacher (1966) *The Last Memories of W. Gallacher*, London: Lawrence & Wishart.

Gordon Gardiner (1938) *Notes of a Prison Visitor*, London: Oxford University Press.

Sheila Garvie (1980) *Marriage to Murder: My Story*, London: Chambers.

Charles George Gordon (1921) *Crooks of the Underworld*, Geoffrey Bles.

J.W. Gordon (1932) *Borstalians*, London: Martin Hopkinson.

Major B.D. Grew (1958) *Prison Governor*, London: Herbert Jenkins.

Tom Hadaway (1986) *Prison Writers: An Anthology*, North Shields: Iron Press.

M. Hamblin-Smith (1934) *Prisons*, London: Bodley Head.

Richmond Harvey (1937) *Prison From Within*, London: Allen & Unwin.

T. Edmund Harvey (1941) *The Christian Church and the Prisoner in English Experience*, London: Epworth Press.

Anthony Heckstall-Smith (1954) *Eighteen Months*, Allan Wingate.

Joan Henry (1952) *Who Lie in Gaol*, London: Gollancz.

Norman Howarth Hignett (1956) *Portrait in Grey*, London: Frederick Muller.

Archie Hill (1973) *A Cage of Shadows*, London: Hutchinson.

Archie Hill (1984) *An Empty Glass*, London: Hutchinson.

Billy Hill (1955) *Boss of Britain's Underworld*, Naldrett Press.

Jack Hilton (1935) *Caliban Shrieks*, Cobden Sanderson.

Alfred Hinds (1966) *Contempt of Court*, London: Bodley Head.

William Holt (1934) *I Was a Prisoner*, London: John Miles.

Harry Houghton (1972) *Operation Portland*, London: Rupert Hart-Davis.

Howard Journal (1955) 'Prison and After. The Experience of a Former Homosexual', Vol IX. No. 2.

David Jardine (1978) *In Jail with Jesus*, Belfast: Christian Journals.

Peter Jenkins (nd) *Mayfair Boy*, Pinnacle Book.

Jock of Dartmoor (nd) *Human Stories of Prison Life*, London: Readers Library.

Joanna Kelley (1967) *When the Gates Shut*, London: Longman.

Charles Kray (1976) *Me and My Brothers*, London: Everest.

James Leigh (1941) *My Prison House*, London: Hutchinson.

Ronald Lloyd and Stanley Williamson (1968) *Born to Trouble: Portrait of a Psychopath*, Oxford: Cassirer.

Frank Longford (1974) *The Grain of Wheat*, London: Collins.

Gordon Lonsdale (1966) *Spy*, St Albans: Mayflower-Dell.

Netley Lucas (1925) *Crooks: Confessions*, New York: Doran.

W.F.R. Macartney (1936) *Walls Have Mouths*, London: Gollancz.

De Witt Mackenzie (1930) *Hell's Kitchen*, London: Herbert Jenkins.

Donald Mackenzie (1955) *Fugitives*, London: Elek.

Yolande McShane (1980) *Daughter of Evil*, London: W.H. Allen.

John McVicar (1974) *McVicar by Himself*, London: Hutchinson.

Jonathan Marshall (1974) *How to Survive in the Nick*, London: Allison & Busby.

Richard P. Maxwell (1956) *Borstal and Better*, London: Hollis & Carter.

Patrick Meehan (1978) *Innocent Villain*, London: Pan.

L. Merrow-Smith and J. Harris (1962) *Prison Screw*, London: Herbert Jenkins.

Kate Meyrick (1933) *Secrets of the 43*, London: Long.

Alastair Miller (1976) *Inside, Outside*, London: Queensgate.

A.Mitchell-Innes, (1932) *Martyrdom in Our Times*, London: Williams & Norgate.

Terence and Pauline Morris (1963) *Pentonville: A Sociological Study of an English Prison*, London: Routledge & Kegan Paul.

Andrew Keith Munro (1972) *Autobiography of a Thief*, London: Michael Joseph.

Nee Gud Luck in Dorham Jail (1985), Beamish: Pit Lamp Press.

Hippo Neville (1935) *Sneak Thief on the Road*, London: Jonathan Cape.

Frank Norman (1958) *Bang to Rights*, London: Secker & Warburg.

Frank Norman (1970) *Lock 'em Up and Count 'em*, London: Charles Knight.

Muriel Norroy (1939) *I Robbed the Lords and Ladies Gay*, London: Methuen.

Jimmy O'Connor (1976) *The Eleventh Commandment*, Guernsey: Seagull.

Patrick O'Hara (1967) *I Got no Brother*, London: Spearman.

Maurice O'Mahoney with Dan Wooding (1978) *King Squealer*, London: W.H. Allen.

Dr Samuel Ingleby Oddie (1941) *Inquest*, London: Hutchinson.

Dr Grace Pailthorpe (1932) *What We Put in Prison*, London: Williams & Norgate.

Tony Parker and Robert Allerton (1962) *The Courage of His Convictions*, London: Hutchinson.

Tony Parker (1965) *Five Women*, London: Hutchinson.

Tony Parker (1967) *A Man of Good Abilities*, London: Hutchinson.

Tony Parker (1970) *The Frying Pan*, London: Hutchinson.

Tony Parker (1973) *The Man Inside*, London: Michael Joseph.

Audrey Peckham (1985) *A Woman in Custody*, London: Fontana.

Personal Column: A Testimony of Crime (1952), London: Staples Press.

Jim Phelan (1940) *Jail Journey*, London: Secker & Warburg.

Jim Phelan (1948) *The Name's Phelan*, London: Sidgwick & Jackson.

Ron Phillips (1974) 'The Black Prisoner's Subjective View' *Race Today*, June.

Albert Pierrepoint (1974) *Executioner Pierrepoint*, London: Harrap.

Sir Sidney J. Pocock (1930) *The Prisoner and the Prison*, London: Alston Rivers.

Harry Pollitt (1940) *Serving My Time*, London: Lawrence & Wishart.

Philip Priestley (1981) *Community of Scapegoats: The Segregation of Sex Offenders and Informers in Prison*, London: Pergamon.

Walter Probyn (1977) *Angel Face*, London: Allen & Unwin.

PROP (nd) *Don't Mark His Face*, London: Preservation of the Rights of Prisoners.

Red Collar Man (1938) *Chokey*, London: Gollancz.

Lieut. Col. C.E.F. Rich (1932) *Recollections of a Prison Governor*, London: Hurst & Blackett.

Dr Guy Richmond (1975) *Prison Doctor*, Surrey; BC Nunaga.

Robert Roberts (1968) *Imprisoned Tongues*, Manchester: Manchester University Press.

S.K. Ruck (ed) (1951) *Paterson on Prisons*, London: Frederick Muller.

Pablo Salkeld (1949) 'The ugly head', *Horizon*, July.

Alfred Salt (1955) *Jottings of a JP*, London: Christopher Johnson.

Raphael Samuel (1981) *East End Underworld. Chapters in the Life of Arthur Harding*, London: Routledge & Kegan Paul.

Siegfried Sassoon (1984) *Collected Poems 1908–1956*, London: Faber & Faber.

Sir Harold Scott (1959) *Your Obedient Servant*, London: Deutsch.

Emmanuel Shinwell (1955) *Conflict Without Malice*, London: Odhams Press.

Mary Size (1957) *Prisons I Have Known*, London: Allen & Unwin.

George Smithson (nd) *'Gentleman George': Raffles in Real Life*, London: Hutchinson.

Michael Sorenson (1986) *Working on Self-Respect*, London: Peter Bedford Trust.

Ruby Sparks (1961) *Burglar to the Nobility*, London: Arthur Barker.

James Spenser (1934) *Limey Breaks In*, London: Longmans Green.

F.A. Stanley (1938) *A Happy Fortnight*, London: Peter Davies.

A. Stevens (1952) *Father to Son. Extracts from the Letters of Philip Guy Stevens*, Shrewsbury: Wilding & Son.

Jim Stockton (1968) *Runaway*, London: Hutchinson.

Jago Stone (1975) *The Burglar's Bedside Companion*, London: Everest.

Brian Stratton (1975) *Who Guards the Guards?*, London: PROP.

Robert Sykes (1967) *Who's Been Eating My Porridge?*, London: Frewin.

Allan K. Taylor (1949) *From a Glasgow Slum to Fleet Street*, London: Alvin Redman.

Wally Thompson (1956) *Time Off My Life*, London: Rich & Cowan.

Toby (1979) *A Bristol Tramp Tells His Story*, Bristol: Bristol Broadsides.

Tom Tullett (1966) *Inside Dartmoor*, London: Frederick Muller.

Nicholas Tyndall (1967) *Prison People*, Reading: Educational Explorers.

John Vassall (1975) *Vassall – The Autobiography of a Spy*, London: Sidgwick & Jackson.

John Vidler with Michael Wolff (1964) *If Freedom Fail*, London: Macmillan.

Marjorie Wallace (1986) *The Silent Twins*, London: Chatto & Windus.

Henry Ward (1974) *Buller*, London: Hodder & Stoughton.

Warden (1929) *His Majesty's Guests: Secrets of the Cells*, London: Jarrolds.

Des Warren (1982) *The Key to My Cell*, London: New Park Publications.

H.W. Wicks (1938) *The Prisoner Speaks*, London: Jarrolds.

Peter Wildeblood, (1955) *Against the Law*, London: Weidenfeld & Nicolson.

Margaret Wilson (1931) *The Crime of Punishment*, London: Harcourt.

Stuart Wood (1932) *Shades of the Prison House*, London: Williams & Norgate.

H.J. Woods (1926) 'Religion in the city of cells', *Congregational Quarterly*, July.

Zeno (1968) *Life*, London: Macmillan.

INDEX

Note: authors' names nave been printed in bold.